**W9-CLM-201**

*HYPNOTIC RECOLLECTIONS*
The History of The Development of
Hypnotism as a Separate and Distinct
Profession in the 20th Century
By Dr. Dwight F. Damon

Published by
      Advanced Studies Consultants, Inc.
      PO Box 1738 - Merrimack, NH  03054

Copyright©2011. Advanced Studies Consultants Inc.
ISBN-978-1-885846-17-4
4th Edition Copyright©2019. Advanced Studies Consultants Inc.

Cover Design, Interior Design & Production: Melody Damon Bachand

All rights reserved. No  part of this book may be reproduced in any form or by any
electronic or mechanical means including information storage and retrieval systems
without permission in writing from the publisher, except by a reviewer, who may
quote brief passages in a review.

TM

# Introduction

Freedom is not free—someone had to earn it! The definition of freedom is: "The acceptance of responsibility for the rewards and consequences of a person's own choice."

As anyone who is involved in hypnosis knows first hand, freedom must be constantly re-earned. There are always those naysayers and competitors who will demand conformity and uniformity to their way of thinking, instead of your own as an independent, conscious, reasoning adult with developed skills above and beyond what others may have learned. Each of us has the responsibility to be actively involved in the totality of our occupation and lives by standing firm against any attempt to restrict our choice of thinking. The strength of our species is not conformity and uniformity, but individuality and uniqueness. Apathy and complacency indicate we have given up the fight to determine what is right, true and correct for ourselves and those we share our lives with.

Dr Dwight Damon has created a masterpiece of information bringing to our awareness the trials and tribulations of those who have preceded us in our recent past, of this century and the last. These predecessors have created new techniques, tested old, developed skills and fought for their and your rights to engage in the occupation and location of your own choice, as only those with an absolute commitment to hypnosis can imagine. He has afforded everyone an opportunity to re-explore the old trails and simultaneously explore and blaze new trails for the betterment of society as a whole and of ourselves. This magnificent work is the new standard of hypnosis history. It fills in the blank, recent segment of our lives and occupations, which has never been recorded before. This is a publication we will treasure forever.

Virgil Hayes
02/30/11

## Dwight F. Damon, DC, DNGH, OB

National Guild of Hypnotists founding/charter member 1950
President - National Guild of Hypnotists, Inc.1986 - 2011
President - National Federation of Hypnotists
(NFH 104, OPEIU, AFL/CIO-CLC) 1994 - 2011
Associate Editor - *Journal of Hypnotism* 1951-1954
Associate Editor/Columnist - *Herald of Psychology* 1949 -1950
Editor/Publisher - *New Journal of Hypnotism*® 1986 -1988
Editor/Publisher - *Journal of Hypnotism*® 1988 - 2011
Founder, Executive Editor/Publisher - *Hypno-Gram*® 1987 - 2011
Motivation and hypnotism author/teacher, editor/publisher
and columnist since 1950's
Founder/President - Success Seekers® Clubs and
Ideas For Success Seminars® 1970 -1973

-Entertainment-
TV Personality WOC-TV 1956 -1959 & WMUR-TV 1960 - 1980

Books for the entertainment industry:
*Making Magic Your Business*
*TV's Original Balloonatic*©
*Balloonatrix*©

Books in progress:
*The Granite Showman*
*HYPNOmotivation*©

# Preface

Welcome, dear reader, to a lifetime of memories about hypnotism. As you read this book, you will experience our growth as a separate and distinct profession through the past 60+ years. You will also have an opportunity to meet the heros, villains, and characters who played a part in our contemporary history.

But, most of all, I hope you will gain a greater appreciation of how we reached our present status as a profession, and how much more we have to accomplish in the future.

Sometimes it seems as if we've achieved *in spite of*, but I prefer to think we've achieved *because of*. I'm sure you're wondering because of *what*? Well, just read the book and you'll soon know the answers.

In this age of electronic editing we have become used to "enhanced" photos and printed materials, but what you will find in the following chapters is not enhanced at all—the photos and print articles have come from my personal archives of almost sixty-five years …

The "recollections" mentioned in the book title have come from the deep recesses of my memory with occasional assistance from several friends and colleagues who also still have good recall.

I invite you to join me on a nostalgic regression to 1947 in New England when I bought my first book about hypnotism, Konradi Leitner's *Master Key To Hypnotism*, and then attended my first class at the Boston Hypnotism Center with Dr Rexford L. North in 1949. That is when my fascination, or "love affair," with hypnosis began. I remember it as if it were yesterday, and I would like to have you accompany me on a journey through those years as I recall experiencing them. If you enjoy reading about it just half as much as I enjoyed living it, I know you will have had a good time … because I certainly did!

Dwight F. Damon

7/2011

# Contents

# Chapter 1
## Why *Hypnotic Recollections?*

Many scholarly books are available regarding the work of the pioneers of hypnosis/hypnotherapy, such as Milton Erickson and others, who followed in the footprints of Mesmer, Braid, Charcot, et al. Most of the books on the history of hypnotism were written about those early practitioners and their ideas. Then, there is much written about those in more recent times, such as Freud, Cooke, Van Pelt, Erickson, etc. The book you now hold in your hands is devoted primarily to the 20th Century history of a different professional group—the hypnosis professionals who are *not* a part of the licensed community of mainstream health care. To paraphrase author Robert Heinlein, "A generation (of hypnotists) which ignores its history has no past—and no future."

Our researchers (recollectors) are helping to present facts and fallacies of what could be called, *The Development of Hypnotism as a Separate and Distinct Profession in the 20th Century*—which is really too long a title. Although it is an accurate description for this book, I feel *Hypnotic Recollections* is more to the point. Our contributors are not merely researchers, but also "recollectors" who, for the most part, actually experienced the real-life information which they contributed to this book.

So, rather than presenting just a formal, fact-filled, *History of the Development of Hypnotism as a Separate and Distinct Profession in the 20th Century, Hypnotic Recollections* became the working title as we gathered reminiscences of professional hypnotists to address the subject more intimately. These hypnotic recollections and hard facts, combined with past experiences, give us a vivid oral history of the era of 1945-2011. It has been collected, researched, and is now presented for the first time in written format.

To be as complete and accurate as possible requires not only a great deal of research, but also interviews with and oral recollections by those who were active in the field as long as 65 years ago to back my recollections and those of others. I've spoken to hypnotists who belonged to many different organizations ... some who had retired long ago and never thought about hypnotism since ... some who had been reported as deceased, and even one who had been in a witness protection program. It was important to get information from all of these folks and combine it with printed material we have in my archives from those years.

Do you know which hypnotist was married to a movie star? Which one invented an artificial heart? Which one did time for putting a contract out on a competitor? Which one is a TV star? Which one busted the "Gypsy" ordinance in Orlando, Florida? Which one was said by sports writers to reputedly have an "evil eye"? Which one lost battles with the FDA and the IRS? Which one tried to legally change his first name to "Doctor"? … And, which one actually did?

Do you know about the many battles with the "elitist" group of licensed health professionals … about the legislative battles we've fought and won … which of our groups fought unfair legislation and which group simply claimed the credit for any positive accomplishments?

If you haven't been in the profession for 65 years, you probably don't know all of this, as well as other interesting facts about our professional development. After you read *Hypnotic Recollections* we hope you will pass this information down to future generations of hypnotists and, most of all, we hope you'll have a greater appreciation for what has been achieved.

*Hypnotic Recollections* presents both the good and the bad, but more importantly, the *true* facts about the art, science, and philosophy of what the "elitists" commonly refer to as the "lay hypnotists." Lest we receive a label of being a sensationalized version of our hypnotism history, let's start by presenting the basis of our professional development.

I told you why this history is needed, but perhaps you wonder why I became the "chosen one" to write it. Well, the truth is that I seem to be the only one still standing who can remember back to the beginning of the era we're discussing. When I started working with Dr Rexford L. North, I was at an age when my enthusiasm was all-encompassing. I experienced, absorbed, and therefore can recall so much that it seems as if it was only a short while ago, not 65 years, that I began my interest in hypnotism and life as a hypnotist.

Along the way, as I have been writing and researching the late '40s and early '50s, I have often reached out to long-time friends and colleagues in the field to substantiate my recollections. Colleagues such as John Hughes, Arnold Levison, and Maurice Kershaw have received my calls to check their memories or personal libraries regarding the correct year, name, or place in verifying what I recollect.

So, there are numerous "recollectors" I want to give credit and thanks to for helping me be complete and factual with the contents of this book. What you are reading are oral recollections, which are now becoming historical facts that will be available for future researchers.

My hope is that you will find this information as exciting as I did when I actually experienced it during the past 65 years. You may feel that it is slanted towards covering more about the National Guild of Hypnotists, but the truth is that it has been the Guild, its officers, and members that made it possible for me to conceive, believe, and achieve our "Big Idea"—*a separate and distinct profession*—the practice of hypnotism in which *we help ordinary, everyday people with ordinary, everyday problems.*

When the National Guild of Hypnotists was founded in 1950-51 the membership was roughly 90-95% stage hypnotists and hobbyists, and 5-10% office practitioners. Now, 61 years later, the balance has switched to the exact opposite, with stage hypnotists being the smaller percentage. The Guild, however, still recognizes its heritage, which was the seed from which our profession sprouted.

In the late '40s and early '50s, women in the field of hypnotism were virtually unheard of until Joan Brandon on the East Coast and Pat Collins on the West Coast established themselves as professional stage hypnotists. We'll discuss these two ladies more in another chapter, but being able to meet and become acquainted with professionals of this caliber made a distinct impression on me at my young age. In addition, my work on the *Journal of Hypnotism* and my role as a "roving reporter" while serving as a radioman in the US Coast Guard took me to many places I might not have traveled to otherwise.

When I was attending Emerson College, I played all sorts of venues with my hypnotic act; banquets, sleezy night clubs, and theaters. When I served in the Coast Guard I also performed in other countries,various US cities, USO clubs, and officers' or non-com clubs. When I went back to college on the GI Bill, hypnosis shows and classes helped put food on our table. So, you see, I have a longtime love affair with the world of hypnotism, and thankfully a long memory that will help me to share some wonderful history with you.

In reading *Hypnotic Recollections* please keep in mind that in the late '40s and early '50s photo-copiers hadn't been invented and many popular-selling hypnotism "books" were, for the most part, actually mimeographed booklets, which sold for $1 - $3. A 10-week hypnotism course, meeting once a week, was $50, payable in weekly installments. Television was in its infancy and there was no Internet or e-mail. It was an era of rent controls, price controls, and families living on wages of $40 or $50 a week. However, it was still an era of live entertainment in theaters and nightclubs, many of which featured stage hypnotists, but which were on the verge of fading away, as I will discuss a bit further on.

## 079.157.010 - HYPNOTHERAPIST
Alternate Title: Master Hypnotist
Alternate Title: Hypnotist
As defined in
*The Dictionary of Occupational Titles*

Published by
The United States Department of Labor

"Hypnotherapist induces hypnotic state in client to increase motivation or alter behavior or alter behavior pattern through hypnosis. Consults with client to determine the nature of problem. Prepares client to enter hypnotic states by explaining how hypnosis works and what client will experience. Tests subjects to determine degrees of physical and emotional suggestibility. Induces hypnotic techniques of hypnosis based on interpretation of tests results and analysis of client's problem. May train client in self-hypnosis conditioning."

*Several hypnotists are credited with placing this definition in the Directory of Occupational Titles in 1973 (see pg. 48). The title is still accepted although other professional titles have also been established, e.g. Consulting Hypnotist. The newer Consulting Hypnotist title was developed to give exclusivity to the profession and avoid overlapping with other licensed health professions who utilize hypnotherapy as a modality in the practice of psychology, medicine, psychotherapy, etc*

*As far as who gets credit for the listing it shouldn't make any big difference since "Bookie" (187/167-014) and "Strip-Tease Dancer" (151.047-010) are also included among the hundreds of occupations that are listed in the directory.*

*No updates of the Directory have been published since 1973.*

# Chapter 2
## The Art, Science, and Philosophy of the Practice of Hypnotism

When a document of this kind is written it could be to satisfy the academics and intellectuals in other professions, who may consider themselves qualified to judge what we do. This judgement is normally based on the protocols of their practices, which are not acceptable in this situation. The Art, Science, and Philosophy of the practice of hypnotism document was not written to impress, or to justify. It was also not written to control practicing hypnotists. It was written because the practice of hypnotism, although said to be thousands of years old, has just finally emerged in the 21st century as a separate and distinct profession and there is a need to develop our own protocols regarding the principles and practice of our profession.

You may ask why, in *Hypnotic Recollections,* are we discussing the art, science, and philosophy of hypnotism? Where did it come from? Was it channeled to me from those who have passed on ... Dr Rexford L. North ... Ormond McGill, Harry Arons, Charles Tebbetts, or even Dr Maxwell Maltz? Have the voices of the ancients: Mesmer, Braid, Elliotson, Coué, and the temple priests of Egypt and Greece come to us with the wisdom of the ages? The answer to all these questions is no, but we need to lay the groundwork to understanding and appreciating what our pioneer hypnotists have achieved in the interest of both practitioners and clients. When documents of this type are presented they are the result of thoughtful teamwork, and I have a group of top professionals on my team as president of the National Guild of Hypnotists. My past and present cabinet members are: Jacob Bimblich, MA, BCH, CI, OB; Shaun Brookhouse, MA, CMI, DNGH, OB; Anthony DeMarco, LLB, FNGH, OB; Elsom Eldridge, Jr., EdM, OB; Larry Garrett, CH, OB; Reverend C. Scot Giles, DMin, OB, and Richard Harte, PhD, CMI, DNGH, OB, all of whom have the best interest of our profession at heart.

*The Art of Hypnosis*: As professional hypnotists we are concerned with achieving maximum results for each and every client who comes to us for help with a problem. From the beginning or our education and training we must strive to attain the intellectual and practical knowledge, combined with hands-on experience, that allows us to confidently and competently assess a client's presenting problem with a thorough intake interview that provides us with his or her desired goal. Once information is acquired, we must provide the proper induction, programming, and comfortable emergence to achieve optimal results.

*The Science of Hypnosis*: Since there are many theories of how and why hypnosis occurs, we must keep abreast of advancements made by researchers, but never lose track of the fact that not everything in life can be explained in the laboratory. The mind/body connection and the knowledge that each human body contains a self-contained chemical factory, extensive communication network, impressive mental and physical defenses, and an innate operating system, encourages us to work in harmony with all of these built-in resources as we guide a client into self-hypnosis and feed back, as positive suggestions, positive programming derived from his or her initial interview.

*The Philosophy of Hypnosis*: First and foremost, we must do no harm. The mental and physical well-being of each client is the prime requisite of every ethical and professional hypnotist. We must always maintain a strictly professional relationship with a client, avoiding any impropriety. Clients who present with obvious medical or psychological problems should be accepted only with a written referral from a licensed health-care professional.

I believe that the professional practice of hypnotism and the resultant state of hypnosis are normal and natural to life and must not be presented as mysticism or pseudo-science in any manner. In keeping with our philosophy, our goal must be to help ordinary, everyday people with ordinary, everyday problems.

As the author/recollector of these personal remembrances and facts, I was actually involved with the hypnotism era of 1945-2010, and it has been a matter of comparing many various interviews with my own life experience in my goal to be as accurate as possible in recollecting that 65-year time span.

This book not only is about another era, but is also about a special professional hypnotism genre, which the elitist establishment (licensed health professionals) often disparagingly referring to "lay hypnotists." As far as *that* label is concerned, we find that a definition of "lay," according to *Webster's New World Dictionary* is, *"not belonging to or connected with a given profession; nonprofessional,"* and doesn't describe the several thousand male and female professional hypnotists around the world who help ordinary, everyday people with ordinary, everyday problems on an ongoing basis.

Decidedly, the majority of hypnotists who are in practice also conduct themselves as professionals, which is, according to *Webster's, "a person who does something with great skill."*

The primary definition of "professional," according to *Webster's,* also is: *"of, engaged in, or worthy of the high standards of a profession,"* and the definition of "profession" is *"a vocation or occupation requiring advanced education and training, and involving intellectual skills, as medicine, law, theology, engineering, teaching, etc."*

One man's "Big Idea" that developed in the 1980s through the National Guild of Hypnotists and has finally become a reality on entering the present century, was that the professional practice of hypnotism is not an *industry*, but a *profession.* As you read *Hypnotic Recollections,* it is my hope that it will give you a better appreciation of what actually has transpired during the past half century or more in the development of the art, science, and philosophy of the practice of hypnotism to create a separate and distinct profession.

*Hypnotic Recollections* has actually been a work-in-progress for the past 60 years, and includes personally experienced bits and pieces, collected as an oral history. I want to acknowledge my "recollectors" who helped me put the bits and pieces together: Joann Abrahamsen, Jacob Bimblich, Norbert Bakas, Cal Banyan, Maureen Banyan, George Baranowski, Paula Baranowski, Roy Cage, Anthony DeMarco, Elsom Eldridge, Larry Garrett, Marilyn Gordon, Sandi Graves, Richard Harte, Martha Harrison, Virgil Hayes, Jeff Higley, John C. Hughes, Marx Howell, Roy Hunter, C. Scot Giles, Shirley Kein, Jerry Kein, Maurice Kershaw, Al Krasner, Layne Keck, Arnold Levison, Joe B. McCawley, Patricia MacIsaac, Caroline Miller, Curtis Drake Morley, Don Mottin, Ed Morris, Don Rice, and all those who helped with even the slimmest clue to assist me in my quest for all the facts. All of these hypnotists gave me help tracking down people I wanted to reminisce with. They helped me to find out if certain people were even still alive and to clarify events that I needed extra help in detailing or authenticating.

For accuracy, I must state that even though this book uses the word *history* in its subtitle (*Hypnotic Recollections - The History of The Development of Hypnotism as a Separate and Distinct Profession in the 20th Century*), there are no references to sources, since this is an oral history compiled over half a century. I have been careful to track many stories to verify their truthfulness and have succeeded for the most part, or I did not include the recollections in the book.

Teachers have always taught their hypnotism students about the Sleep Temples, Mesmer, Braid, Charcot, Esdaile, et al. Some zealous teachers even mention the possibility that hypnosis occurred with Adam and Eve according to the stories of the Bible and the Talmud. Dr John C. Hughes has written, among other books, *The Illustrated History of Hypnotism,* a scholarly text, which was cited by prominent psychologist/best-selling author, Dr Edith Fiore, as "a monumental history … charting the development of hypnotism from ancient times to the start of the modern era," which is where we start our journey.

Professor Maurice Kershaw, in Canada, has amassed a wonderful research library of rare hypnotism first-editions and also presents an outstanding lecture on our profession's ancient history.

The monumental work of these men is important for our understanding of how *hypnosis* has evolved through the ages. However, until now, we haven't been introducing students to the history of the development of *hypnotism* as a separate and distinct profession in the United States since the end of World War II. This, I believe, is also very important because it is *our* history and it will continue to be created as today's hypnotism graduates become the new pioneers and carry on the legacy that has been passed down to them.

What wonderful chapters will be added to the saga? Will we continue with our own educational processes? Will we have many more post-secondary approved schools? Will there be our own educationally recognized colleges, or perhaps specialized curricula in main-line degree-granting institutions? Will our present-day practitioners continue to strengthen the profession we have worked so hard to establish?

I believe that all these things can happen, but I can't guarantee it. I am willing, however, to predict that someday a student working on his or her PhD thesis will use this book to research the facts as presented in these pages. And although they might not be found anywhere else in print, we wouldn't have included them if we didn't believe they were true.

We are hypnotists, not prognosticators, so we can only wait and see what the next 65 years will bring. As professional hypnotists, however, we also know that if you can conceive an idea, and believe it, you can also achieve it. Rear Admiral Alan B. Shepard, Jr., who holds the distinction of being the first American to journey into space, often told of how, even as a youngster growing up in Derry, NH, he wanted to be the first man to travel in outer space, and it came to pass. He conceived, believed, and achieved. We have done the same to create our profession, and will continue in the future.

The successful professionals we have interviewed didn't just affirm, conceive, or aspire to achieve, they took action steps to accomplish their goals. Patricia MacIsaac, busy consulting hypnotist and my co-author of *HypnoMotivation®*, can tell you personally that "positive thinking without positive action is worthless." You will realize that as we trace the development of our profession in the United States during the past 61 years.

We might ask why it is that the majority of practitioners are not readily team players. Why do they become islands unto themselves in so many ways? Could it be because almost everyone who studies the art, science, and philosophy of hypnotism starts out with the same negative subconscious desire ... not necessarily a desire to be in a helping profession ... not really to build a lucrative income as a hypnotist ... not actually to help mankind with our wonderful modality?

If it isn't any of the reasons mentioned, what is it that most everyone has in the deepest recesses of their minds that leads them to study hypnotism? Very simple … new students want to learn *to hypnotize themselves and others.* I believe that is usually the basic reason–*to learn to hypnotize themselves and others*—probably stemming from beliefs they have about hypnotism … the common myths we all know about. However, later, as professional hypnotists, they will spend time removing these same myths about hypnosis from the belief systems of others.

 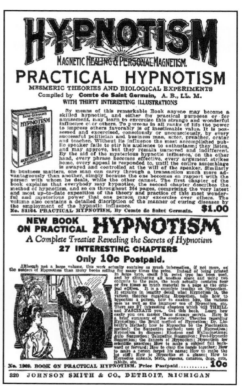

*In the early 1900s you could purchase a how-to book on hypnotism for as little as ten cents (see pages 15-16)*

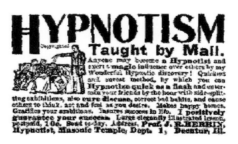

9

# MASTER COURSE in *Hypnotism*

### BY HARRY ARONS

#### HYPNOTIST, LECTURER, WRITER

only **$1.98** Postpaid

*Photo Illustrated*

**SHOWS** *you*

HOW TO ..
- Hypnotize quickly
- Hypnotize by phone

*TELLS you* • Hypnotize in public for money
- Hypnotize individuals and groups

**ALL SECRETS REVEALED IN THIS SPECTACULAR PHOTO ILLUSTRATED BOOK!**

An expert hypnotist takes you into a new, strange world — reveals in simple, direct-to-you language the methods . . . techniques . . . practices of the professional hypnotist. Jealously-guarded "tricks-of-the-trade" are laid bare before your eyes . . . you learn how suitable subjects are hypnotized a: a glance or a snap of the fingers, by phone or even by mail . . . you'll have at your fingertips the conditions and inner secrets behind the electrifying, almost unbelievable hypnotic feats of the masters. Profusely illustrated with see-how photographs of beautiful models undergoing hypnosis . . . complete — yet concise and to the point . . . the MASTER COURSE IN HYPNOTISM is designed especially for people who want to learn how to hypnotize — as quickly and easily as possible!

**A PSYCHOLOGIST SAYS**

The MASTER COURSE IN HYPNOTISM "is a fine, authoritative course on the subject".

Dr. Werner C. Michel

**A PSYCHIATRIST SAYS**

Your book "gives the best methods I know, in a concise and clear manner".

Siegfried A. Low, M. D.

**NOW EASIER TO LEARN**

It's simpler than you think to learn hypnotism. You don't need to be a master-mind, or to have any special powers. Most earnest persons of good intelligence can learn how to hypnotize to some degree. It's just a matter of knowing the methods and developing a knack or flair through practice. Send only $1.98 for the MASTER COURSE today . . . it may prove your "Open Sesame" into a world of new opportunities for fun and profit!

**MONEY BACK GUARANTEE**

# POWER PUBLISHERS, 790 Broad St., Newark 2, N. J.

---

# HYPNOTISM, SUCCESS and YOU

It is a tragedy indeed that most people "muddle" through life without ever having known the exaltation of success or the exhilaration of public recognition. The pain and futility of this sombre drama is heightened by the fact that this sad condition could have been avoided had the individual had an understanding of the powers of the human psyche and the principles through which these powers could be released.

There is no "magic" in the art of successful living. Self-confidence, positive attitudes, personal magnetism, and happiness are attained through the application of positive and specific principles of constructive thinking that are "suggested" to the subconscious mind through the medium of hypnotism. It is therefore the hypnotist and his medium, hypnotism, which is the "key" not only to the release of this wonderful "Life Force," but also to the direction of that force for better living, success, and ultimate recognition in our highly competitive society.

The way to attain these highly desirable ends and to increase your earning capacity at the same time is to enroll with Melvin Powers at the Wilshire School of Hypnotism, and so become another one of his highly successful students.

Stop being a failure! Enroll now. Happiness can be yours! Enroll now.

**YOUR LIFE CAN BE A SUCCESSFUL EXCITING ADVENTURE!** Take our course and be convinced! The course can also be taken with Dr. Rexford North in Boston. Those living in the East will find his course thorough and most satisfactory.

For those who cannot take the course in person, we suggest the text book for the course, *Hypnotism Revealed*, by Melvin Powers. It will be the best one dollar investment you ever made.

Send for

**"Hypnotism Revealed"**
Priced at $1.00

Address all correspondence to:

## WILSHIRE SCHOOL OF HYPNOTISM
Dept. HJ
1334 Wilshire Blvd.
Los Angeles 17, California

---

# LEARN HYPNOSIS AND SELF-HYPNOSIS
### With Frank Shames and Richard Harte

A workshop course specifically designed to teach techniques of hypnosis and self hypnosis and their applications in the helping professions - sales, business, sports, and self-improvement. Because of the individualized instruction and practice sessions the group is limited to ten.

Dates: March 12, 13 & 14 Time: 9 am to 5 pm each day
For reservations or further information, call 490-0721
Alpha Hypnosis Programs, 201 East 37th St. NY, NY 10016

---

*OLDEST SCHOOL IN THE MIDDLE WEST*

# HYPNOTISM INSTITUTE of CHICAGO

Personal Instruction Under Direction of
EDWIN L. BARON, Ph.B.

Graduate, Loyola University — Post-Graduate, University of Chicago

*(Featured in LIFE, TIME, LOOK, NEWSWEEK, CORONET, Etc.)*

**Hypnotism Institute of Chicago**

64 West Randolph St.    Chicago, Ill.

*In the 1950s hypnotism advertising started upgrading and book prices were now up to $1.98 for a "Master Course in Hypnotism."*

# Chapter 3
## Early Years of Education in Other Professions

Before organized education in the "professions" entered the picture around 1918, you could become a "professional" doctor, lawyer, or dentist by attending night school. Surprisingly, even in the 1970s, you could still obtain a law degree by correspondence through the Blackstone School of Law. Medicine, chiropractic, osteopathy, dentistry, optometry, and podiatry also have all gone through the phase of short-term training in their formative years in the United States, but these professions now require hands-on, classroom experience, not night school, mail-order courses, apprenticing, or Internet training.

We must remember that many present day professions in the United States started out much as hypnotists did. In early rural America, dentists pulled teeth and cut hair in the same chair ... physicians became "doctors" by riding with a "doc" who was already established ... and lawyers "read" for the law. Part of the folklore about the prestigious Mayo Clinic is that the founding Mayo Brothers' grandfather became a "doc" in that quaint do-it-yourself fashion of an early era, by riding with and assisting a "doc." So, as the country was spreading out it was basically a matter of apprenticing to a mentor who was already recognized professionally in order to learn and earn your own professional title.

As these other professions have evolved, their educational standards have naturally kept pace, and the day could come when educational standards for hypnotism practitioners could be on par with the various licensed health professions.

In the meantime, there is a large group of pioneers who have laid the groundwork for our profession. They have been, and currently are, advancing the art, science, and philosophy of the professional practice of hypnotism. These are the people who will make it happen.

Until the hypnotism profession is widely accepted and there is more of a demand for full-time practitioners, many hypnotists are maintaining the status quo of two careers, but there are still many who aspire to be full-time practitioners now.

It is imperative that those who have already established their professional practices through experience and client results should be willing to carry the responsibility of continuing the growth of the profession through mentoring and sharing with newcomers. Dr Richard Harte and I were recently discussing the fact that back in that era professional hypnotists were very secretive with each other about techniques, fees—everything—they acted more like rivals than colleagues! We have moved way beyond that attitude in this modern age of Internet sharing of information, continuing education, professional publications, and large professional conventions.

If a city should have a lot of professional signs for consulting hypnotists' offices gradually appearing it's only natural that the public will notice. I would say that people seeing this would assume there are more consulting hypnotists opening offices because they help a lot of clients in that town or city, and there is a need to be filled. A number of the same observant public would also assume that all these consulting hypnotists must get results or they wouldn't be opening offices. This perception would then help to build the acceptance, anticipation, and belief that make for successful clients. Would this be a good thing for everybody? Of course!

Now, you may not agree with what I just stated about more practitioners being a good thing, but I saw this happen in the early '60s when the practice of chiropractic was not yet licensed in Massachusetts, but the town of Salem, NH, which was right on the border had no MDs . . . just 28 chiropractors with busy practices.

Our educational concepts have grown immensely, along with our development as a profession, particularly during the past quarter century. Many hypnotism texts are updated annually, CDs, DVDs and MP3s have been added, and classroom hours increased. Consequently, we continue to see more competent and confident graduates coming into the field. However, successful professionals I have interviewed through the years didn't just affirm, conceive, or aspire to achieve, they took action steps to accomplish their goals. Once again, *positive thinking without positive action is worthless.* You will see this as we trace the development of our profession during the past 60 plus years.

It is quite obvious that we have reached a "tipping point" in the practice of hypnotism as a profession while moving into the 21st century. Now, by knowing where we came from, we should be able to build on it and continue to expand. In this day and age, we should be open to sharing and helping each other, not like the earlier days when hypnotists kept their supposed secrets from colleagues. The truth, of course, is that there is really nothing new —just improvements, modernizations, if you prefer.

So, if we are to grow even more in the profession that has been established by the "good old boys," we need to work together for the common good and get away from the mistake of believing our own personal publicity. After all, how many people can actually be "The World's Greatest Hypnotist" at the same time? If you check the Internet, you'd be surprised at how many think they are!

Over 60 years ago, Dr Rexford L. North cautioned me to avoid the "hypnotists' disease of believing your own publicity." He was talking to me as a stage hypnotist, but I think that even professional hypnotists need to start thinking of the common good of the profession as well as their own personal practices.

Egocentric personalities and non-conformist attitudes restrict practitioners' true ability to advance. Perhaps those practitioners need a few sessions as clients of a competent hypnotist to effect a change in their own professional and personal lives. Unfortunately, the profession, by its nature, seems to develop more individualists than team players, and a lot of them succumb to the "hypnotists' disease" mentioned by Dr North ... *believing their own publicity.*

If every practitioner was actively dedicated, enthusiastic, and passionate about the art, science, and philosophy of hypnotism, think of how much faster the reality of a separate and distinct profession could have been achieved. Keep in mind while reading this book that the study of hypnotism, and particularly the professional practice of hypnotism, has always attracted independent thinking individuals, for the most part. However, when this type of individual *does* become a team player, there is a dynamic relationship that benefits all concerned parties.

Let's think for a minute about why John Doe is attracted to studying hypnotism. Is it because from the time he was a child he wanted to be a hypnotist when he grew up? Not too likely, wouldn't you agree? Is it because he wants to use this wonderful tool to help mankind? Very possible, if he has done a lot of reading and research about the profession. Or, is it because he is just naturally curious and believes the myths that came from books and movies ... which, by the way, he will later spend his professional life telling his clients aren't true?

Well, if he was exposed to those myths of hypnotists "having control," etc., couldn't his inner self (subconscious) want him to learn to hypnotize himself and others? There's nothing really wrong with that desire if it brings the interested party to study with an instructor who teaches his or her students the ethical art, science, and philosophy of hypnotism. They need to seek out an instructor whose graduates learn to use this wonderful tool to help themselves, their families, and those who will become clients.

*In the late 1940s/early 1950s the images used to sell how to books and publicize hypnotism articles in magazines was decidedly suggestive. These images perpetuated the age-old myths and public beliefs about hypnotism.*

# Chapter 4
## The Beginning of a New Era for Hypnotism

Can you learn to hypnotize from a book? Well, sort of, but it really is a lot easier to have personal instruction, so that you have an experienced hypnotist to guide you and critique what you are doing. My first interest in learning hypnotism was with Konradi Leitner's book, *Master Key To Hypnotism*, purchased through the mail from an ad in a pulp magazine. I was a student at Cushing Academy in Ashburnham, Massachusetts, and practiced, often unsuccessfully, on fellow students, faculty members, and dorm masters who were willing to volunteer.

For the most part, prior to the late '40s and '50s, people learned to hypnotize from a book or from someone who was already accomplished in the art. As you'll see, the actual establishment of live, organized classes, using written notes and hands-on demonstrations, didn't become common until after World War II. Then the practice of hypnotism started to grow to what it is now, 60 plus years later, a separate and distinct profession.

Before television, there had been a lot of venues for hypnotists and there were many successful stage hypnotists who played them. However, those stage hypnotists who were interested in additional income started thinking ahead about how to make additional money by sharing their knowledge and providing the inquiring public with the "secrets" of hypnotism. Many of these hypnotism entrepreneurs also became successful teachers and publishers of hypnosis materials for the general public.

Pulp magazines of that era had full-page ads which urged readers to "*Learn to Hypnotize Yourself and Others.*" The magazines were, for the most part, comic books or fiction magazines popular from 1896 through the 1950s, printed on cheap wood pulp paper with ragged, untrimmed edges. At 10¢ each, they had a wide readership.

Ads were prevalent for booklets and mail-order courses from such authors as Konradi Leitner, Bruno Furst, David Lustig, Walter Gibson (author of the "Shadow"), Rexford North, Harry Arons, Melvin Powers, Nelmar, etc., all of whom published and sold mostly through mail order companies they owned, such as The Hypnotism Center, Power Publishers, Nelmar Publications, Nelson Enterprises, and Wilshire Publications.

For many years, the "dream book" of magic, jokes, novelties, and things to buy or plans to build was, for most youngsters, the *Johnson Smith Company's Catalog of 5000 Novelties*. It is interesting to see, in our hypnotism museum, the 1914 edition of this catalog and an ad for a booklet of *25 Lessons in Hypnotism, with Magnetic Healing and Personal Magnetism,* listed for 25¢. A succeeding catalog in the late '30s and early '40s listed the same little hypnotism booklet, now expanded to 264 pages, including "Thirty Interesting Illustrations," selling for $1.00. However, probably for the budget-minded student, the catalog still listed 10¢ and 25¢ booklets of 25 lessons. Just think, in those days, for as little as $1.25 a customer could assemble a hypnotism library, without even being charged for postage and handling!

Prior to that time, the American public's concept of hypnotism was generally based on books and movies, such as the 1919 German silent film, *The Cabinet of Dr Caligari*, and other stories that appeared in books and on the silver screen. The mystique of hypnotism provided many more stories as movies started to talk and the film industry grew.

These stories usually featured mysterious powers possessed by hypnotists, who were often depicted as being somewhat evil, and used their "powers" for nefarious and/or evil activities. Come to think of it, that first book I bought was from an ad featuring a mysterious-looking hypnotist with sparks shown coming from his hands, which were pointed at a rather sexily dressed (for the time) young lady. I was probably 14 or 15 years old at the time, but the ad did catch my eye and the artwork could have been part of the motivation to purchase the book with money from my meager savings.

It was all pretty mysterious, and of course, the professional hypnotists wanted to keep it that way to enhance their success as entertainers. The hypnotism profession as we now know it in the US hadn't even been envisioned, so stage hypnotists were primarily responsible for keeping hypnotism alive and active during all those years before the Second World War, and even into the '50s and '60s.

There had been numerous stage hypnotists in America in the late 1800s and early 1900s, along with phrenologists, magnetic healers, and even hypno-healing practitioners. One hypnotist who still stands out as having a positive and beneficial approach was Emil Coué, known for his famous self-empowering phrase, "Tous les jours, a tous points de vue, je vais de mieux en mieux." "Every day, in every way, I am getting better and better." He was very popular when he came to America and spread his message personally in the early 1920s. As a side note, I might mention how Coué's concept played a part in my personal life some 80 years after he formulated it and brought it to America.

The phrase was powerful self-hypnosis then and still is today. In 2006, my late wife Maggie was battling cancer when peritonitis occurred and her progress became even more threatened. I made posters for her hospital room, positioning them where she could easily see them and repeat the Coué mantra. When she, to all appearances and tests, pulled through that episode, her oncologist and the nurse supervisor asked if they could reproduce the posters for use on that floor. I told them about Coué and said I was sure he would be more than happy if they did. Maggie had pulled through the very serious peritonitis situation, but unfortunately it reoccurred again a short time later and her body was just too depleted for another positive response.

In the world of hypnotism nothing really changed, improved, or advanced until WW II ended, late in 1945. Dramatic changes were about to occur in the real-world application of hypnosis methods in the medical and psychiatric wards of VA hospitals. Physicians and therapists were treating WW II veterans for "shell-shock," which is now referred to as Post Traumatic Stress Disorder (PTSD). Basically they were still using psycho/medical treatments developed years before with veterans of the First World War.

However, a new approach showed promising benefits with the use of hypnosis to treat these mentally injured warriors. It opened the eyes of physicians, psychiatrists, psychologists, and others to some very positive results for their patients. It was this work using hypnotic intervention with WW II veterans that aroused much more professional interest, and many more licensed health professional who were already skilled in the art started using hypnotism techniques in their practices.

Emile Coué
1857-1926

*Couéism caught the public interest and spread from Europe to America in the early 1920s.*

17

*In the 1940s and 50s, before TV, there were night clubs, theaters and many venues for the stage hypnotist.*

# Chapter 5
## Stage Performers Become Teachers

Between 1945-1955, as show venues faded away due to the new entertainment showplace (TV), show business didn't provide as much work for professional hypnotists. Even nightclubs were starting to book fewer live acts as they struggled to stay in business with the new competition of TV. With fewer bookings, more stage hypnotists put their knowledge and experience to good use teaching others how to hypnotize.

Before television, there had been an abundance of live bookings and many successful stage hypnotists to play them, but there always were a number of performers who developed an extra stream of income teaching, publishing, and selling hypnosis instruction. So, it came to be, in that era, that many licensed health professionals learned the rudiments of hypnotic techniques from stage hypnotists.

Even as many performers throughout the US were getting off the road and teaching the basics of hypnotism to eager students, most still performed in their local and regional venues. Seasoned and knowledgeable showmen also became the pioneers of the new hypnotism profession, which would emerge more fully in coming years.

Harry Arons, Dave Elman, Rexford North, Melvin Powers and many East Coast hypnotists had been regulars at the "Borscht Belt" resorts in the Catskills and nightclubs in Atlantic City, New York, Boston, and Montreal. Others, such as John Calvert, Tex Morton, The Great Pauline (Joseph Poulin), Flint (Herbert T.), Ormond McGill, Rajah Raboid (Maurice P. Kitchen), and many more had appeared across the country in vaudeville and large theaters. But now vaudeville was almost completely dead and those large theaters were installing wide screens, which eliminated large show stages. It was the development of television plus wide-screen movies that was changing the professional lives of stage hypnotists and other entertainers.

Coming on to the scene with a family connection to many different acts through my parents' entertainment agency, was exciting for me. I had been performing magic professionally as "New England's Youngest Professional Magician" since the age of thirteen, and worked through my teens in big theaters as those venues were phasing out live attractions.

When I studied and consequently went to work with Dr North, the nightclubs were following the demise of live theater shows. We were probably the last show to play the ATC theater circuit in New England, which still had stages suitable for our Hilarious Hypnosis show or our midnight spook show.

I was privileged to know showmen such as Ormond McGill, John Calvert, and Virgil (Virgil Mulkey) who presented large illusion shows on world tours and had hypnotism segments in their shows. They were very accomplished hypnotists as well as magicians. McGill often made hypnotism the major part of his show, while Calvert, who had also had gained fame in movies as the "Falcon," featured large illusions, and usually only a short comedic hypnotism presentation with several volunteers standing "in one" before the main curtain. This gave his stage crew time to set the next magical illusion, but the hypnotism was also a full-evening show when required. Virgil and his lovely wife Julie, told me that hypnotism was their "ace in the hole" in case something happened to their big show equipment and they still needed to fill a date.

The idea of teaching caught on and there were hypnotism books and courses being offered all over the country by hypnotists who usually based their curricula on someone else's course they had attended or "picked up" and copied. There was really nothing wrong with this because most of the courses were not copyrighted and basically all of them were teaching the same core principles of hypnotism.

Ormond McGill authored the first authoritative book on stage hypnotism, *The Encyclopedia of Genuine Stage Hypnotism*, which was published by Abbott Magic company in 1947, becoming the definitive book of instruction on stage hypnotism. It was responsible for thousands of magic hobbyists and other individuals learning to be stage hypnotists, and it continues to be a popular-selling book almost 65 years later.

A world-traveled showman, McGill also easily moved into the more clinical side of hypnotism through his abilities as a researcher, historian, and author of books and columns. Generously sharing his knowledge, he was an exception to the rule in a very jealous and back-biting profession. Ormond was definitely a gentleman and a gentle man in everything he did. He never had a bad word to say about anybody, even those who cheated him on business deals or took advantage were forgiven.

After writing *The Encyclopedia of Genuine Stage Hypnotism,* he wrote other books for the Boston Hypnotism Center, Westwood Publishers, and some major publishers. A prolific and knowledgeable author, McGill produced over 50 books and articles on hypnotism as well as other subjects which drew his interest during his long life (1913-2005). When Delight, Ormond's wife and partner, passed, West Coast magician Chuck Mignosa partnered with him on shows and also acted on his behalf as much as a natural son would have done.

In 1986, when Ormond McGill, Arnold Furst, and I renewed our friendship from the early Hypnotism Center days, a small number of us were devoting our energies to rebuilding the National Guild of Hypnotists membership. The organization had all but died out when Dr North disappeared and there was no longer his leadership.

Did these changes in show business mean the end of stage hypnotism (demonstrational hypnosis) had arrived? Not by a long shot! Was it enjoying a resurgence in popularity? Not really, but audiences still enjoyed hypnotism shows, and organizations such as NGH still had a place for stage hypnotists in their memberships. The Guild could almost be called a "secret" group, not by choice, but because there were only a handful of us who kept in touch, hoping someday to reorganize.

Many of the ancient myths still prevailed with the public in those years; that a hypnotist has the "power" to make people do certain things … that you might not be able to "come out" of hypnosis, that you will tell your innermost secrets, and so forth, and, of course the idea that when you are hypnotized in a stage performance you don't remember what you did on stage. Chatting with Ormond at one of the early NGH conventions, he and I laughingly agreed that one attribute in many stage volunteers might be classified in the DSM-IV as "convenient amnesia."

Arnold Furst, author of *Hypnosis for Salesmen,* was a very active hypnotist advocate and teacher on the West Coast. As a magician and hypnotist he had entertained US servicemen in the South Pacific on USO tours from 1943 - 1946, and during the post-war years he formulated a new approach to teaching hypnosis. Heading back to the Orient, he supplemented his hypnotism shows on US military bases by teaching hypnotism to physicians, dentists, and psychiatrists in civilian hospitals.

Working with a translator in his classes, Arnold became a faculty member at the Hypnotism and Psychological Institute of Tokyo. Furst also enlisted the cooperation of Lester T. Kashiwa, MD, for additional case histories in his book, *How to Prepare and Administer Hypnotic Prescriptions.*

It was said in jest by professional acquaintances on the West Coast that because of Furst's frugality he transported his show, which consisted of a tuxedo and a briefcase, on tramp steamers. He always laughed about the image, although he once said to me that it was somewhat true. In 1955, however, he upgraded his mode of travel as manager of an extensive 2-year world tour of his friend Ormond McGill's hypnotism/magic stage show.

There was room for everybody to teach, although there weren't too many who were interested or had the ability to conduct formal classes. The busiest courses were based in larger metropolitan areas, as in the case of North in

Boston and Arons in New Jersey. Arons also used mailings to licensed health professionals and organized classes in various cities where he could line up his required minimum number of students to make it profitable.

North soon expanded beyond Boston, adding a weekly Carnegie Hall classroom rental in New York City. He soon found the weekly train travel too hectic and the additional financial overhead too draining on his Hypnotism Center in Boston, so NYC was discontinued after a few months.

Dave Elman (born Kopelman), a former vaudeville hypnotist and variety performer, had become the emcee/host of "Hobby Lobby," a popular network radio show broadcast on the CBS, Columbia, and other radio networks in New York City from 1937-'48. Elman had gained the title of "Dean of American Hobbyists" with the show's popularity. I recall listening to it faithfully, as it was rated as one of the top network programs of that time.

During World War II, while working in their NYC Hobby Lobby office late one evening, his wife's attention was drawn to a window in a nearby hotel, where it seemed that someone was playing with a light switch, turning it on and off. Dave reportedly saw that it was more like the dots and dashes of Morse code and called the FBI. Agents spoke with the Elmans and then went to the hotel and arrested Nazi spies, who were giving signals to others relative to US shipping. His son, Larry, told us recently that the Elman family required 24 hour FBI protection when overt threats and attempts were subsequently made on their lives.

It was shortly after this, in 1949, when Dave Elman organized his first course of instruction in hypnotism, similar to Harry Arons' tactic of teaching only licensed health professionals. The curriculum was based on Bernheim, Monroe, and others, with modifications for the health professionals he would be teaching to use in their practices. Just as with Arons' classes, the exclusivity of only licensed health professionals being allowed in class proved to be very popular. However, it was not until years later when his book was republished by Westwood, that the Elman induction and approach to office hypnosis became widely known beyond his medical graduates and was introduced to our practitioners. Currently, his son, Colonel Larry Elman (ret.), who had assisted his dad in the early days of teaching the course, is reviving the Elman name and methods through seminars and workshops.

There was good news on the horizon, though. As TV started to reach more homes, producers were in search of talent to provide entertaining shows, and more promotion-minded stage hypnotists turned to the new medium, scoring some good appearances on top shows.

As I remember, the first hypnotist booked to appear on a major TV show was Ormond McGill, on *Art Linkletter's House Party,* a daytime CBS West

Coast TV show in the early 1950s. He also did several appearances on Art Linkletter's, *People Are Funny Show*, as well as numerous appearances on other television shows.

About the same time, Dr Franz Polgar performed on the CBS TV *Arthur Godfrey Show* from NYC, and other East Coast programs. Polgar was not really a theater-oriented hypnotist, but had established a stellar reputation and repeat business presenting his shows for colleges and community-oriented groups along the East Coast.

Both of these outstanding showmen capitalized on the TV exposure. McGill publicized his "Concert of Hypnotism" in Canada and on the West Coast, and Polgar promoted his lecture-type shows on the East Coast. Naturally, their advertising featured "As seen on TV" or "Direct from TV" and enhanced their marketability to the attending public and prospective show sponsors. These two hypnotists adapted well to working on TV, appeared regularly on a number of shows, and opened the door of this new entertainment medium to other professional stage hypnotists. In fact, Dr Franz Polgar later had his own 15 minute TV show for a short time on CBS TV.

Living back in New England after serving in the US Coast Guard, I became acquainted with Polgar through the Hypnotism Center, and we often picked him up to drive him to nearby dates, as he usually traveled by train or bus from his home base in New York.

So, it would appear that McGill and Polgar were the pioneer hypnotists in modern television. However, the National Association of Broadcasters, in 1965, adopted rules that hypnotism could only be shown, in fiction or fact, in the context of a drama or as a demonstration, as long as the actual induction wasn't seen or heard by the viewing audience. A year or so later, Dr Herbert Spiegel, a New York psychiatrist who advocated the use of hypnosis by MDs as a therapeutic tool, gave a couple of demonstrations at Columbia Medical Center, hypnotizing volunteers via television from a separate location. He warned that the television industry had to guard against the unethical use of "mass hypnosis" to spread any exclusive agenda.

Whether the National Association of Broadcasters was influenced by Spiegel's demonstrations I'm not sure, but their code was changed in 1966. It now stated that hypnosis could only be depicted in the course of a TV drama and the hypnotic trance state could only be shown as part of the story line. Obviously this ruled out the appearance of stage hypnotists on television, but judging from the many who have been on TV programs during the past couple of decades, the rule has been either abolished or ignored.

Previous to this, in the late '40s and early '50s, we often used radio to hypnotize a subject who would "sleep" in an hypnotic trance in a store window as a publicity stunt, either for a local theater appearance or for a mattress company. In the case of the theater appearance the young lady would be removed by ambulance to the theater to be "awakened" on stage at the performance. In the case of the mattress company, I recall standing in the store window with the microphone, explaining the hypnotic state to passersby and also extolling the virtues of the Beautyrest© mattress with its independent springs, etc., when we booked a double-header (theater appearance plus a paid product promotion).

*Before Shopping Malls existed people went downtown to shop. A live "Hypnotic Window Sleep" gathered crowds and garnered a lot of free publicity. Pictured here are Dr Rexford L. North, a young Dwight Damon (Upper left & center) and Dr Zomb (Ormond McGill) in action in various locations. (Upper right & lower photos)*

# Chapter 6
## The General State of Hypnotism in the 1940s -'50s

Let's move along ... where was hypnotism as a profession in 1949-1950 years? Well, Harry Arons was advertising his *Master Course in Hypnotism* by mail for $1.98, and a bit more for personal instruction to groups and individuals. A couple of years later, Arons found his niche in marketing "ethical" hypnotism training courses to licensed health practitioners, such as physicians and dentists, at his Ethical Hypnosis Training Center in South Orange, New Jersey. He also was traveling to various cities around the country. Arons will always be remembered for realizing the financial and professional possibilities in training licensed health professionals to use hypnosis with their patients.

In my younger years, pondering on the terms "ethical" and "genuine" hypnotism, I wondered if anyone ever taught "unethical" or "make-believe" hypnotism. Now, in the 21st century, I shudder when I find what could be considered proponents of both, "unethical" and "make-believe" hypnosis, on the Internet and at some small conferences.

If we don't take ourselves seriously as professionals, how can we expect others to do so?

In 1949, Dr Rexford L. North opened the The Hypnotism Center, the first and only hypnotism school in Boston, where he taught ten weekly lessons in "genuine" hypnotism for a tuition of $50—60 years later that would be equal to a very affordable $450.

The fascinating story of how a hypnotist who had lost his hearing, his confidence, and his money, but still conceived, believed, and achieved the goal of creating a hypnotism center to teach others, is an excellent example for all of today's hypnotists. *The Amazing Stone-Deaf Hypnotist - Dr Rexford L. North,* published by HypnoClassics© in 2005, tells the story of this truly unusual and amazing icon of the hypnotism profession.

In late 1950 and the spring of 1951, the National Guild of Hypnotists (NGH) and *The Journal of Hypnotism* began, thanks to Dr North's mail-order list and a list loaned by Arons, who became an associate editor. I was attending Emerson College, but also had become assistant to Dr North and lived at the Hypnotism Center on 26 St. Botolph Street to save money.

From the first discussion, Arons had been skeptical of the idea of an organization for hypnotists, and called it "a foolish idea, and "a waste of postage stamps." However, he wrote numerous articles in the *Journal of Hypnotism* when it became a reality, and a couple of years later started his own organization (AAEH) and magazines (*Suggestion* and *Hypnosis Quarterly*).

The Boston Chapter #1 of the National Guild of Hypnotists had been formed and George Rogers was named chairman, with Arnold Levison elected as treasurer of the new organization. Harry Arons was presented with his membership certificate by Rexford North during one of Arons' visits from New Jersey to the Boston Hypnotism Center, and hypnotism history was about to be made during the ensuing half a century.

Rexford North and I were fortunate to also have Bernie Yanover, who was a great researcher, helping us at the Boston Public Library and elsewhere. We were the entire production staff of the fledgling magazine for hypnotists, but among the contributing columnists to the new magazine were Harry Arons, Maurice Kershaw, Ormond McGill, Melvin Powers, and others. Early editions often contained articles written by mainstream health care professionals such as therapist, author, and researcher Dr Raphael Rhodes. There were also many more, including Herbert Charles, Bruno Furst, and Milford Ellison.

The Hypnotism Center also published two books by Ormond McGill in 1953: *A Better Life Through Conscious Self-Hypnosis* and *The Master Method.* For many years McGill had a difficult time convincing other hypnotists that "all hypnosis is self-hypnosis." This is understandable, since stage hypnotists, particularly, are often afflicted with what North described as "the hypnotist's disease" . . . when they actually start to believe their own publicity," ie: "The world's greatest hypnotist," etc. A similar disease also is commonly found in professional mentalists, and  perhaps it also afflicts those who are elected to government positions of power.

Meanwhile, North continued to hold classes in Boston and also started a series of classes at Carnegie Hall in New York City, where advertising proved to be too expensive. Back in staid New England, newspapers would not accept ads for hypnotism classes or lectures, although in bluenose Boston, the newspapers and radio outlets had no problem about reporting or participating in hypnotic events, so North was still able to generate a lot of interest through personal publicity.

The Boston Hypnotism Center team also produced a 10-lesson home study course in hypnotism, which was the first of its kind, and the first recorded course on 33 1/3 rpm records. We also published *The Herald of Psychology* magazine and numerous hypnotism books, many of which would simply be considered folios in today's world.

In that era before electric typewriters, computers, copiers, the Internet, and quick-print stores, it was the start of something amazing—a profession for hypnotists, and would help bring hypnotism from theater stages into professional offices in future years.

In the early '50s, stage hypnotists, hypnologists, and hobbyists comprised over 90% of the NGH membership, and 10% were clinical practitioners. From the beginning, the handwriting was on the wall—a new profession was going to eventually emerge.

Dr North's articles and live demonstrations with patients were said to be responsible for dental hypnosis being accepted by the medical and dental societies of the Boston area. An article from a Boston newspaper of that era states:

> *"A MEDICAL FIRST - History was made at Quincy City Hospital Feb. 23, 1955, when hypnosis was used as an anesthetic for the first time in Massachusetts. Dr William P. Ridder performed minor surgery on the arm of Elsie McKinley, 23. Dr Naif L. Simon anesthetized the patient with hypnosis during the minute operation. Miss McKinley, a nurse anesthetist at the hospital returned to her tour of duty directly after the operation."*

During the early1950s NGH had established a handful of chapters. The cost of a membership was only $5, but in 1956, this rapidly growing hypnotism association suffered a major setback with the loss of their mentor Rexford North and his strong leadership. Unfortunately, just as it had really started to grow, it became a rudderless ship.

North will be remembered as the inspiration and driving force of what has become the world's oldest and largest hypnotism member organization, the National Guild of Hypnotists (NGH). He was also my inspiration and guiding spirit while attending Emerson College, as I studied and worked with him, eventually following in his footsteps, pursuing the dream. He was truly my mentor, and over fifty years later, when international award-winning Internet guru Ralph Benko credited me on his *pnosis.com* website as being "the founding father of hypnotism as a separate profession," I couldn't help but think of how pleased Dr North would be with what we have accomplished as a profession.

It can be said that there was a great deal of difference in East and West Coast training of hypnotists— different philosophies and styles of hypnotism emerged. Chicago and Mid-West teachers aligned more with the East Coast, where students were taught with the premise that they wanted to learn to "hypnotize themselves and others." It also was more hands-on, experiential training aimed at competence and confidence for the graduate in mastering the *art* of hypnotism. Obviously there is room for both, just as there are different philosophical approaches in many other healing-arts professions.

West coast training since those post-war days has been directed toward more of a therapeutic approach, which some critics refered to as "junior hypno-psychologist training." Because of their focus, West Coast courses also often involve more classroom time to accommodate the ancillary subjects being taught. I recall a COPHO (Council of Professional Hypnosis Organizations) meeting in the mid '90s when a very successful California school owner was enthused about Pell grants increasing his bottom line with student enrollments. Starting in the 1970s, the ancillary subjects added to the hypnotism training had made the entire course at his West Coast school more suitable for tuition aid through government-backed student loans.

Now, in the 21st century, no matter where a person decides to look into training as a hypnotist, he or she could possibly be confused by the many "methods" that are available. For various reasons many school proprietors have taken the basics of traditional hypnosis, added their own variations, and called it something else.

There was Gil Boyne's "Transformational Hypnosis" and Charles Tebbetts' "Parts Therapy," to name a couple which originated on the West Coast. There was also the Dave Elman Induction, which originated on the East Coast in the '40s, but didn't become widely known beyond his medical and dental graduates until almost a half century later. Sometimes the unique titling actually describes the system, such as Cal Banyan's "5PATH,®" which is an acronym for either: Five Phase Advanced Transformational Hypnosis™ or Five Phase Advanced Therapeutic Hypnosis.™

Traditionally, though, the unique selling proposition for hypnotism courses has been,"learn to hypnotize yourself and others." It still continues to be widely accepted as the basic reason that people become hypnotism students, whether they even realize or admit it. The old myths are being dispelled, but the mystique is still present when people think about hypnosis, and even in this enlightened age there is still the primal urge to want to have power over others. Unfortunately, there are professional hypnotists who study, work, teach, and still end up with the hypnotist's disease of believing their own publicity and never really accept the truism that "all hypnosis is self-hypnosis."

Unfortunately, there are also hypnotists who study, graduate, work with clients, teach others, but never fully utilize this wonderful tool for themselves. It's hard to believe, but there are actually professional hypnotists who have never been in an hypnotic state. The argument could be made that an optometrist doesn't need to wear glasses, an obstetrician needn't have a baby, and so forth, to be able to practice his or her speciality. But the ease of accomplishing the many benefits of hypnosis would make one think that every professional hypnotist would be utilizing, at the least, self-hypnosis on a daily basis.

Hypnotists have a wonderful tool for themselves and their families as well as their clients, but with many of them it's like the age-old adage about the cobbler who is too busy to repair shoes for his family or the mechanic who is too busy to repair his own car, and so forth. There are others who aren't too busy, but would just rather enviously watch the successful practitioner who utilizes his knowledge and skill personally as well as professionally and who enjoys the benefits derived from both uses.

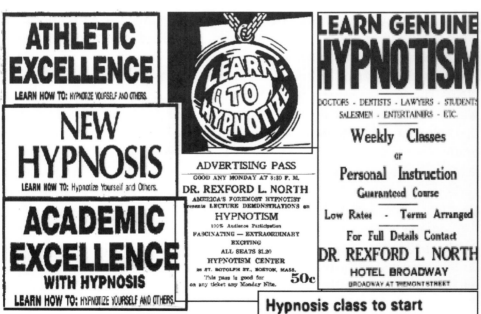

*Hypnotism ads for training in the 1960s and 1970s started to move in a new direction.*

### Hypnosis class to start

The La Verne Parks and Human Services Department will begin a four-weeks self-hypnosis class at the La Verne Community Building Monday at 7:30 p.m.

Frank Genco, hypnotist/hypno-therapist, is the instructor. A free lecture explaining self-hypnosis and its benefits will be given the first hour. The fee is $35. For more information, people may call 596-8700.

Ormond McGill and Dr. Franz Polgar are credited with being the first stage hypnotists to appear on major TV shows in the early 1950s.

*Above—Ormond McGill on the Art Linkletter show "People Are Funny" TV show.*

*Above—Ormond McGill and volunteers on "Art Linkletter's House Party" TV show.*

*Left—Dr. Franz Polgar appearing on the "Arthur Godfrey show."*

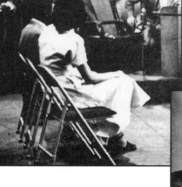

*Right—Pre-show confab of Polgar & Arthur Godfrey.*

# Chapter 7
## Who, What, Where & When On The East Coast

In 1949, Harry Arons and Rexford North both had hypnotism courses and books they were marketing and, since they were both located on the East Coast, it was inevitable that they would eventually meet up and find they had a lot in common. Both were ambitious and both were cautiously friendly, but in time neither of these men ever really liked ot trusted the other, according to those who knew them. They coexisted as friendly competitors, one might say, without too much emphasis on friendly.

The National Guild of Hypnotists (NGH) however would change all that in the future. North's first Boston hypnotism class, which was to graduate in the fall of 1949, had three local college students, Dwight Damon, Frank Anderson, and Berchman Carville, who were to later become charter members of the National Guild of Hypnotists in 1950, and in 1986 spearheaded the NGH's re-birth.

Also in that class were the chief of psychiatry at Massachusetts General Hospital, a court officer, and several men who just wanted to learn to hypnotize themselves and others, as the ads said. But, interestingly enough, there were no female students in those early years.

As classes grew in the late '40s and early '50s, the Hypnotism Center of Boston became the Mecca for hypnotists from all over the globe. North and his group of graduates also founded the first national hypnotism member association, the National Guild of Hypnotists.

Martin T. Orne and Theodore X. Barber, who both later gained fame in psychological circles regarding hypnosis, were local college undergrads and became "regulars" at classes and chapter meetings.

Later, Orne became widely known as a "hired gun," testifying quite often against so-called "lay hypnotists" in legal cases. Curiously enough, when deposed for a trial his curriculum vitae always included that he had studied at the Boston Hypnotism Center under Rexford L. North, who was considered a "lay" hypnotist.

In late 1950 and the spring of 1951, the National Guild of Hypnotists (NGH) started up and began *The Journal of Hypnotism*, thanks to North's mail-order list and a list loaned by Arons, who became an Associate Editor. From the first discussion Arons had been skeptical of the idea of an organization for hypnotists, and called it "a foolish idea, and "a waste of postage stamps." (As noted in Chapter 6)

George Rogers was named chairman and Arnold Levison treasurer of the

NGH. Harry Arons was presented with his membership certificate by Rexford North during one of his visits from New Jersey to the Boston Hypnotism Center. Hypnotism history was about to be made during the ensuing half a century.

I became Dr North's right-hand man and we were the entire production staff of the fledgling magazine for hypnotists. Among the contributing columnists to the new magazine were Harry Arons, Maurice Kershaw, Ormond McGill, and Melvin Powers. Early editions often contained articles written by mainstream health care professionals, such as therapist, author, and researcher, Dr Raphael Rhodes. There were many more: Herbert Charles, Bruno Furst, Milford Ellison, and others.

In 1956, the *Journal of Hypnotism* suddenly become a tabloid newspaper. The reason was unexplained, but I assumed it was probably financial. Renamed *Hypnotism* in the fall of 1956, the publication ceased publication entirely when Dr Rexford L. North vanished without a trace.

After serving in the US Coast Guard I had decided to return to college with help from the GI Bill and moved my family to Davenport, Iowa. There, while attending Palmer Chiropractic College, I also taught and performed hypnotism classes and shows to supplement my government stipend. We had been writing monthly, but correspondence suddenly stopped from North back in Boston, and his unexplained disappearance remains an unsolved mystery to this day. Fifty-five years later, I still hear occasional theories of what happened, and there are always those who assure me that *they* will solve the mystery. Those of us from that era have accepted the fact that it will remain what it was then … a mystery.

During the 1950s, NGH had established a handful of chapters, but in 1956 the relatively new hypnotism association suffered a major setback with the loss of their mentor, Rex North, and his strong leadership. A dozen or so members of the original NGH Boston chapter remained in touch and kept the dream of someday making the NGH a meaningful organization again. With this very small group of like-minded comrades, the NGH could almost have been a "secret" society until the '80s when it would experience a re-birth with the same nucleus of dedicated charter members who had kept the dream alive.

# Chapter 8
## Outstanding Personalities of the '40s - '50s

In 1949 a new car cost $1650 ... gas for the car was 26¢ a gallon ... postage stamps were 3¢ ... and Harry Arons advertised his *Master Course in Hypnotism* by mail for $1.98.

In 1952 Dr Rexford North's 10-lesson *Modern Hypnosis* course text was $5, *How To Make Money With Hypnotism* by Arons was $2, and Ormond McGill's *The Master Method of Hypnotism* was offered by mail to "Discriminating Hypnotists" for $2. Seems like things were looking up in the marketing of hypnotism instruction to the public!

Of course, these men charged more for classes and personal instruction. Arons was to find his niche, however, in marketing weekend courses to licensed physicians, dentists, and others from his Ethical Hypnosis Training Center in Newark, New Jersey, and Rexford North was doing weekly lecture-demonstrations and classes at the ever-growing Boston Hypnotism Center.

Dave Elman, who had a career as a stage hypnotist, became well-known as the host of the *Hobby Lobby* show on the Mutual network from 1937-1948. When the show went off the air he concentrated his efforts on teaching hypnotism to physicians. So then, both Arons and Elman were giving hypnosis training only to licensed health professionals. This approach, some say, may have partially contributed to the label of "lay hypnotist" that some doctors and psychologists gave to hypnosis professionals in the decades that followed.

Walter Sichort and his Ultra Depth© hypnosis came on the scene in the '40s, upstairs over a flower shop he owned in Blackwood, New Jersey, when he began teaching hypnosis at his Relaxology Institute. Sichort referred to his work as "relaxology." He told me years later at a meeting in Chicago that he used the term relaxology to avoid any laws that might pertain to hypnotism. With his long-time assistant, Sara Zane, Sichort lectured and demonstrated the deep hypnotic coma state he claimed was akin to that used by Dr James Esdaille in India during the 1880s.

With the death of his assistant Sara, Sichort continued to lecture at conventions, but no longer did actual demonstrations of the Ultra Depth© state. Whether he was too emotionally upset over her death or just unable to find another suitable subject with the outstanding innate ability to achieve the coma state was always a questionable issue. However, his demonstrations of how to teach a person self-hypnosis were always effective and well received. Sichort also headed up the New Jersey Hypnotist Union Local # 474 in 1971-'72. After his passing in 2000, James P. Rainey registered the name Ultra Depth,© and continues to lecture and teach his mentor's work.

Across the Hudson River, in New York City, there was a lot of hypnotism activity in the mid '40s. The Institute of Applied Hypnology was operated by Clark R. Bellows, Jr, MsD, who declared himself at that time to be the "Dean of American Hypnotists." Bellows wrote *Hypnotism For Fun And Health* and developed a following for his classes in New York City, accepting all who were interested, not just licensed health professionals.

Dr David F. Tracy, was employed supposedly as a "psychologist" to the St. Louis Browns in 1949 but his real job was to use hypnotic techniques to improve the team's sports performance. Based in NYC, he later worked with the New York Rangers and the St. Francis College basketball team. Tracy also taught hypnotism courses in NYC during that era, attracting students who read his book, *The Psychologist at Bat,* which told about his experiences as a psychologist/hypnotist in the world of professional baseball. In 1952, Tracy also wrote *How To Use Hypnosis,* "for everyday use in selling and advertising," and, *How To Sleep Without Pills.*

Dr Bruno Furst, psychologist and world famous memory expert, taught hypnotism courses at his center in NYC from 1939-45. Although he started teaching hypnotism classes when he emigrated from Germany, Furst was a master of memory and gave wonderful demonstrations and shows of this skill until his memory courses soon became the main focus of his professional life. He was best known as the author of *The Practical Way to a Better Memory.* He was dubbed by the press as "the hypnotist who remembers." His memory course is still in print but his hypnotism course is long forgotten, except by an occasional recollector from that era.

North got together with Bruno Furst when he was presenting his course at Carnegie Hall, and Furst came to visit the Hypnotism Center to see if he could set up a memory course with us in Boston. There really wasn't a meeting of the minds between North and Furst, which made me happy since I had been targeted as the one to learn the method and present the course at our location. Frankly, I had enough to do and remember, and I was at an age when I needed a little free time to do it. Nevertheless, the time spent working with Dr North did give me a firm foundation for future endeavors in life, which would require 24/7 dedication to business.

Ralph Slater was playing at a theater just off Broadway in 1952 after his publicity-loaded court case in England, which is discussed elsewhere in this book. I was stationed at the Federal Building at the time and picked up a ticket from the USO to see the show. Since I was a "roving reporter" for the

*Journal of Hypnotism,* I attempted to set up a post-show interview and found that Slater was definitely affected by the "hypnotists' disease" mentioned previously in this book. He said we could speak after the show, but he needed me to come up when he called for volunteers because it always looked good to have servicemen in uniform on the stage. Since I really wanted to see the show, not be in the show, I politely declined and he said OK, but when he called for volunteers he pointed me out and asked the audience to encourage me with their applause ... so I was a good sport and went up on stage.

His show, from my point of view as a participant, wasn't any better than I had seen or actually done in my own professional career, but I went along with it. He got plenty of mileage out of me as the only uniformed sailor on stage and probably in the whole darn theater, which was about half full.

Finally my chance to "escape" came when he declared an intermission and walked off stage, leaving all of the volunteers sitting there. I tried to do it in a non-embarrassing way for him, as I slid slowly out of the chair toward the floor. Audience members, concerned that I would get hurt, I guess, started to shout. As I reached the floor, opening my eyes and standing up, Slater was there in a flash, with a pleading look and a wink of the eye, so I "went back into trance" for the rest of the show, which, thankfully, was a shorter segment.

Our subsequent backstage "interview" turned out to be a brief harangue about everybody who was a professional hypnotist in New York City. Frankly, it didn't make a good article, so we never ran it. Before I left he showed me his book, *Hypnotism and Self-Hypnosis,* and asked if I had read it. When I replied that I hadn't had the opportunity, he offered to *sell* me a copy! I politely pled poverty as a serviceman and years later I ended up with two copies in my library anyway, so I'm glad I saved the money.

The Coué Institute had a brief '50s resurgence. I was still on temporary duty in the Federal Building in NYC and decided to pay a visit. Located in an older residential hotel not far off Times Square, it was a one-man operation, but had no real connection with the famed Emil Coué, simply using the title and teaching the principles. I recall the very large entry/living room of the establishment and the soft-spoken proprietor, who seemed pleased to have company to discuss hypnosis. The gracious host knew about the *Journal of Hypnotism* and, after a nice chat, gave me a couple of Coué Institute brochures and a book on how to memorize the Morse code as I was leaving. Sixty years later while working on this book, I checked our library for a clue to the gentlemen's name but found only the Morse code memory booklet ... authored by M. A. Ree ... very clever!

Professor James "Jimmy" Grippo was a well known New York and Florida hypnotist who managed boxer Melio Bettina early in his career and was able to guide him to the World Light Heavyweight title. It was said that he hypnotized Bettina, telling him he would be courageous, bold, feel no pain, and would be a conquerer in his matches. Tiger Jack Fox claimed, after losing to Bettina in 1939, that he was a victim of the "evil eye" of Grippo.

Actually, "Jimmy" Grippo was often said by sports writers to be giving certain boxers the "evil eye" when seated at the ringside corner of one of his favored boxers. Many boxers, managers, and handlers believed, and tried unsuccessfully to have him banned from ringside seating during important bouts. This gave Grippo and the boxing game a lot of free newspaper space. More than anything else, Grippo should be remembered as a man who knew how to get his name in newspapers, magazines, and the movie theater news-reels.

I never met Grippo, but did see much of his publicity in the newspapers and in theater newsreels. He also became well-known as a close-up magi-cian, entertaining at Caesar's Palace in Las Vegas in the '60s, in addition to his hypnosis work in the world of professional boxing.

Years later, in the 1980s, John Halpin, longtime operator of the American School of Hypnosis in New York City, was pretty well thought by others to be on retainer as boxer Mike Tyson's hypnotist. Without the "evil eye" reputation and with the condition that it all be kept confidential, Halpin acted in a very ethical manner, always declining any comment regarding rumors or answering any questions about Tyson.

In the early '50s, W.C. Weber established the Hypnotic Research Institute in Bridgeport, Connecticut. He published *Scientific Hypnotism,* a small pamphlet-type magazine/newsletter, and lectured around the country to hypnosis groups/magic clubs. He was active until the mid '50s, contributing articles to the AAEH *Hypnosis Quarterly* until a fall-out with Arons and AAEH. Weber was acknowledged for his very scientific explanations of how the body reacted in hypnosis and what hypnosis really was.

Also outside the New York City area, but still on the East Coast, Dewey Deavers opened his hypnosis studio in downtown Pittsburgh, Pennsylvania in the post-war era, to teach hypnotism classes and work with clients. Deavers had a rather unusual theory that male hypnotists should consult with men, while women should consult only with female hypnotists. Thus, he worked with men, while female clients saw his associate, Peggy O'Neil.

Although well-known regionally, Deavers never wrote a book, so most hypnotists who learned the art after 1980 never heard about him. He submitted the following article, which we ran in the January 1952 *Journal of Hypnotism.*©

## Somnambulist Resists Improper Suggestions
by Libbie Volpie, Assistant at Dewey Deavers Studios

(This is a factual account of a genuine, non-laboratory hypnotic test, which may help to answer some questions in Herbert Charles' article: Man Loses Savings—Hypnotism To Blame? in the July issue of the *Journal of Hypnotism*)

By a coincidence, at about the time this article was published, we had at the Dewey Deavers Studio in Pittsburgh an attempted abuse of hypnotic power, to cause a subject to act contrary to her own interests. This attempt was unsuccessful. The conditions of this were so extraordinary that I think Mr. Charles' requirements will be more than satisfied. Everything can be substantiated by several independent witnesses.

This is what happened: A young woman, in the deepest stage of somnambulism, was approached by an unscrupulous hypnotist, without the knowledge of the operator in charge. The suggestion was given, "Whenever you look into my eyes, you will do whatever I tell you to do." A few minutes later, she was awakened from the trance. The unscrupulous operator then approached her again, told her to look into his eyes, and commanded her to get into his car. She refused to do so.

I will give a detailed report of how this occurred. But first let me point out the remarkable factor in this case. Here an unscrupulous hypnotist had an opportunity to reach a somnambulist who is already in a deep trance. Yet his suggestion is rejected because the subject senses that it is undesirable.

### Here is the story:
On June 16, 1951, Mr. Dewey Deavers gave a demonstration of somnambulism for his students and clients. The subject, Marjorie Antonini, had been hypnotized by Mr. Deavers before, both for therapeutic purposes, and for demonstration. Her husband, Robert Antonini, had performed in shows staged by Mr. Deavers. He was hanged, using a genuine gallows and rope, but prevented from sustaining any injury by a post-hypnotically induced catalepsy of the neck muscles. Even the four-year-old son of the Anoninis had been hypnotized by Mr. Deavers. I mention this to show that the subject had absolute confidence in Mr. Deavers, and no inhibitions whatever against hypnotism. She was normally a deep somnambulist, completely responsive.

On this occasion, one stranger was present. He was a professional man in good standing, who was an ardent amateur hypnotist. He had just recently come to Pittsburgh, and was eager to meet hypnotists here. As a courtesy, he was invited to this demonstration, which invitation he was soon to abuse.

Mrs. Antonini was hypnotized, and put through all the somnambulist routines: catalepsy; automatic motion; anaesthesis; hallucinations, both positive and negative of sight, sound, touch, temperature, etc.; regression to the age of four; and many other phenomena. Then the climactic suggestion was given: That we were all going to a restaurant and that she would go along, remaining in a trance. Her behavior would be normal in every way. The pupils of her eyes would be normal, she would watch out for traffic, take care of her child, order her own food, and carry on conversation in a normal way with members of our party.

The entire group then went to a near-by restaurant, Mrs. Antonini in a profound trance, but acting and talking normally. While we ate, members of the group tested Mrs. Antonini in various ways, and were satisfied both as to the depth of trance, and the normalcy of response.

Mr. Deavers then circulated among the group, to be sure that all had an opportunity to test Mrs. Antonini for themselves. In the few minutes that this was going on, the unscrupulous operator, Mr. ------ sat down next to Mrs. Antonini, and asked several personal questions, such as where she lived, where her husband worked, etc. She became very disturbed, although she had answered similar questions freely to others. Apparently, she sensed a sinister motive in this man. Mr. ----- then made the suggestion: "Whenever you look into my eyes, you will do exactly what I tell you to do." He then told her to wake up. We learned later that he believes a post-hypnotic suggestion cannot be remembered if the subject awakens immediately after it is given.

Mr. Deavers returned to find Mrs. Antonini very agitated, while Mr. ----- was giving contradictory suggestions to wake up and go back to sleep. He did not know of the post-hypnotic suggestion that had been made, and was annoyed at what he thought was simply meddling by an incompetent amateur.

Mr. Deavers woke the subject, and the group dispersed. Mrs. Antonini, now completely awake, walked toward the streetcar stop, with her small son. Suddenly Mr. ------ appeared out of a side street. He commanded her to look into his eyes, then told her to get into his car, as he would drive her home.

Mrs. Antonini became confused and disturbed. She did not remember or respond to the post-hypnotic suggestion that she would go into a trance when he commanded. It took another trance to get her to recall consciously that such a suggestion had been given. She pretended to acquiesce, until she saw her streetcar coming. She then broke away from him and boarded the streetcar.

When she arrived home, she called Mr. Deavers. She was disturbed by "something unpleasant" that had happened. She remembered the incident on the street, but could not recall what had led up to it. Mr. Deavers hypnotized her over the phone. She then recalled being given the post-hypnotic suggestion by Mr. -----. Everything she said was verified by investigation.

Mr. Deavers, of course, took steps to prevent Mr. ----- from ever doing this again, but handled it discreetly, to avoid reflecting public discredit on hypnotism.

I think this should satisfy Mr. Charles' requirements for genuine evidence that a hypnotic subject can not be induced to do anything against his own best interest.

Norbert Bakas, a close friend of Dewey Deavers, also began his long career in Pittsburgh after WWII. Norb tells of building a hypnotism practice while charging a fee near that of the minimum hourly wage of that time, while most area hypnotists were doing sessions without even charging a set fee. Working with well-known professional athletes and also teaching occasional classes, he has been a true devotee of the hypnotic arts and was instrumental in organizing the first hypnotism union, Local 469 OPEIU. His book, *Self-Hypnosis; Your Golden Key to Self-Hypnosis and Self-Healing,* was self-published in 2010, and he is still active in the field.

In the late '50s, in Orlando, Florida, a very dedicated local hypnotist, Joe B. McCawley, went up against the so-called "Gypsy Law." This law, or ordinance, required seers, fortune tellers, phrenologists, psychics, and so forth to pay an exorbitant license fee of $1250 for an annual business license. The intent of this kind of law, which was prevalent throughout the South, was to keep those whom they felt were itinerant gypsies out of their towns and cities. Unfortunately, there was no license provision for practicing hypnotists, so when Joe applied for a business license he was also regarded with the same disdain as the seers and psychics and given a choice of that kind of license, or one as an entertainer. He decided to fight City Hall.

In 1958 McCawley, an AAEH member, had opened a referral-only practice in Orlando, but being denied a business license as a hypnotist had riled him. The fact that he would have to get a license as a psychic, medium, tea leaf reader, or scalp interpreter upset him. McCawley persevered with the endorsement of several prominent physicians and dentists who were already referring their patients to him. After numerous official hearings, an amendment to the existing ordinance was enacted. City Hall finally issued the first "Ethical Hypnotism" license for "pre-conditioning of patients for physicians and dentists." He was charged $25, which was the same fee that physicians and dentists paid for their business licenses, not $1250, the fee for "seers and fortune tellers."

Joe B. McCawley was now the first licensed ethical hypnotist in the United States. The date was May 25, 1959, although the license was temporary until a city ordinance was prepared on September 30, 1959. Orange County also issued a county license to accompany this Orlando city license.

In addition to being one of the founding members of the Florida Association for Professional Hypnosis and maintaining a busy referral practice, McCawley also taught many students in his Ethical Hypnosis Training Center of Florida, which he opened in 1959-60. In a recent interview for the *Journal of Hypnotism* I asked Joe B. why, in published photos over the past 50 years, he is never shown smiling. He replied that he has always been smiling and happy, *on the inside*, because he was doing what he really liked— the practice of hypnotism!

The Florida Association For Professional Hypnosis was founded in 1959-60 by Joe B. McCawley, Martin Segall, Ted Van Antwerp, Betty Gedrottis, and Ernie Deutsch, to help protect practicing hypnotists in the state and continue legislative efforts on their behalf.

McCawley continued his efforts regarding state-wide legislation. In 1960, the Florida Association for Professional Hypnosis connected with Florida's Attorney General, Richard Ervin, requesting that a law be prepared to recognize and protect professional ethical hypnotists and the public. It was an uphill battle but, shortly thereafter, the Florida Hypnosis Law of 1961, Senate Bill 3927, was enacted. Patterned after an AAEH model bill, it was *"AN ACT relating to hypnosis for therapeutic purposes; declaring legislative intent; providing definitions; prohibiting the practice thereof, except by, or under the supervision of a person licensed to practice certain branches of the healing arts; providing penalties; providing an effective date ..."*

Gerald and Shirley Kein founded Omni Hypnosis Center in 1979, in Fort Lauderdale, Florida after many years of practicing hypnotism part-time. In 1985, Jerry Kein developed a hypnotism training curriculum based on what he had learned over the years through practical experience with clients and from former teachers and mentors. He presented classes regularly in Fort Lauderdale.

After Jerry experienced a heart attack, they moved to DeLand, Florida and started training classes at their Omni Hypnosis Training Center. The National Board of Hypnosis Education & Certification (NBHEC), was founded in 1989 by the Keins, and they held conferences in Daytona Beach in 1994/95/96, but made a decision to merge the group with NGH in 1996. It is currently an affiliated organization.

According to state records, the Florida Society of Professional Hypnotherapists, founded in 1986, and the American Nurse Hypnotherapy Association, also founded in 1998 by Gerald and Shirley Kein, are no longer active at this time. Jerry Kein is a regular columnist for the *Journal of Hypnotism,*® a board member of NFH 104 OPEIU AFL/CIO CLC, and an examiner for the NGH Board Certification.

Jerry Kein in DeLand and Charles Francis in Fort Myers became very active in Florida legislative matters, with many trips to the state capitol regarding the practice rights of hypnotists in Florida. Working together, Francis and Kein were two dedicated individuals defending the Hypnosis Law from sunsetting, and fighting attacks by other licensed groups against hypnotists. They followed in the footsteps of Joe B. McCawley, who had fought earlier for the rights of Florida hypnotists to practice freely.

Charles Francis, who was a professional journalist before becoming interested in a career in hypnotism, was the editor of the *Hypno-Gram*© from 1995 to 2005, when a decline in his health necessitated cutting back. In addition to his successful practices in Fort Myers and West Palm Beach, Florida, he wrote *Counseling Hypnotherapy*, a highly acclaimed book in the profession. He also co-authored *Scripts and Tips,* with Dr John C. Hughes. Charles is now retired and living in New Mexico, and as a generous gesture to the profession he grew to love more than any other he had experienced, assigned all his author copyrights and royalties to the National Guild of Hypnotists.

Chaplain Paul G. Durbin, a Methodist minister, served as Director of Clinical Hypnotherapy at Methodist Hospital in New Orleans, Louisiana. He served on the hospital staff since 1976 as Director of Pastoral Care and from 1999 as Director of Clinical Hypnotherapy. He is a retired military chaplain who last served as Army National Guard Special Assistant to the Chief of Chaplains, Army, with the rank of Brigadier General. Durbin is the author of *Human Trinity Hypnotherapy,* published in 1993, and *Kissing Frogs: Practical Uses of Hypnotherapy,* published in 1996.

In the windy city of Chicago, Illinois, there was a hypnotist who was a master at getting publicity for himself and for hypnosis. Edwin L. Baron, PhB, taught 6-week courses for aspiring hypnotists at his Hypnotism Institute of Chicago in the '50s, and his knack for self-promotion and hypnotism publicity kept him in the public eye, as attested to by feature stories in Chicago newspapers and national publications such as *LOOK* and *LIFE.* His publicity coups were beneficial to the profession as they always cited the many positive aspects of hypnotism.

On November 4, 1957, Baron started a 5-day hypnotic sleep at the Hypnotism Institute of Chicago with a female client, in conjunction with three local physicians. The client who had been seeking help "suffered from insomnia which limited her sleep to less than two hours a night, and she had an emotionally caused rash on her left hand," according to a published report on the project in the Vol. IV No. 2 issue of *HYPNOSIS.*

In addition to the three consulting physicians there were also several nurses and volunteer female hypnotism students to assist, so there was somebody with the client at all times. A pre-induction Roshach test was given to the patient and, to detect any physiological changes which might occur, she was also given basal metabolism tests, electrocardiographs, pulse rate counts, and blood pressure examinations before, during, and after the experiment.

The patient was kept in hypnosis for five days, and afterwards she reported that "the things that irritated her before the treatment no longer bothered her." She also reported that she was "sleeping normally and had added two more pounds with her new-found appetite. There was no reappearance of a rash on her left hand."

The public learned about this unique project from a photo spread and stories in *LIFE* and other magazines, which brought the use of hypnosis for medical purposes to the attention of readers around the country. This hypnotic hibernation therapy for an emotional disturbance was monitored medically and achieved success for the client, and publicity for Baron and the profession.

In the 1950s, Sidney Schneider founded the Chicago Hypnosis Training International School, one of the first AAEH approved schools. Schneider received an honorary doctor of science degree from Union University Graduate School for his development of the Brain Wave Synchronizer in 1956. This medically-approved device proved effective for inducing hypnosis in clients who were normally resistant to hypnotic induction.

The Brain Wave Synchronizer was used in hospitals, clinics, and many hypnotists' offices. It was particularly useful with reticent clients who didn't want to give up control in order to enter the hypnotic state. The only drawback was that the device used a flashing strobe light, which could possibly cause a seizure in clients with epilepsy or other similar conditions. However, several recollectors to this book used the device with clients and report positive results and no side effects. Although not widely used or even available today, there are still some units used in various offices, and two models are in the historical collection of the NGH.

The Brain Wave Synchronizer was purchased by hospitals, clinics, and many hypnotists for office use. All rights to the Brain Wave Synchronizer are now owned by Art Leidecker, well-known Chicago hypnotist and former owner of Leidecker Institute in Chicago. Leidecker originally became interested in hypnosis during the 1950s, but his desire to learn more didn't emerge until early retirement after several other successful careers. In the mid 70s he developed a successful practice and hypnotism school, the Leidecker Institute.

Stanley V. Mitchell, a moving force in local professional hypnotism, maintained a private practice in Chicago from the '40s into the '80s. He was active with AAEH, World Congress of Professional Hypnotists, and the Mid-America Conference, and also involved with researchers at Northwestern University working with individuals who had experienced UFO sightings.

Larry Garrett has probably had the longest-running hypnotism presence in Chicago at this time, having started in the 1960s as a student of Fred Schiavo.

As the new guy on the block, Larry found that the deeply-entrenched AAEH group wasn't very welcoming to newcomers. However, keeping his goals in sight, he went from doing stage shows to a store-front office in 1997, then to a larger practice in conjunction with a physician/hypnotist.

In 1997 he bought and rehabilitated an entire old building into a modern Wellness Center. One of the attributes displayed by Larry Garrett is to welcome all hypnotists to the area, even providing a place where they can see clients by the hour and utilize the facilities of a first-class professional wellness center. This gives many area hypnotists a professional office at a very low overhead.

His travels to Iraq to hypnotize a "business man," with US government approval, during the travel embargo to that country is told in his book, *Healing The Enemy.* It is fascinating to read about his experience of finding the client was actually Uday Hussein, the evil son of Sadam Hussein. His debriefing by CIA and FBI agents after each of two trips and his presence in Baghdad when "9/11" occurred is gripping—almost like being there with him as you read it.

Solomon and Hyman Lewis practiced and taught in the Detroit, Michigan area in the post WW II era. The brothers founded their Michigan Hypnosis Institute in 1958 as a state chartered school offering 10-week hypnosis courses. As staunch members of AAEH, they also organized a very success-ful 1959 AAEH convention in Detroit. *Self-Hypnosis Dynamics,* written by Hy in the '50s, was popular enough to be republished by Borden Publishing in 1962.

Sol Lewis was very much interested in past lives after the Bridey Murphy story broke in 1956, but Harry Arons and the AAEH frowned totally on the concept of past lives. They asked Sol to resign, but he told them they would have to "kick him out" … so they did. He joined NGH, participating in the first convention in Danvers, Massachusetts in 1988, and becoming one of our most popular presenters.

We all admired Sol Lewis for his dedication to hypnotism and our "Big Idea" of a separate and distinct profession. Through the years he was a pop-ular teacher and socially, at conventions, he captivated colleagues with his many stories, often told with a sly smile and a "believe it or not" attitude. As a German POW he was able to pass himself off as being of Italian ances-try, not Jewish, and his ability to use self-hypnosis also helped him to survive being in the prison camp.

The Quad Cities (Davenport/Bettendorf, Iowa, and Rock Island/Moline, Illinois) had some hypnotism activity in the mid-1950s. I was enrolled at Palmer Chiropractic College in Davenport and supplemented my GI Bill by teaching a 10-lesson course in hypnotism using the Boston Hypnotism Center text. I know it sounds ridiculous that it was *Ten Lessons for Ten Dollars*, and actually guaranteed, at that, but in 1956 you could feed a family of four for $12 for a week … I know, because I did!

John Hughes, also a veteran, enrolled on the GI Bill at Palmer College and joined me in teaching the weekly hypnotism classes at the Helping Hands Club, located down on the levee. We updated the Boston Hypnotism Center course while teaching it to fellow students, faculty members, and the general public. We called the course *Power Hypnosis*. Each class ran on Sunday afternoons at the rented lecture hall. Later, I had the Sunday use of a local dance studio, which the proprietor offered in lieu of paying for the course.

John Hughes connected with a promoter and expanded his personal horizons by teaching courses and doing shows in other cities throughout Iowa and Illinois. In the ensuing years after graduation, he built a sterling reputation as research editor of the *Journal of Hypnotism*® and for his research into the history of hypnotism. John also wrote several very popular hypnotism books: *Autosuggestion - Your Key To A Better Life, Hypnotism: the Induction of Conviction, The World's Greatest Hypnotists, The Roots of Hypnotism in America, The Illustrated History of Hypnotism,* and co-authored *Scripts and Tips*, with Charles Francis. He currently enjoys his retirement in Las Vegas, observing the profession via the Internet, and as a featured columnist and Research Editor of the *Journal of Hypnotism*.

Col. B.J. Palmer, developer of the chiropractic profession, as a young man had been friends with Joseph Poulin, a stage hypnotist billed as The Great Pauline.

"BJ," as he was known, spread the word about the new profession of chiropractic through his many show business friends and was a great fan of circuses, magic, and all kinds of show business, with extensive contacts in all these fields.

Because of this, once we became acquainted, he was generous with his approval and personal support of my activities on the local entertainment scene. He owned WOC TV across the street from the campus and proved to be very helpful to me in getting publicity as well as paid television appearances as a magician/hypnotist, which helped my hypnotism classes and shows.

Another Palmer student, S. Paul Albert, originally from Maine, performed as "Martel" in Rock Island nightspots. Albert also taught hypnotism classes at his Martel Institute of Hypnology. So, in the mid 1950s, there were three professional hypnotist/college students teaching and doing shows in the Quad Cities area.

Wendel Loder, a Rock Island graduate of Martel's, assumed teaching when

Paul Albert graduated from Palmer College and returned to Maine. Loder established a long-running private practice starting in 1958-'59. He was known for mandating that all of his students must have experienced hypnosis to *his* personal satisfaction in order to successfully graduate. One of his most successful graduates, Ernest Telkemeyer of Geneseo, Illinois, became a well-known conference presenter and recipient of many awards and citations for his work.

The '60s were a time of stage hypnotists experiencing a resurgence of bookings at fairs and outdoor events, and a relative new venue opened up playing school assemblies, mostly through the mid-western states. It was also a time when female hypnotists Pat Collins and Joan Brandon were making it big in nightclubs in NYC, Vegas, and the West Coast, which we will discuss in another chapter.

*Pat Collins  leading female nightclub and stage hypnotist on the West Coast.*

*Joan Brandon leading female nightclub and stage hypnotist on the East Coast.*

### SLEEP WITH PAT COLLINS!
THE HIP HYPNOTIST

CRESCENDO

WRITER OF MANY BOOKS AND AN AUTHORITY ON THE SUBJECT OF

## HYPNOTISM

SCIENCE OF SELF-HYPNOSIS

THE ART OF HYPNOTISM
BY JOAN BRANDON

Books by
Joan Brandon

## MISS PAT COLLINS
### ANSWERS YOUR QUESTIONS ON
# HYPNOSIS

Q. WHAT IS HYPNOSIS?

A. "Hypnosis is an artificially induced passive state in which there is an increased amenability and responsiveness to suggestion and command, provided that these do not conflict seriously with the subject's own conscious or unconscious wishes." — Dorland's Medical Dictionary, 1974 edition.

Q. CAN ANYONE BE HYPNOTIZED?

A. YES, as long as they want to be. A willing, strong-minded person makes the best subject. The higher the I.Q. the better.

Q. CAN A PERSON BE LEFT IN AN HYPNOTIC TRANCE?

A. NO, there has never been a case recorded of a hypnotized person failing to return to normal. Should the hypnotist, for any reason, fail to tell them to wake up, they would eventually fall into a regular sleep, which would bring them out of it.

Q. CAN YOU BE MADE TO DO ANYTHING WHILE HYPNOTIZED?

A. NO, you will not say or do anything that would be against your moral or ethical code.

Q. DO DOCTORS USE HYPNOSIS?

A. YES, leading physicians and dentists throughout the country use hypnosis.

Q. CAN YOU STOP SMOKING OR LOSE WEIGHT THROUGH HYPNOSIS?

A. YES, these along with many other annoying or undesirable habits are treated very successfully through the use of hypnosis or self-hypnosis.

Q. WHAT FEELING DO YOU HAVE WHEN HYPNOTIZED?

A. That of a profound relaxation and remembrance. You are not asleep or unconscious because you can hear all sounds and are not in a regular sleep. Upon awakening you will remember all of the suggestions given you, unless you do not want to remember. When you awaken you are full of energy as though you had been asleep for many hours and usually obtain a feeling of self-confidence never before reached. In general you feel as though you have been through one of the most relaxing experiences of your life!

Q. CAN ANYONE VOLUNTEER TO GO ON STAGE?

A. YES — Sometimes it takes two or three times before you relax properly — you are welcome as many times as you wish. It's fun and interesting to find hidden talents in people.

Thank You — Come Back Again — Every Show is Different — Because the Personalities Are Different!

### The Hilarious Hypnotist

*LIFE goes into a trance with Pat Collins*

*Joan Brandon and Pat Collins both had a knack for getting lots of publicity for themselves and hypnotism in general.*

# Chapter 9
## The West Coast Story

The main players in California in the 1950s-1960s were Melvin Powers' Wilshire School of Hypnotism, Gil Boyne's Hypnotism Training Institute of Los Angeles; Dr William J. Bryan's American Institute of Hypnosis, and Dr John Kappas' Hypnosis Motivation Institute. There were also numerous lesser-known schools, especially in the Los Angeles and Bay areas.

Ormond McGill was a lifetime resident of Palo Alto, California, and when not traveling with his stage show, was very active on the California scene. He was also involved in operating a California hypnotism school during the 1950s-1960s, but most of his regular teaching, when not touring the world on stage, was at the ACHE conventions and Randal Churchill's Hypnotism Training Institute.

When NGH re-grouped, the "Dean of American Hypnotists" came back to teaching specialized continuing-education tours around the US and at the annual NGH convention. He was always highly honored by all hypnotism organizations, but especially by NGH, because of his long-term association with the group. In fact, since 1996, the "Ormond McGill Chair," a finely hand-crafted, laser-inscribed, hardwood chair, has been awarded to the convention faculty member of the year voted best presenter of the previous year.

About 1947, Melvin Powers (born Melvin Schwartz) moved from the Boston area to the West Coast, where he started the Wilshire Book Company, located on Wilshire Boulevard in Los Angeles. In 1949, Powers wrote and published *Hypnotism Revealed*, followed by *Self Hypnosis* and *A Practical Guide to Self-Hypnosis*, which sold hundreds of thousands of copies over the ensuing years. He was a talented author and also a knowledgeable publisher and marketer of hypnosis books, in addition to operating the Wilshire School of Hypnotism.

Powers told me in a 1988 interview that he always thought of himself as a hypnotist who sold books, until 1963, when he obtained the paperback publishing rights to Dr Maxwell Maltz' popular book, *Psycho-Cybernetics*. Then he started to think of himself as a *millionaire publisher* who was also a hypnotist—the book sold over three million copies.

Gil Boyne (born Mark Gilboyne) originally started as a stage hypnotist in the late 1940s on the East Coast before moving from Philadelphia to California in the early 1950s, where, using his stage name, he was to make his mark on the emerging profession of hypnotherapy. He continued performing stage shows and also made inroads with motion picture personalities, being dubbed in his promotional materials as "Hypnotist to the Stars."

In 1959, Boyne was hired as a technical director for a motion picture entitled *The Hypnotic Eye* and although it was an exploitation B film, not a box office blockbuster, this movie represented an unprecedented association between Hollywood and hypnotism professionals. Moviemakers had actually consulted a professional hypnotist regarding a movie that involved hypnosis in the plot.

Boyne established a private practice in Hollywood in the 1950s and was the originator/author of *Transformational Hypnosis*, a method he taught at his school. He published this textbook as well as books written by Ormond McGill, Dave Elman, Charles Tebbets, and others, through his Westwood Publishing Company.

Gil Boyne's Hypnotism Training Institute of Los Angeles was one of the first schools to use visual aids in addition to actual demonstrations. His students viewed videos of Boyne in session with clients using *Transformational Hypnotism* techniques. He was an advocate of longer training hours than those used on the East Coast, and there was constant friction among hypnotism organizations because of this.

Boyne truly influenced the practice of hypnotism in the 20th century in a number of ways. He claimed to be responsible for establishing a listing for the profession of hypnotism titles in the 1973 *Directory of Occupational Titles* published by the US Department of Labor, but there has long been an opposing claim that Dr John Kappas was responsible for the listing, and Norbert Bakas believes that it was two hypnotists in Pennsylvania. Nevertheless, the definition remains in force and unchanged today, but the controversy still remains as to who was actually responsible for it. Since there were several titles listed, i.e. hypnotherapist, master hypnotist, hypnotist, perhaps Boyne and Kappas or the individuals from Pennsylvania were all equally responsible for one or more of them.

The complete definition in the *Directory of Occupational Titles* was *"Hypnotherapy induces hypnotic state in clients to increase motivation or alter behavior or alter behavior pattern through hypnosis. Consults with client to determine the nature of problem. Prepares client to enter hypnotic states by explaining how hypnosis works and what client will experience. Tests subjects to determine degrees of physical and emotional suggestibility. Induces hypnotic techniques of hypnosis based on interpretation of tests results and analysis of client's problem. May train client in self-hypnosis conditioning."*

West Coast hypnotists who operate schools gained a reputation for whistle blowing on colleagues who taught courses without having post-secondary education state licensing. This occurred even when a hypnotist who was a certified instructor moved across the country, not even intending to teach in his new location. Often state laws on post-secondary education exempts classes with a small enrollment or tuition under a certain level, so state licensing is not always necessary, but leading organizations encourage it for their certified instructors.

Hypnotists sometimes check each other's ads in the yellow pages for anything they might point out as being false advertising. All of this petty stuff is bothersome and slows things down somewhat in pursuing the Big Idea of being a *profession*. Occasionally, there is a case of deceptive or false advertising which is submitted for action by an ethics committee. NGH seems to be the one organization that has a bona fide ethics committee consisting of two ministers, a lawyer, a nurse, and a psychotherapist.

Through the years, there have been antagonistic attitudes between organizations that really were unnecessary. For example, in a phone conversation in the early 1990s, when Gil Boyne (West Coast - ACHE) called me (East Coast - NGH) to tell me how I should be running the National Guild of Hypnotists, the end of the conversation went something like this:

> Damon: *"Well, thanks for the call, Gil, but we'll make any changes because we think they are needed, not because you think they are, but in the meantime, I'm glad that we can be friendly."*
>
> Boyne: *"I don't want to be your friend!"*
>
> Damon: *"Well, I don't want to come to your house for supper either, but you know what I mean ... the Guild has always tried to maintain friendly relationships with all other professional groups."*
>
> Boyne: *"Didn't you hear what I said? I don't want to be your friend!"*
>
> Damon: *"Then why do you call me all the time?"*
>
> (Boyne then hung up the phone)

Gil Boyne became active in legislation in California, Utah, Indiana, and other states, and for the most part, he preferred to operate independently, rather than in conjunction with any other hypnotism organizations.

For many years, Boyne actively attacked other hypnotism organization leaders, Dr A.M. Krasner of ABH and Dr Dwight Damon of NGH became his favorite targets. To his credit, in 2002, Boyne publically apologized for his behavior toward us with the following recorded and printed apology:

## A PUBLIC APOLOGY (LONG OVERDUE)
### From GIL BOYNE

In 1980 I founded the American Council of Hypnotist Examiners for the primary purpose of developing a curriculum which would become a standard for certification of hypnotherapists. This included a substantial increase in the hours of classroom training before certification could be granted.

In October 1987, Dwight Damon, Director of the National Council of Hypnotists, offered to promote a three day master class for me in New York. I accepted and was featured on the cover of the *Journal* of the National Guild of Hypnotists. A feature article was written about my career and my creation of Transforming Therapy ™.

The seminar was held in New York in May, 1988, and was well attended by more than sixty hypnotherapists, mostly National Guild of Hypnotists members. Since the National Guild of Hypnotists' requirement for certification was far less than the 200 classroom hours required by the American Council of Hypnotist Examiners, I decided to use the seminar as a "bully pulpit" to attack the certification policy of the National Guild of Hypnotists, and to speak of the merits of the American Council of Hypnotist Examiners training and certification policies.

I proceeded to vigorously attack the training policies of the National Guild of Hypnotists in a hostile manner while engaging in argumentative discussions with class members. This was an unethical decision and I have regretted it many times since.

The action was a product of egoism and unthinking arrogance on my part. Of course, I created numerous enemies, many of whom have since become dedicated adversaries. For many years since then, the two organizations have savaged each other to the detriment of the profession.

For more than 25 years there were numerous legislative efforts to restrict the practice of hypnotherapy to state licensed medical and mental health practitioners. All of them were defeated!

I am convinced that the defeat of these legislative bills was influenced by;

(a) the efforts of a few dedicated political activists

(b) many successful case histories which created a great number of word-of-mouth testimonials which led to numerous media stories of the benefits of hypnotherapy.

(c) the ever-increasing number of practitioners trained by the major schools and associations in America.

In the forefront have been the schools and instructors of the American Council of Hypnotist Examiners, the National Guild of Hypnotists, and the American Institute of Hypnotherapy

Although there are others, I am focusing on these three because they have trained the greatest number of students, many of whom have become highly skilled professional hypnotherapists and instructors.

The American Council of Hypnotist Examiners continues to question the certification of students who have completed only brief and superficial introductory courses, and are immediately told they are competent to begin a practice.

However, the National Guild of Hypnotists has gone on to develop many instructors/trainers who offer continuing education programs sponsored by the National Guild of Hypnotists. In addition to initial training and continuing education programs, the final development of professional competence is gained by the practical experience of working with clients.

Although our organizations advocate different policies and principles for training, we have common purposes--to continue the growth, progress, understanding and creative uses of hypnotherapy, the profession we love so well. Just as in politics, we can agree to disagree in some areas and yet form and nourish lasting friendships on a foundation of shared interests. For too long, the American Council of Hypnotist Examiners has been an exclusive organization. The time has come for us to become fully inclusive!

I recognize and appreciate the fact that the long-range vision and plans of Dr Damon, Dr Krasner, Tad James and I have common origins, purposes and goals.

As an initial step toward reducing discord and antagonism, I offer my heartfelt apology to all that I have offended and alienated with my words and deeds. This apology is especially directed to Dr Dwight Damon and Dr Al Krasner since they were most often the target of my attacks.

Together with the officers and members of the American Council of Hypnotist Examiners, I wish to be on public record that I am committed to the full professional acceptance, recognition and appreciation of our colleagues in the National Guild of Hypnotists and the American Institute of Hypnotherapy.

With Respect to All,


Gil Boyne, CEO Emeritus
American Council of Hypnotist Examiners


Three years after the public apology, in a newspaper interview during a 2005-06 Connecticut hypnotherapist's trial on a sex charge, Boyne took the opportunity to attack Dr Dwight Damon and the NGH as being the reason the problem could occur. The defendant happened to be an NGH member, which had nothing to do with the case. He was found guilty of the charges and deported to England.

NGH was able, with the assistance of NFH 104, OPEIU and the AFL/CIO state chairman, to participate in the creation of a reasonable and fair law which covers all hypnotists, including stage performers. The law also classified hypnotists with licensed health providers, mandating any sexual charges against practitioners to be treated as felonies.

In spite of some personal failings, it should be acknowledged that Gil Boyne definitely had a major role as leader, teacher, author, and legislative activist in the profession. It appears, though, that he wanted to be the only one in the profession in any of these roles. Born in 1924, Gil Boyne died in London, England, in May of 2010, but he definitely left a lasting legacy to the profession.

Has this attitude changed between organizations a quarter of a century later? Not really, especially since a person can be maligned around the world with a few key strokes on the Internet in a matter of seconds. Nevertheless, great progress has been made because most professional hypnotists really do practice what they preach to their clients—positive results from a positive attitude.

Dr William J. Bryan, Jr., a medical doctor, minister, and attorney, founded the American Institute of Hypnosis (AIH) with associates, in California, on May 4, 1955. A flamboyant character, he had legitimate degrees in medicine, law, and religion and definitely knew how to woo the media to get personal publicity and promotion. He developed a system of electronic hypnosis and the Bryan method of hypnoanalysis. Among his many credits was as a consultant on the movies *Tales of Terror, The Manchurian Candidate,* and the cult classics *Dementia 13.*

As I recall, Bryan was a student of Gil Boyne's and most of his exploits were before the Internet and instant communication as we know it today. He was a magnet for the press, but most of his publicity was confined to the West Coast and Las Vegas.

An exception would be when Bryan started working on high profile, headline-grabbing legal cases with attorneys such as Melvin Belli and F. Lee Bailey, and he was credited with being responsible for the confession of the "Boston Strangler," Albert DeSalvo.

Attorney Melvin Belli, who was big on demonstrating evidence in ways that hadn't been seen in courts previously, used charts and films dramatically to influence jurors, and obviously thought that Bryan was a natural for this kind of presentation. The book that seemed to really help Bryan's credibility was a book that F. Lee Bailey wrote, called *The Defense Never Rests.*

In one trial, a judge decided that Bryan was not qualified as a forensic hypnosis expert, and this was later affirmed by the California Supreme Court. Bryan claimed that he had been licensed to practice medicine in California since the early 1950s. He admitted on the stand that he was not a psychiatrist, but the surprising thing was that he admitted he had only become involved in hypnosis less than a year before this trial and had never appeared in any court previously as an expert, especially never to testify about someone's state of mind at the time of a crime. They said he was not credible, so Bryan took steps to make himself credible—he wrote a textbook, *The Legal Aspects of Hypnosis.*

Later in his career, authors of one of the many RFK conspiracy books alleged that Bryan was responsible for inducing Sirhan Sirhan, through posthypnotic suggestion, to shoot RFK. Other conspiracy theorists repeated this claim, but Bryan denied this then died suddenly, before he could initiate libel suits.

During his career, Bryan was the author of *Religious Aspects of Hypnosis; The New Self-Hypnosis*, with Paul Adams, *The Chosen Ones; The Psychology of Jury Selection*, and *Media Sexploitation; The Hidden Implants in America's Mass Media–And How They Program and Condition Your Subconscious Mind*.

It was well-known that he had a number of legal problems concerning female clients in the late '60s, and once he was extradited from California to Nevada for charges involving an 18-year-old girl in Las Vegas.

In 1978, Bryan was found dead in a Las Vegas hotel room, reportedly from natural causes, although even with a coroner's report, there was later speculation as to the actual cause of his demise. All in all, William Joseph Bryan, Jr. was a flamboyant and enigmatic character in the field of hypnotism for almost a quarter of a century, 1955-1978.

Hypnotism Motivation Institute (HMI), located in Tarzana, California, was founded in 1968 by Dr John Kappas, author of *The Professional Hypnotism Manual, Relationship Strategies, The ESP Attraction, Improve Your Sex Life Through Self-Hypnosis,* and several other books. Dr Kappas died in 2002, and is survived by his wife, Florence Henderson, a popular TV actress who starred as the mother on "The Brady Bunch," a very popular TV series. She is also known as a certified hypnotherapist, and continues her career as a popular and active television star.

As principals in the ownership of HMI, Kappas, his son George, and the Hypnotherapists' Union Local # 472 were involved as defendants in a class action suit during the late 1990s. The suit was launched by a former student, Jeffery Higley, in the spring of 1999, in Los Angeles Superior Court. According to public record, the suit alleged an inferred promise in the school's advertising materials of employment and career opportunities after graduation. Part of the lawsuit also concerned the fact that students of HMI were required to join the hypnotists Union.

HMI is now directed by George Kappas and provides training leading to graduation as a certified hypnotherapist. The American Hypnosis Association (AHA) and Hypnotists Union local # 472 are also closely connected with HMI.

The American Institute of Hypnotherapy (AIH), not to be confused with the earlier American Institute of Hypnotism (AIH) operated by Dr William J. Bryan, Jr., was founded in Santa Ana, California, by Dr A.M. Krasner in 1982, four years after Dr Bryan's death. Al Krasner had also migrated from the East Coast, where he had a professional practice in Warwick, Rhode Island. He soon had 19 offices operating in the LA area, He is the author of the popular book on hypnotism, *The Wizard Within*, which was published in 1990 -'91. It may be apocryphal, but it was said that the book title was chosen in response to Gil Boyne's constant public referral to Al Krasner as the "Wizard of Oz."

For a number of years, AIH was approved by the California Bureau for Private Postsecondary & Vocational Education to grant PhD and DCH degrees. In subsequent years, the PhD degree program was eliminated, but the DCH (Doctor of Clinical Hypnotherapy) program remained in place. At one time these degrees were available by distance learning as well as in class in California.

AIH was sold in 1995 to a former student and staff member, Dr Tad James, who is known for his work in the field of NLP and as the creator of Time Line Therapy®. Tad James is the author of *Hypnosis: A Comprehensive Guide, The Secret of Creating Your Future*®, and *The Lost Secrets of Ancient Hawaiian Huna.* Drs Tad and Adriana James currently operate the Tad James Company, specializing in Neuro Linguistic Programming training.

Mathew "Matt" James, son and former collaborator of Tad James, now operates AIH. He is listed as president of Kona University, formerly known as American Pacific University.

Banyan Hypnosis Center for Training & Services in Tustin, California, is operated by Calvin Banyan, MA, BCH, CI, DNGH, a licensed psychotherapist. In 1996 Cal, with his wife and business partner, Maureen, established the Banyan Hypnosis Center in Coon Rapids, Minnesota. They soon enlarged their services and became Banyan Hypnosis Center for Training & Services. Eventually they relocated to California, which provided a better base for hypnotism certification classes there and in Singapore.

Cal Banyan formulated a process called *Five-Phase Abreactive Therapeutic Hypnosis*, which is known as 5-PATH®. He is a certified instructor for the NGH and co-authored *Hypnosis and Hypnotherapy* with Gerald Kein. He is without doubt one of the most enthusiastic boosters of hypnosis in general, and a very prolific user of the Internet to spread the word.

In 1978, Boyne graduates Randal Churchill and Marleen Mulder founded the Hypnotherapy Training Institute in Corte Madera, California. It was one of the first licensed hypnotherapy schools in the state. Currently, in 2010, after Gil Boyne's passing, Churchill became president of ACHE, a West Coast hypnotism member organization originally started by Boyne.

Since 1968 Churchill has built a reputation as an intuitive, highly supportive therapist. He is the originator of Hypnotic Dreamwork™ and the author of *Become the Dream, Regression Hypnotherapy: Transcripts of*

*Transformation*, and *Catharsis in Regression Hypnotherapy*.

David Quigley, BA, who was trained in 1980 by Churchill, operates a state licensed post secondary school, the Alchemy Institute of Hypnosis, in Santa Rosa, California. During the 1990s Quigley wrote *Alchemical Hypnotherapy*, which is based on a system of hypnosis for healing that he developed in conjunction with somatic healing, a way of using hypnosis to help a client enhance the body's ability to heal itself.

*John C Hughes*

*Arnold Furst*

*Ormond McGill*

*Outstanding stage hypnotists who were also knowledgeable and dynamic teachers.*

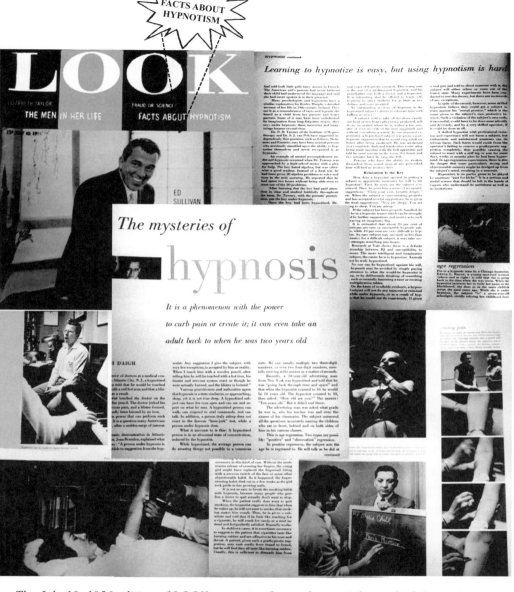

The July 10, 1956 edition of LOOK magazine featured an article in which hypnotists Edwin Baron of Chicago and Joan Brandon were featured with age-regression and anesthesia demonstrations.

Author Ralph Daigh concluded, "Hypnotism is no parlor game to be played just for kicks. It is a serious and useful science that should be left in the hands of experts who understand its usefulness as well as its limitations."

# Chapter 10
## Hypnotism in College Settings

Maurice Kershaw, MA, DNGH, who, in his native England, studied with Dr Sidney J. Van Pelt, emigrated to Canada and established a private practice in Montreal in 1953. In addition to conducting his own classes, Professor Kershaw also taught a block of three full-credit courses in hypnotism for pre-medical and dental students at John Abbott College of McGill University. In the past 60 years, perhaps this was one of the most significant inroads in advancing hypnotism—the first full college credit courses in the field.

Retiring after 24 years of teaching at McGill, Professor Kershaw had developed the training syllabus and curricula to such a degree as to be able to teach it to other hypnotism instructors in workshops and via a printed and recorded NGH course, *How to Teach Hypnotism Courses in Colleges.*

Ed Hightower, BS, DNGH, a highly-respected hypnotist and instructor, was one of the first to have a certification program accepted by a college when he introduced the NGH Hypnotist Certification curriculum at Edgar Mevers College, a senior college of the City University of New York, located in Brooklyn.

There have been numerous community colleges around the country which have given credits for hypnotism courses, but it has not yet moved into the higher levels of academia, and probably won't for many years until the profession is more firmly entrenched and has proven itself through its own practitioners.

Most hypnotism instructors simply rent facilities in the evening for classes, although several have established more official connections as a part of the adult learning or continuing-education offers of an institution.

Although there are undoubtedly many adult-education courses being taught in community colleges nationwide, there is no complete list available at this time.

### Alternative Training, Certifications, and Degree Programs

A note of concern regarding alternative degrees might be in order in this chapter. Although it has not been a major problem in our profession, there has been some activity with non-accredited doctorates. According to media stories, there is a problem of bogus degrees in many fields of endeavor, including education, law-enforcement, and local and federal government.

John Bear, PhD, having established himself as an authority on diploma mills since 1974, has published his well-known manuals on obtaining alternative education, *How To Get The Degree You Want*. Bear formerly included a section in his books, as an exposé or factoid, which gave detailed information about diploma mill locations, etc. Recently he decided not to include the information, since so many readers were using it to purchase diplomas or degrees, even with the knowledge that they were bogus.

It should also be noted that in recent years Bear has been attacked by proponents of distance-learning, noting that his real name is John Andrew Klempner, and criticizing his information because he does state in his manual that he has been a paid consultant to various schools, such as: Columbia Pacific University, Fairfax University, and others. Yet, on the whole, his work is widespread, acknowledged, and quoted.

In recent years the US government operated project "DipScam," an FBI diploma mill task force which exposed the problem affecting many professions. There have been and still are some spurious degree mills operating in the few states that haven't clamped down on the educational requirements for post-secondary education institutions.

Turned down by the court when he tried to legally change his first name to "Dr" there is a hypnotist who simply calls himself "Doc" as he operates his Internet business, although we have never seen any mention of the source of his personal doctorate.

Being able to receive an advanced degree in various studies from mail order promoters who use names similar to legitimate colleges and universities has been around for years. Fortunately, it has not touched the profession of hypnotism extensively.

Yet, every so often, there have been PhDs and other hypnotherapy "doctorates" in the past 25 years, which could be obtained simply for life experience or by reading and submitting book reports, and payment of "tuition."

In the mid 1950s there were, for example, the College of Applied Psychology in Miami, Florida; National Institute of Hypnology in Charlotte, North Carolina; and New York College of Psychiatry in NYC. All were offering courses and degrees and were shut down by authorities. One "Dean" (proprietor) ended up doing time for wire fraud, probably due to the fact that "students" could simply send money and receive their diplomas by return mail.

According to the Internet, ABC's 20/20, and John Bear, in the mid '80s, Columbia State University was operated by Ronald Pellar, a professional hypnotist aka Dr Dante, who is mentioned elsewhere in this book. The "institution of higher learning" was definitely one of "distance learning." Pellar oversaw it long-distance from his $1.5 million luxury yacht in Mexico. There was no faculty, no curriculum, no classes, no courses, no tests, no library, no educational facilities, no campus, and no academic accreditation, according to the US government. There was just a mail drop office in Louisiana receiving the money, forwarding it to Pellar, and sending diplomas to the "graduates."

According to public testimony by a former employee, the operation grossed about $20 million between 1996 and 1998, offering bachelor, masters, and doctoral degree programs in a variety of fields with degrees granted supposedly earned on students' life work, but mostly their ability to send their tuition money. Pellar was arrested on his yacht in Mexico, tried, and once again did time in prison. This operation wasn't necessarily aimed at hypnotists, it just happened to be operated by one. It was widely covered in the press and on TV show such as "20/20."

I attended a free introductory evening presented by "Dr Dante" at Detroit's Cobo Hall in the early '90s. The full page newspaper ads had told of the wonders and opportunities of becoming a hypnotherapist. We were interested in what his approach was, since he also offered free training and membership in a group of hypnotists who were going to work with cancer patients.

Going into Cobo Hall to the lecture room he was to use, I passed several lobby blowups of Dante with various well-known stars in Vegas and Hollywood. One featured him with Lana Turner, the movie star he was married to for a short time.

I had flown to Detroit to attend, but I felt a bit conspicuous since I was the only attendee wearing a tie, suit jacket, and carrying an attaché case, having come directly from the airport.

Dante took pleasure in mentioning several times about "doing time" regarding his attempt to put out a contract on a competitor. As I recall, he also seemed to take great delight in mispronouncing hypnotherapist as 'hypno the rapist." Ever the showman, he finished the presentation by doing a full-body catalepsy on an audience volunteer.

There are other mentions of Dante in our chapters on stage hypnotists and also diploma mills. Not too long ago, there was a TV interview with him in his California trailer court home. He said he was living on his social security, and things didn't look good, but one thing I noticed was that he still had the strong voice of a professional stage hypnotist and showman, even though everything else seems to be long gone from his life in the spotlight.

There really haven't been any major scandals in hypnotism certification for quite some time, although there are always fast-buck operators and less than scrupulous practitioners in every profession.

However, there was the previously mentioned class action suit brought by students against one well-established hypnotherapy institute a few years ago which was, among other things, directed toward the school's alleged promise of finding employment or starting a profitable professional practice on completion of the training. Of course, this can happen to any post-secondary school in any field.

As this book is being written, the federal government has been preparing a bill regarding "for-profit" schools of all types. Tuition fees, which are often government-guaranteed student loans, and inferred employment opportunities by student recruiters have apparently caused problems country-wide. Legislation of this type would impact only a small number of schools training hypnotists.

Although post-secondary school laws vary from state to state, they often allow small classes to be taught without a school being state licensed, but reputable hypnotism organizations encourage their instructors to be in compliance, whatever the case may be in their particular state. Prospective students should always ask for names and contact information of previous students so that they can be sure graduates of previous trainings were fully satisfied.

*Ronald Dante was married to movie star Lana Turner—her 8th husband. In 1969, six months into the marriage, Dante filed for divorce citing extreme cruelty. Turner claimed he stole money and jewelry from her.*

*In 1974 Dr Dante attempted to put out a "contract" on Dr Michael Dean, a rival night club hypnotist. The supposed hit-man was actually an undercover policeman. Dante was tried and served time.*

# Chapter 11
## Hands-On Training vs Books & Electronics

It should be noted that many instructors and schools have experimented with distance-learning, but the institutions that have grown in number of satisfied graduates who continue in the profession have stayed with the traditional methods of hands-on training. Although distance learning has become popular for other studies, it is generally acknowledged that hands-on instruction is still the best approach for hypnotism certification training. At the time of this writing, a strict protocol is being researched and developed as some trial classes have been conducted and studied.

The goal for conscientious schools is to produce graduates who are competent and confident and have actually hypnotized, under supervision, volunteer clients and classmates. In view of this, on-line courses and home-study videos don't have the advantage of personal instruction, demonstration, and monitored hands-on practice that can be provided in an actual classroom atmosphere by an experienced instructor.

During the 1960s through the 1990s, even with all the Internet and electronic technology developing, most instructors and schools found that "show and tell" with student hands-on participation still achieves the best training results. An exception to hands-on training, however, would be continuing-education courses for those who are already certified and in practice. NGH instituted continuing-education to the profession in 1990, so each member is required to earn 15 CEUs per year to maintain their *certification* level, and other organizations soon followed suit. This is good, since required continuing-education was introduced so that the profession would be prepared if any future requirements from government agencies should occur.

Generally speaking, most professional hypnotism organizations produce videos, DVDs, tapes, and CDs for members to rent or purchase. Several organizations also publish their publications, etc., as e-zines via the Internet, so the entire profession is moving ahead with the times. One leading school on the West Coast has also experimented with interactive classes, which require a certain amount of electronic capability by the home classroom student, similar to that which is used with house-bound students in public schools. This has not gained wide acceptance at the time of this book being written, possibly because of the set-ups required for students to participate.

During the 1960s through the 1990s, even with all of the Internet and electronic technology developing, most instructors and schools found that "show and tell" with student hands-on participation still achieves the best training results for producing student confidence and competence. Those who know me also know that I feel hands-on is an integral part of teaching new hypnotism students, but they also know that I try to maintain an open mind to progress.

Although video training in the classroom originated years ago with Gil Boyne and his demonstrational videos in classes, only time will tell if there will be more participation in distance-learning and whether it will be as effective as the tried and true methods now in effect.

Obviously, as another generation comes along students are often more comfortable with the electronic training tools used in school and colleges of today. This is where training materials need to constantly be upgraded with DVDs, CDs, MP3s, and Power-Point to be considered for use by instructors. Yet, there is still the inherent factor of "hands-on" that I think will always be a part of the best training modules in a profession which deals in a one-on-one manner between hypnotist and client.

As far as spreading the word, there is no doubt that the Internet plays an important part in telling people about our profession. I recently saw a list regarding those who presently lead the field for Internet presence promoting legitimate recognized hypnotism training. Listed alphabetically were the following: Cal Banyan, Ralph Benko, Georgina Cannon, Carol Denicker, Ron Eslinger, Marilyn Gordon, HMI, Tad James, Wil Horton, Martin Kiely, Jerry Kein, Don Mottin, NGH, Dick Sutphen, Tom Nicoli, Beverly Taylor, Scott McFall, Jerry Valley, and John Weir. I'm sure there are many more not included in that particular list, since the Internet has become a valuable method of advertising services.

Of course, there are also many cut-rate, mail-order, distance-learning courses being promoted on the Internet. Many have very impressive websites and unbelievable offers. However, when a short, downloadable course, normally offered for $995 is on sale for $95, it does make one wonder about what the true value really is with such a large discount. Also, when a so called "certification" course is offered free over the Internet and concludes with an oral exam and a pitch to enroll in a more expansive certification course, it too creates doubt about the credibility of the training.

# Chapter 12
## Associations, Organizations, Schools and Personalities

During the 1950s through the 1970s, not much had changed in the approach to training that had been established in the late 1940s and early 1950s classroom demonstration and hands-on approach. There was predominately very little in the way of texts or written materials, except for the student's own notes and perhaps some outlines or instructor's handouts. Harry Arons used his *Master Course of Hypnotism* textbook for his classes.

We continued using the Boston Hypnotism Center course, which John Hughes and I had used in the mid '50s in Iowa, and when the National Guild of Hypnotists was re-activated in 1986, *Power Hypnosis* became the official text as we presented an introductory course throughout New England. This was a one-day, non-certification intensive that covered the basics and featured hands-on, group participation in guided hypnosis sessions. This very abbreviated course, conducted by us as two experienced hypnotists/instructors, started many attendees on their way to more formal training and certification. Meanwhile, it was a period of testing and actually finding out how much interest there was in learning hypnotism in 1985-'86. We proved time and again that there was widespread interest in learning *how to hypnotize yourself and others*. Our brief, introductory course showed there was a definite interest in studying a more extensive curriculum which could lead to certification.

Harry Arons had written numerous articles as a contributing editor of the *Journal of Hypnotism*© (1951-'52), yet he also considered himself to be a competitor of North and the fledgling NGH. It was apparent that he resented the establishment and growth of the NGH and its *Journal of Hypnotism,*© even though, or perhaps because, he had contributed his mailing list to help launch them both. He had thought that neither project would succeed, but they did. In 1950, when Rexford North asked to borrow his mailing list, Arons had said, "OK, but it's going to be a waste of postage stamps."

The *Journal of Hypnotism*© and National Guild of Hypnotists succeeded, much to Arons' dismay, and he ceased being on friendly terms, taking potshots at North and the NGH in his own publication … it was back to the old "competitors, not colleagues" that I mentioned before.

The *Journal of Hypnotism*© had stopped publication when Dr North suddenly disappeared in 1956, then it was revived in a larger format as the *New Journal of Hypnotism*© when the NGH re-emerged as a viable and growing entity, having been brought back to life in 1986.

When we started our re-activation campaign, we mentioned in our literature some of the well-known hypnotists who had originally been members and that elicited a phone call to me from Harry Arons. He ordered me to not use his name because he had never been associated with the NGH. I calmly told him that he probably didn't remember me because I was just a college student working with Dr North when he and one of his people, Nard King, I think, came to Boston to visit the Hypnotism Center.

I also told him that one of my prize possessions hanging on my office wall (well, that part was a bit of a stretch, since it was in a file drawer in my office) was a picture of Dr North presenting him, Harry Arons, with his certificate of membership. His answer to this was that he would never admit to being a member unless I could produce a signed application for membership. He knew that back in those days we didn't have applications, you simply paid your $5, gave us your mailing address, and received your membership card. He had been given a complimentary membership as an associate editor of the *Journal of Hypnotism* anyway. I did stop using any mention of his name in 1986 though.

Unfortunately, Arons' personality hadn't improved in the 30 years since I had last seen him … he was still not a smiling, friendly man at all. However, I called him a couple of times a year about doing an interview and a *Journal of Hypnotism* cover to honor his contributions to the profession. Finally, in 1997, with the assistance of Terry Buhler, he agreed. Arons was in a nursing home by this time, and I made plans to travel to New Jersey to talk with him, but it wasn't meant to be. He passed before we could set it up, and I ended up doing an article and cover page posthumously, in the December 1997 *Journal of Hypnotism*.

Harry Arons was certainly important in the world of hypnotism, but personally he was a real enigma. In preparing to write this book, I've spoken to Dr Walter Brackelmanns, Joe B. McCawley, Dr Richard Harte, and others. All of those I spoke with had close ties to him and they all gave different impressions, but most were close to mine. Nevertheless, I will say that he was dedicated, or perhaps even driven, in his hypnotic ventures.

As a side note, in 1956, shortly before Dr North's disappearance and the downsizing of NGH, Arons, observing the NGH success, established the Association to Advance Ethical Hypnosis (AAEH). Although some theorists have attempted to tie the two events together, there never has been any real basis for such an assumption other than it was probably an opportune time for it to occur.

The AAEH had overtaken the NGH in membership early in the '60s. As Arons concentrated on teaching and enrolling licensed health care professionals as members, he also opened up to admitting non-licensed "hypno-technicians" to membership.

Licensed physicians, dentists, etc., had for the most part been an untapped market for hypnotism books and courses, and as AAEH had little competition at that time, it took what doctors called the "lay hypnosis" community by storm. Soon, Arons also started his own hypnosis magazine, *Hypnosis Quarterly*, competing with the NGH in yet another way.

AAEH catered to people who wanted to use hypnosis in a licensed health professional capacity. There was an excessively strict code of ethics, which forbade members from doing hypnotic past-life regression, and even required a physician's referral just to help someone stop smoking. A member not licensed as a health professional used the title "hypno-technician."

There was also a myriad of strict rules, even extending to office signage and members' business cards. Arons was definitely concerned about impressing the medical community and the first AAEH president was Dr W. D. Taylor, a physician from Glen Ridge, New Jersey. There were always plenty of "degreed and licensed" members on key committees and the slate of officers.

Certification with AAEH came at the end of a long process of preparation, requiring supervision and an oral examination, which included a demonstration section and case history. Many hypnosis professionals believe that the AAEH was too conservative; however, it maintained strict membership requirements throughout its existence. The list of AAEH officers contains many physicians and dentists, and in spite of the stringent membership requirements, they established a number of member chapters in major US cities.

AAEH held its first convention in 1956, in New York City. There were about 130 hypnotists in attendance, and Jacob Bimblich, who attended, relates that there were only 9 or 10 women present, who were predominately wives of attendees. We'll discuss more about women in the world of hypnotism as the era unfolds.

There were many anecdotal stories about their conventions, such as the following: Through the years, a well-known performing mentalist, "The Amazing Kreskin," has been quoted as saying, "The concept of a 'hypnotic trance' is a myth," yet a printed report from an AAEH convention had a photo of AAEH member George Kresge, later legally known as "The Amazing Kreskin," performing stage hypnotism at one of their conventions.

Harry Arons dropped out of his controlling position in the AAEH in the early years, and everything was left to committees to handle. One staunch AAEH member, Dr Walter Brackelmanns, a practicing psychiatrist and professor at UCLA, was elected president and kept the organization going for many years as membership dwindled. Dr Brackelmanns, who had also lectured at the NGH convention several times, finally assembled his board of directors, and after thorough investigation and thought, it was decided to merge AAEH into the NGH late in 2009. Longtime AAEH secretary-treasurer, Joann Abrahamsen, worked diligently to also transfer archival material to the NGH, which provided additional verification for a number of recollections in this book.

Because of the many AAEH committees and committee members spread around the country, by the '70s, when Arons had stepped back from being in charge, it was difficult for any elected president to quickly gather a consensus in order to take action on important matters. For example, in 1993, D. Corydon Hammond's master plan to eliminate "lay" hypnotists was presented at the American Society of Clinical Hypnosis convention in New Orleans. AAEH President Levine said, when I called him to participate with us, "By the time I can get our group to agree to participate you'll have the situation all taken care of." As much as he saw there was a need, he was unable to take any action. He was right, we (NGH) took care of the situation.

The Hypnotist Examining Council (HEC) was created in 1973 as a California non-profit professional organization engaging in self-regulation of all who utilized hypnosis/hypnotherapy as an integral part of a professional practice. Gil Boyne was elected president of the organization and the primary focus was on formal and appropriate education and training followed by a comprehensive written examination and a practical demonstration of hypnosis skills before a board of examiners. A code of ethics and principles of practice were formulated and adopted.

The American Council of Hypnotist Examiners (ACHE) was also founded in 1980 by Boyne as a national organization to certify hypnotherapists worldwide. Examination and registration was to be done by regional examining boards, with certification by the national parent body. The regional councils were the result of the demand for full participation by experienced and influential practitioners in other states.

Hypnotist examining boards were to consist of no less than 5 and not more than 11 members. All board members were to have no less than three years of professional experience in a profession in which the use of hypnosis was an integral part. The majority of the board, it was determined, must be made up of non-licensees who were identified publicly by the primary professional title of hypnotherapist or clinical hypnotherapist.

It was to be the responsibility of the board to educate, examine and register all applicants who met established requirements, and to conform to and comply with the bylaws, ethics and requirements of the ACHE. Certification was awarded to qualified applicants by the ACHE.

The American Hypnotism Association (AHA) was formed by Dr William Bryan in 1955, and the American Hypnosis Association (AHA) was started in 1973 by Dr John Kappas. Both of these organizations operated in conjunction with schools operated by the founders. The American Hypnosis Association is still active today under the direction of George Kappas.

The Florida Association for Professional Hypnosis (FAPH) was founded in 1959-60 by Joe B. McCawley, Martin Segall, Ted Van Antwerp, Betty Gedrottis and Ernie Deutsch to help protect practicing hypnotists in the state and continue legislative efforts on their behalf.

The International Society For Professional Hypnosis (ISPH) was founded in Boontown, New Jersey in 1969-70 by hypnotism luminaries Frank J. Shames, Leo P. Gendreau, Harry Arons, Martin M. Segall, Joe B. McCawley, Ted Van Antwerp, Melvin Powers, Dr Garland Fross, Robert N. Sauer, and Maurice Kershaw, among others. One of the stated purposes of ISPH was "to be able to engage in activities that AAEH, a tax-exempt, non-profit organization, cannot be part of."

American Board of Hypnotherapy (ABH), a member organization, was founded in 1982 by Dr A. M. Krasner, as an adjunct to his AIH school. This organization was included in the purchase of the American Institute of Hypnotherapy (AIH) by Tad James.

In South Carolina in 1983, Reverend William Curtis, a Presbyterian Minister, was the founder and first elected president of the National Association of Clergy Hypnotherapists (NACH). Curtis envisioned an ongoing educational and support organization to help members of the professional clergy bring the benefits of hypnosis to ministries within institutional settings, including churches, private schools, hospitals, prisons, the military, and pastoral counseling organizations. A real fine southern gentleman, he called me just to wish us luck, when we were getting started in New York City with our second NGH convention in 1989.

In 1998, fifteen years after its foundation, the National Association of Clergy Hypnotherapists voted to merge into the National Guild of Hypnotists. It was the consensus of NACH members that "clergy will have a far greater influence in the 21st century within the NGH." Reverend Curtis in 1988 was the first to receive the newly established NGH "Hypnosis and Religion Award," which had been established by his peers for their special interest group within the NGH. NACH member Father Phillip Vogel spoke for many when he wrote: "Let me give you my analysis. I don't think NACH as it is now and perhaps realistically in the foreseeable future has the 'critical mass' (the numbers of members) to hold together and/or maintain members year after year. I perceive the only viable solution is for NACH to amalgamate with NGH, a nonprofit organization with a membership of over 5000 members (some of whom are clergy and who were not members of NACH). They have the 'critical mass' to be solvent and ongoing. Their convention is a learning buffet. I dare say that clergy interest in our group would be enhanced as members of NGH. We can provide ethical, religious and spiritual perspective and leadership for NGH."

The National Board of Hypnotherapy and Hypnotic Anesthesiology (NBHHA) was organized in 1984 in Glendale, Arizona by Dr Sean Longacre, a graduate of the American Institute of Hypnotherapy. Longacre was the author of *Client-Centered Hypnotherapy and Visualization and Guided Imagery for Pain Management*, six other textbooks and numerous articles about hypnotherapy and hypnotic anesthesiology for pain management. The organization changed its name to The National Board For Hypnotherapy and Hypnotic Anesthesiology in 1989, "to include all aspects of hypnotherapy." After Sean Longacre's passing in 1999, it's not clear whether the organization continued or not. It appears now to be inactive.

The International Association of Clinical Hypnotherapy (IACH/CPHA) was formed as the California Professional Hypnosis Association (CPHA) in 1967 and incorporated as a non-profit in April of 1971. The name was changed in 1989 "to better reflect the expanding membership worldwide," according to an IACH/CPHA newsletter of 1991. Headquarters were in Long Beach, California.

The International Hypnosis Federation (IHF) was founded in 1999-2000 by former airline stewardess and stand-up comic Shelly Stockwell, who is known for staging a group "hypnotizing" of chickens at a large convention on the East Coast in 1999. Stockwell has held a conference in California annually since forming her organization, and has also authored numerous books on hypnotism. An interesting feature of her convention catalog is that it features cartoons of chickens and, in 2011, a picture of Stockwell dressed in a chicken suit. They also feature "funshops" rather than workshops for attendees.

Two organizations, the National Society of Clinical Hypnotherapists (NSCH) and the American Counselors Society (ACS), were founded by the late Dr E. A. Winkler and his wife Dr Pamela Winkler, owners of St. John's University. E. Arthur Winkler's former college locations, according to *Bear's Guide,* were Nebraska, Missouri, and Ponchatoula, Louisiana, under the names of Eastern Nebraska Christian College, Nebraska Christian College, and Midwestern University.

Hypnosis Information Network (HIN) was founded in Bridgeton, Missouri in 1990 by Don Mottin, who soon had five hypnotism offices operating in Greater St. Louis. Don is currently the vice president of NGH, teaches certification classes, Train the Trainer courses, and continuing-education workshops around the country for the organization. He is the author of many workshops, scripts, courses, and how-to kits for professional hypnotists. *Raising your Children With Hypnosis*, a text for professional hypnotists and parents, is popular with professionals and laymen alike.

During 2003-2004, Don Mottin personally demonstrated the power of hypnosis when he encountered a series of health problems while maintaining his office schedule and teaching NGH continuing education workshops around the country. Although he was, to all appearances, an energetic and healthy young man in his early 50s, he was on the road with a cervical fracture, a mild heart attack, and extreme pain. While in the hospital for tests, a heart catheterization precipitated a major stroke, resulting in hospitalization. His prognosis, even after treatment and therapy, was that he would not recover and would always be in a wheelchair. However, even in a wheelchair, he traveled and continued to present at NGH conferences.

Through the power of hypnosis and the mind/body connection Don proved the doctors wrong. His amazing personal recovery prompted the presentation by colleagues of the unique "Hypnosis Iron Man" award in 2005. His personal experience also prompted creation of his widely acclaimed "Working With Stroke Survivors and Rewiring the Brain" workshop for consulting hypnotists and other professionals, which was acclaimed as the "Premier Continuing-Education Workshop of the Year" in 2010.

Hypnotism Training Institute graduates such as Wendal Churchill, Virgil Hayes, Marleen Mulder, David Quimby, Tim Simmerman, and Charles Tebbetts went out on their own to operate training schools with variations of the Hypnotism Training Center name in whatever city they were located. Most ACHE school operators remained loyal to Boyne through the years until the new century (2000) when several pulled away and made other affiliations for personal and professional reasons.

The American Association of Professional Hypnotherapists (AAPH) was founded in 1980 in California. Its purpose was to support hypnotherapists in establishing and successfully operating their own hypnotherapy businesses. California hypnotherapist Josie Hadley was the first president and, although she passed, the organization is still active, with an Internet website for members.

Dr Anne Spencer, an AIH graduate, formed the International Medical and Dental Association (IMDHA) in Royal Oak, Michigan in 1985. It was set up as a membership organization, and it is believed that the State of Texas at one time used the IMDHA Internet membership list to issue Cease and Desist orders to its members practicing in that state. After 25 years in practice, Anne Spencer retired in 2006 with the sale of the organization to Robert and Linda Otto.

International Association of Counselors and Therapists (IACT) was founded in 1990 by former NGH instructors Steven LaVelle and his wife, Jill, operating out of Florida. Small annual conventions were held, usually on the East Coast, and they also published a magazine, *Unlimited Human*. Jill became the sole owner of IACT in the late 1990s, and in 2006 sold the organization and magazine to Robert and Linda Otto who merged it with IMDHA, as the International Alliance of Professional Hypnotists (IAPH).

IMDHA/IACT/IAPH, headquartered in Lacyville, Pennsylvania is headed by Robert and Linda Otto. They publish *Unlimited Human* as an e-zine and hold annual conventions for their members. The Ottos had been successful hypnotists, traveling around the country doing one- day smoking cessation and weight management group presentations during the 1980s. During the 1990s Robert Otto served five years as president of the IHHFG.

The National Association of Certified HypnoCounselors (NACH) was organized in 1993 in New Jersey by Anthony DeMarco and John Gatto, the dedicated duo who championed the 1994 New Jersey Hypnocounselor Law. With the help of the union (NFH #104 OPEIU AFL CIO CLC) and at great personal expense, and countless hours of work, they shaped new legislation in the state of New Jersey which now protects the profession and established a new title, "Hypnocounselor." The state had been challenged several times before by Harry Arons and others, but this time a regulation of the NJ Board of Psychological Examiners granting an exemption to practice hypnotism was passed into law, thanks to the untiring efforts of these two NGH/NFH members, who have also operated the first state-licensed post-secondary vocational school of hypnosis in New Jersey since 1991—the Academy of Professional Hypnosis, in Union, New Jersey.

The International Hypnosis Hall of Fame (IHHF) in Bluebell, PA came on the scene in the early 1980s to honor outstanding hypnotism professionals. Penny Dutton Raffa, a pleasant and enthusiastic supporter of the practice of hypnotism and its practitioners, was president of the IHHF. The annual convention attendance was usually around 125-150 and featured presenters who had been nominated for induction into the Hypnosis Hall of Fame.

Raffa also started an affiliate association, The International Hypnosis Hall of Fame Guild (IHHFG), as support for the IHHF. She had a vision, which never came to pass, of creating an actual museum, but she continued to hold annual conferences and awards ceremonies until 2000, when they were discontinued. Penny Raffa also authored a limited edition, self-published, autobiography, *From Psycho to Psychic*.

The Hypnotism Educational Council International (HECI) was formed in 1980 by Charles Tebbetts after an acrimonious falling-out with Gil Boyne over book royalties and other matters. Tebbetts had taken Boyne's training during the 1970s and established a private practice in Los Angeles, where he developed a technique based on the teachings of Paul Federn, which he called "Parts Therapy." Tebbetts also wrote *Miracles on Demand* and *Self Hypnosis and Other Mind-Expanding Techniques*; both were initially published by Boyne's Westwood Publishing.

After this parting of the ways with Boyne, Tebbetts republished *Miracles On Demand.* However, a complete press run of this excellent hardbound book, last I knew, was sitting in a warehouse due to legal claims of two parties to whom, it was said, Tebbetts sold the rights.

By the end of the decade, Tebbetts was now known as "The World's Oldest Hypnotherapist." Charles Tebbetts and his wife were living in Washington state, where he established his school and conducted classes.

While attending the NGH Convention in 1992, Tebbetts suffered a fatal heart attack the day before his pre-convention workshop. Since we were meeting in Nashua, NH, we were able to immediately arrange for physicians to handle his case. It is interesting to note that the physicians involved in his ICU care later told me that, through conversation with his widow, they found he had more severe symptoms than he let them know about. He was masking them with self-hypnosis, and they told me that if they had a true evaluation they would have been better able to manage his case and possibly save his life.

However, Charlie, in an heroic effort not to disappoint anyone, used self-hypnosis to mask any pain or discomfort he felt while in the ICU. Roy Hunter jumped in at the convention to present the workshop for his mentor, and continues the Parts Therapy work today. Hunter is the author of *The Art of Hypnosis, The Art of Hypnotherapy, Hypnosis for Inner Conflict Resolution,* and *Mastering the Power of Self-Hypnosis*.

The World Congress of Professional Hypnotherapists (WCPH) was founded early in 1980-81 by Barrie Konicov, an entrepreneurial hypnotist who is said to have sold several million hypnosis tapes of various titles. The FDA raided his offices due to the claims he made regarding the efficacy of his tapes. A one-time Libertarian candidate for the United States Congress, Konicov was also listed by *Atlantic* magazine as one of the ten biggest tax scofflaws of the 20th century, according to Wikipedia.

Also, according to the Internet, the Internal Revenue Service pursued charges against Konicov and in 2001 he was convicted on income tax charges. Konicov was sentenced to 87 months in a federal penitentiary plus three years probation. The judge also ordered Konicov to pay his back taxes of $11,311.81. Reportedly he acted as his own attorney, and as in the case of Ralph Slater in England in the 50s, it was said that he caused himself problems with the judge due to his behavior in court.

Roy Cage of Forth Worth, Texas was prominent in the formation of the National Society of Hypnotists (NSH) in 1984. Although a small group, they were a dedicated core of professional hypnotists who met annually, usually in Las Vegas, to study and discuss the profession. Cage served as president and "sparkplug" of the group. He is also credited with the original concept of establishing a coalition of all hypnotism organizations to work for the common good. His idea was acted on and COPHO was started at an ABH meeting in California in 1989.

The Texas Association for The Hypnosis Institute (TATHI) was formed by Frank Monaghan, hypnotist and school operator in the Dallas/Fort Worth area in the early '70s into the mid '80s. Monaghan was best-known for his limited edition book, *The Waking Sleep*, in which he stated that "hypnosis is not a state of unconsciousness but is definitely a form of sleep, since the individual's body is more relaxed that in physiological sleep."

The National Association of Transpersonal Hypnotherapists (NATH) was established in 1989 as a transpersonal hypnotherapy member organization. Founders are Allen S. Chips, DCH, PhD, author of *Clinical Hypnotherapy: A Transpersonal Approach*, *Script Magic*, and *Killing Your Cancer Without Killing Yourself*. Together, with his wife Dee Chips, BSW, MHt, CRM, author of *Inspirational Poetry* and *The Power of Reiki,* they also operate the American Holistic University and hold annual conferences in Virginia Beach, Virginia.

Although located in Montreal, Canada, Professor Maurice Kershaw is included in this book because so much of his time was spent working with AAEH and NGH, developing the profession in the US When the NGH Certification Board was established, Kershaw became the chairman and chief examiner, and has been a frequent convention faculty presenter on "Pediatric Hypnosis," "Geriatric Hypnotism," and "How to Teach Hypnotism on a College Level. " Kershaw is also internationally known for his research and oral presentations on the history of hypnotism.

Georgina Cannon, Reverend Tim Jones, and Debbie Papadakis from Ontario, Canada, with their teaching and media availability have also helped considerably to establish our profession in the US, and Canada.

On January 3, 1990 Hypnobirthing and an idea for a Hypnobirthing© Institute came into existence when Marie Mongan's grandson became the first baby born using this technique. Reportedly, the hospital personnel were in awe. They had seen women experience gentle birthing before, but they knew that this birth was not to be dismissed. What they were seeing was not a fluke, but a birth that had been carefully and lovingly planned, prepared for, and achieved.

What those hospital personnel also witnessed was the official birth of HypnoBirthing The Mongan Method, a process that would have a place in the history of hypnotism, as Marie Mongan went on to register the name and create a training program that grew considerably during the '90s. Her program draws practitioners from both the hypnosis profession and the medical field worldwide.

Although she has been a long time Certified Instructor for the NGH, her primary focus has been involved with her growing organization. Because of the numbers of successful births by mothers using the Mongan Method, her organization became international long before the end of the decade.

The National Society of Hypnotherapists (NSH) was founded in California by Dr Irene Hickman, an osteopath who then became a consultant to the group.

The HypnoFertility Foundation originated in Colorado to address the need for fertility and birth by hypnosis assistance for infertility sufferers in the US and abroad. Board certified consulting hypnotists and directors are Lynsi Eastburn, author of *It's Conceivable! Hypnosis for Fertility*, and Art Leidecker, author of *From Scratch and On a Shoestring*. They were both operators of licensed hypnosis schools and have taught programs internationally. Specific hypnotic procedures complement both natural and medically assisted fertility and birth in their methodology.

# Congressional Record

Hon. William H. Zeliff, Jr.
of New Hampshire
In the House of Representatives

*Tuesday, May 11, 1993*

Mr. ZELIFF Mr. Speaker. New Hampshire State Representative Dennis H. Fields recently brought to my attention the activities of the National Guild of Hypnotists. At the request of Representative Fields, I am sharing his information with my colleagues.

The basic objectives of the National Guild of Hypnotists are: 'to provide an open forum for the free exchange of ideas and to actively pursue due recognition of the importance of hypnotism for mankind.' The National Guild of Hypnotists is pledged to constantly strive to establish and maintain a high code of ethics and to encourage continuing education and high standards for all individuals and organizations in the field of hypnotism and hypnotherapy.

Advisory board members have been enlisted from the major healing arts and other professions to provide a comprehensive pool of professional opinions and philosophies. A strong code of ethics guides members as they serve the public and other professionals. Researchers find the National Guild of Hypnotists to be a valuable resource for books, audiotapes, and videotapes and their widely read publications, the Hypno-Gram and Journal of Hypnotism.

Hypnosis has been used through the ages, but first started to be used more widely after recognition as a valid therapy by the British Medical Association in 1955 and the American Medical Association in 1958. The U.S. Department of Labor recognizes the occupational title of 'hypnotherapist,' and hypnotherapy is rapidly gaining recognition as a separate and distinct profession.

The National Guild of Hypnotists has initiated and constantly upgrades basic and postgraduate educational resources for the benefit of students, practitioners, and the general public. Alternative therapies studies rank hypnotherapy as one of the most highly favored by the general public.

Annually, a thousand or more hypnotists come from around the world to New Hampshire for what has become known as the world's largest and friendliest hypnosis convention and educational conference. During the 42nd year of the National Guild of Hypnotists, we should commend and encourage them by recognizing their outstanding past accomplishments and wishing continued growth to this unique organization and its dedicated members.

# Chapter 13
## ReBirth of NGH

The first "presenters" we brought to the East Coast under NGH auspices in mid '88 were Arnold Furst and Ormond McGill, with workshops in New York City, Boston, and Newark, N.J. Although Randal Churchill, on the West Coast, challenges our claim to dubbing Ormond "Dean of American Hypnotists," Elsom Eldridge and I still believe it was our doing, or it was at least a simultaneous or serendipitous happening.

The next workshop instructor we brought out to the East Coast was Gil Boyne. As he explains in his apology, elsewhere in this book, it proved to be an adversarial two days, which attendees were not necessarily aware of, but which created a difficult time for those of us who had to deal personally with him.

Instructors who were utilized by the National Guild of Hypnotists were Steve and Jill LaVelle ('86-'90), and George Bien (Bienkowski) ('89 -'94). The LaVelles and Bien both presented the new training in those years as a 3-day weekend course of instruction leading to certification as a registered hypnotist (RHy), but the need for an even longer course of instruction was still there. It is interesting, though, that many of today's successful consulting hypnotists started their careers as students in the basic weekend courses many years ago. The intensive courses often ignited a desire for more training and knowledge, and often led to a career as a professional hypnotist.

Assured that there was a need for more thorough training, the NGH readily moved in that direction. In 1990 we recruited Dr Richard Harte, who had succeeded Harry Arons as the owner/director of Power Publishers and the Ethical Hypnosis Training Center. Harte was appointed NGH training director and developed the first basic and advanced core-curriculum for our emerging profession. His project brought the original courses of Arons and North together with modern additions to provide this basic core curriculum, which is annually kept current through independent evaluations, additions, and revisions. The classic approach to learning and practicing hypnotism still remains, with the goal of producing competent and confident graduates.

Often those who want to appear to be knowledgeable, but who were not even in our field as the curriculum was developed, are apt to say it was just a rewrite of the Arons course. However, the truth is that it was the genesis of today's most popular training materials and a composite of courses taught by many hypnotists in the late 1940s and early 1950s. There were additional up-to-date additions by Dr Harte, and through the years important contributions have been made by other well-known hypnotism educators such as Dr

Shaun Brookhouse, Fiona Biddle, Reverend C. Scot Giles, Don Mottin, and others who contributed their input as the world moved into another century. Updated texts, CDs, DVDs, MP3s, specialty booklets, and downloadable e-books have all been added.

Within a short time, interested students were able to take two college semester courses (100 hours) leading to designation as a certified hypnotherapist (CH). We had continual attacks from Gil Boyne, who wanted everybody to present 300 hours of training as he did. However, many of the hours of his training involved students in class watching recorded video demonstrations by Boyne with clients.

As the NGH and the profession have spread around the world, teaching materials have also been translated into over a dozen languages, making the National Guild of Hypnotists actually international in scope. Through NGH certified instructors, there are currently members in 72 countries who have taken the equivalent of two college semesters, or 100+ minimum hours, of hands-on training, plus homework assignments which provide more than the minimum required hours, often amounting to 100-150 hours, and leading to the title of Certified Consulting Hypnotist (CH). According to NGH headquarters in New Hampshire, even as cutting-edge teaching materials are added the philosophy remains the same—*show and tell*—instructor demonstrations and actual hands-on student practice with volunteer clients. The goal is to provide a solid foundation to insure the competence and confidence of each graduate.

The NGH core-curriculum has received commendation and validation by many educators and post-secondary organizations. Each year since its inception in 1991, the NGH core-curriculum has had annual updates and additional new study aids, such as DVDs, CDs, and additional text books added to remain state-of-the art.

So as not to infringe on licensed health professionals and to avoid restrictive laws, the certified hypnotherapist (CH) title became Consulting Hypnotist (CH) in August of 2006, and is currently in popular use. Nevertheless, in some areas, particularly on the West Coast and in other countries, there are many practitioners who still use the Certified Hypnotherapist title. Some states, such as Florida, have laws concerning "therapeutic hypnosis" or title laws, such as New Jersey's Certified "Hypnocounselor," so there is not standardization across the board with all organizations.

# Chapter 14
## The Dawn Of A New Era— The "Big Idea"—
## A Separate and Distinct Profession

Earlier we mentioned students in Dr Rexford L. North's first Boston Hypnotism class who would eventually play an important role in the development of NGH and the profession. They were Frank Anderson, Berchman Carville, and myself. Although not in that group, Elsom Eldridge, Jr., who had been a student of mine, would also play a key role, as you will see.

On mustering out of my service during the Korean conflict, I decided to keep the work of my missing mentor, Dr Rexford L. North, alive, but found quickly that it was a difficult proposition placing ads about hypnotism classes in New Hampshire newspapers. I could only purchase very brief ads, which were accepted reluctantly only because my family had advertised with the local newspaper for over thirty years and were also personal friends of the publisher.

Instead of returning to Emerson College in Boston I enrolled in Palmer Chiropractic College in Davenport, Iowa, where I received my degree as a doctor of chiropractic in 1959. My plans included opening a clinic in Merrimack, New Hampshire, but state board exams were not scheduled for a year. Having started on the air at WOC-TV while a student in Davenport, I dropped in to the local TV station and established my own weekly children's show on WMUR TV, an ABC affiliate in Manchester, New Hampshire. It was a live Saturday morning show and ran for close to 20 years. I also established my chiropractic practice and started a couple of other businesses. I guess you would call it multi-tasking now, but in those days it didn't have a special name.

Frank Anderson, on his discharge from the service, continued studying the emerging field of electronics and soon was developing instrumentation and devices for use by professional hypnotists and others during the '80s. He also developed a hypnotism practice in a suburb of Boston and later in Epsom, NH.

The third member of our trio, Berchman "Bert" Carville, had amazed physicians and military medics during his service in the Korean conflict when he suffered injuries from a grenade. During treatment for his new injuries, he used self-hypnosis and autosuggestion instead of any chemical anesthesia or drugs while having the shrapnel removed.

Carville had become a multi-linguist working for the US government in a job he would never discuss, but which took him around the world to many exotic locations. In his travels he also worked with hypnotism and published the same hypnosis book in many different languages. His mail address changed quite often. Sometimes it was an APO and other times Naval or Air Force bases. When we occasionally saw him he never did disclose what his job actually was, except that he worked for the US government.

We three Boston Hypnotism Center classmates also had kept in touch with other former NGH members, never wavering in our desire to rebuild the National Guild of Hypnotists sometime in the future. The future came in 1986 through a hypnotism enthusiast, friend, and former student, Elsom Eldridge, Jr.

Key factors in the 1986 comeback of NGH were the resources of the Achievement Center, owned by Eldridge, a longtime friend and hypnotism student of mine. He had built an extremely successful seminar business that covered the entire United States, and it was operated through the technology of computers, located in his offices in New Hampshire.

One day I visited his Achievement Center and it was an *aha* moment for me, his mentor when we were younger. The roles now reversed when my former student explained how computers could help me in revitalizing the NGH. It was fascinating, to say the least.

The decision was made by our few remaining NGH stalwarts to build the professional organization that had originally been envisioned 36 years earlier in 1950, now using successful non-hypnotism related member organizations as models.

Utilizing computer technology and old fashioned perseverance, the NGH grew to thousands of members in many countries by the end of the 20th century, and in 2011 now represents well over 12,000 members in 72 countries.

When the decision was made to reactivate the *Journal of Hypnotism*® in 1986, Dr John Hughes was named research editor. Since there had been a 30-year lapse between issues, it was decided to call the publication *The New Journal of Hypnotism* and it remained as such until September 1988, when we returned to the original title as the *Journal of Hypnotism*®.

NGH held its first convention in 1988, and it was attended by about 250 members. The rapidly growing organization featured a firewalk for interested participants and highlighted presenters such as Sol Lewis, Charles Tebbetts, Ormond McGill, Frank Anderson, Dwight Damon, Elsom Eldridge, Steve LaVelle, and Jerry Valley. Elsom and I were busy introducing the presenters, and he became the conference director, a position he has held for over a quarter of a century.

Former member and *Journal* columnist Maurice Kershaw was returning from an AAEH convention and stopped by the NGH convention on his way back to Montreal. He came back into the fold and resumed writing his *Journal* column after a 32-year hiatus.

As a longtime friend of mine, Ormond McGill came back on board as an integral member of the NGH team, presenting weekend workshops across the US He was soon to be recognized internationally as the "Dean of American Hypnotists." Back with friends at NGH he did workshops, wrote books, authored a regular column, produced many CDs and DVDs, and remained a loyal member until his passing in 2005 at the age of 93. In addition to his career as a world-traveled magician and stage hypnotist, Ormond McGill also was a skilled hypnotherapist and a student of Eastern mysticism. He wrote numerous books about hypnosis, meditation, and self-hypnosis, with many being published by the National Guild of Hypnotists. Most of all, Ormond McGill was a gentleman and a gentle man.

To date, no other hypnotist has matched McGill's prodigious output of books concerning hypnotism. He also wrote on many other subjects and was considered an authority in many specialties, even to having a rare species of butterfly he discovered officially named for him.

At the sixtieth anniversary NGH convention in August of 2010. four of the original 1950-51 charter member were present at the president's table, Dr Arnold Levison, the first NGH treasurer; Professor Maurice Kershaw, longtime columnist; Dr John C. Hughes, Research Editor; and myself, Dr Dwight Damon, President. However, there are many hypnotists who have come into the field in recent years and who will carry on the work now that we are firmly established, not as an industry, but as a distinct profession.

The National Guild of Hypnotists is the oldest and largest hypnotism member organization and has led the field since its re-birth in 1986, finally gaining us recognition as a separate and distinct profession. Once again, younger members of the Guild are making great strides in this brand-new profession, that is thousands of years old and more historical facts will be added by those who follow in the footsteps of the old guard.

Women have become an integral part of the profession as seen at the most recent NGH convention when 63% of attendees were female and 37% were male.

Many specialties have emerged in the past quarter century, and now consulting hypnotists are proud to say that they *help ordinary, everyday people with ordinary, everyday problems of life.* We consult with licensed professionals in the medical, dental, and mental health fields, as well as with members of the general public.

# Power Hypnosis Hypnotherapy

**A Two Day Seminar With Ormond McGill**
Dean of American Hypnotists

## Miami

## St. Louis
April 23-24, 1988

## Boston
March 26-27, 1988

## Chicago
May 21-22 1988

The Dean of American Hypnotists, Ormond McGill's POWER HYPNOSIS HYPNOTHERAPY SEMINAR — Demonstrations • Class Participation • Hypnomeditation • Hypnoanalysis • Power Hypnosis • Hypnosis for Talent Advancement • Profound Hypnosis • Vital Energy Techniques • Past Life Regression • And much, much more • With the Added Bonus of Ormond McGill's Evening "Concert of Hypnotism"

National Guild of Hypnotists
P.O. Box 308
Merrimack NH 03045

first class

### 3 Invitations

1. Don't Miss Ormond McGill's "Power Hypnosis Hypnotherapy" Two Day Weekend Seminar

NGH Continuing Education Classes
Instructors:
Ormond McGill — Arnold Furst
Donald Mottin — Gil Boyne

Plan Now to attend our
Continuing Education Weekend with

## GIL BOYNE

May 27-28-29, 1988 • New York City

**ADVANCED CLINICAL HYPNOSIS**

Gil Boyne's unique teaching methods have attracted students from every state in the United States and from 14 foreign countries. His totally new approach is a departure from traditional methods and techniques such as NLP and Ericksonian hypnosis.

This course is guaranteed to excite your imagination and stimulate your thinking, and may even transform your basic beliefs about hypnotherapy, as well as change your beliefs and attitudes about this exciting profession.

Three full days will be crammed with new techniques, including instantaneous induction. You will learn a pragmatic philosophy that focuses on results and not theories. Practical demonstrations, videotaped case histories, live therapies with class members, rapid age regressions are all included — and much, much more. Here is practical training for practical therapists who want to maximize their results.

**Tuition $445 (Guild Members: $395)**
To Register: Phone (603) 429-9438
or Write NGH, Box 308, Merrimack, NH 03054

A 2010 NGH CONTINUING EDUCATION WORKSHOP

## REWIRE THE BRAIN THROUGH HYPNOSIS
## THE ANSWER FOR STROKE SURVIVORS

*Presented by Don Mottin, CI, DNGH, OB*

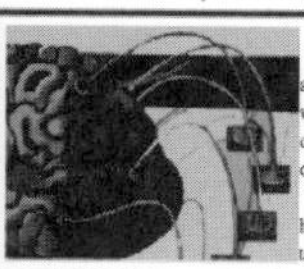

What is a stroke? In very simple terms a stroke is a brain attack. This takes place when blood flow is cut off to a certain part of the brain. Without blood flow a portion of the brain will die.

The good news is that we can actually help rewire the brain. Imagine what could take place if the brain could start learning a new function. For years, neurologists have known that the brain has the ability to repair itself.

When does hypnosis fit into this procedure? There are literally dozens and dozens of behaviors that can be affected after a stroke. You will learn to work with over 20 different symptoms. Here is your chance to give something very valuable to another individual.

A full workbook with scripts, techniques, and affirmations will give you the confidence you need to be a success when working with stroke survivors.

### Who Should Attend

[text partly illegible]

Have questions for Don?
Email him at dmottin@hotmail.com

Class 9am - 4:30pm

GUARANTEE

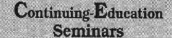

# Continuing Education Seminars

*Rapid Induction Techniques*
*and*
*Hypnotic Prescriptions for Hypnotherapy*

A FOUR-HOUR SEMINAR CONDUCTED BY

## Arnold Furst

Author of
"Rapid Induction and Self-Hypnosis"
"How to Prepare and Administer Hypnotic Prescriptions",
"The Hypnotic Approach to Successful Salesmanship"

| NEWARK | NEW YORK | BOSTON | HARTFORD |
|---|---|---|---|
| SATURDAY | SUNDAY | MONDAY | TUESDAY |
| June 13, 1987 | June 14, 1987 | June 15, 1987 | June 16, 1987 |
| 1pm to 5pm | 1pm to 5pm | 6pm to 10 pm | 6pm to 10 pm |
| HOWARD JOHNSON'S LODGE | BEST WESTERN MIDWAY HOTEL | HOWARD JOHNSON'S MOTOR LODGE | HOLIDAY INN |
| | | | |

SEMINAR TOPICS

Guild Members Only $55 if pre-registered before June 10th, Otherwise, $65 at the door.

# Chapter 15
## Legislative Action Through the Years

Without a doubt, the most important individual regarding legislation concerning the practice of hypnotherapy and hypnosis during this era was Reverend Scot Giles, a clergyman and the legislative liaison officer of NGH and NFH. Trained at Lombard Theological School at the University of Chicago he has a doctorate in Mental Health Ministry and maintains a private practice in Wheaton, Illinois.

Reverend Giles also directs a program called "I Can." The first medically approved program of its kind in the US for hypnotic intervention into cancer is based at LaGrange Hospital in LaGrange, Illinois.

In preparing this chapter of the book I am referring to the extensive notes compiled by Reverend Giles and filed with NGH through the years as well as our personal conversations, plus participation by myself and others in legislative matters. Scot Giles joined the NGH in 1992 and attended his first convention in 1993. Days after he got home he learned that the Illinois Clinical Psychologist License Act had changed into "Practice Protection."

Up until then health care license laws had been "Title Protection Laws" that merely protected a title. For example you could only call yourself a "Licensed Clinical Psychologist" if you held a license under that law. However, other people could do the same sort of things as a Licensed Clinical Psychologist, provided they just did not call themselves by that title.

However, a series of court decisions made it clear that there was a problem with "Title Protection License Laws." In a number of decisions, they were deemed an unconstitutional restriction of Freedom of Speech. Courts were ruling that only "Practice Protection License Laws" were fully legal.

A "Practice Protection Law" does not just protect a title. It does protect the title but also sets out a list of practices that only someone licensed under that law can do.

Medical Doctors have had such laws for decades. For example, only a Medical Doctor can perform surgery. No one is free to do surgery without a license just because they don't use the title "Medical Doctor." The practice of surgery is protected and restricted to those who hold that license.

As a result, all over the country, Clinical Psychologist groups began to change their "Title Protection Laws" into "Practice Protection Laws."

It was easy to do. In most cases they only had to change a few dozen words in the law. All of the Psychology Laws already contained a list of Psychological Practices, and in just about every state, "hypnotism," "hypnosis," or "hypnotherapy" were on that list.

That meant the moment any state changed its Clinical Psychologist License Law from "Title Protection" to "Practice Protection" only licensed Psychologists or people with similar licenses could do hypnotism.

The American Society of Clinical Hypnosis (ASCH) realized this change would put what they called "lay-hypnotists" out of business. They just needed to help this process along and since the American Society of Clinical Hypnosis is headquartered in Illinois that state was one of their first targets.

Although a newcomer to the Guild and to the professional practice of hypnotism, Scot Giles had been using hypnosis as a tool in his pastoral counseling.

As a new member of NGH he was suddenly exposed to some of our problems and called me to see what he could do. He assembled a team of other hypnotists, as they were the only people he knew who had reason to oppose the change in the Psychology Law. They wrote an exemption bill and put it in. They worked hard and it lost by only one vote, but now Scot was encouraged to try again.

By this time we realized the extent of the problem which had now also appeared in other states, and coincidently we were in the process of organizing a political organization, NFH #104, that was part of the OPEIU, AFL-CIO, and Scot Giles became our legislative liaison officer. This made all the difference for him, as previously he had a hard time getting in to talk to legislators. However, the very day we officially became part of the union he recalls that he found himself taking a Senator out to lunch. He comments that it's been said that America has the best government that money can buy, and maybe there is some truth to that. The AFL-CIO definitely gets more attention than the National Guild of Hypnotists or any other hypnotism organization.

An Illinois legislative team of committed hypnotists came together, composed of Ernest Telkemeyer, Arthur Leidecker, Wendel Loder and Scot Giles. With OPEIU AFL-CIO help they arranged a meeting with the Director of the Illinois Department of Professional Regulation, and they, with the President of the Illinois AFL-CIO sitting at the table, agreed not to enforce the Psychology Law against us so long as we had a bill pending in Springfield to make hypnotists lawful practitioners.

That meant the committee had to put at least one bill before the Illinois Legislature, every year, without fail, until one of those bills passed. In practice, they ended up putting many more than only one bill each year.

So, six bills later, the submitted law passed in 1997 as an exemption to the Psychology License Act provided hypnotists practiced within certain limits.

The first round of corrective legislation had failed by a single vote, but the volunteer committee of hypnotists persisted and, in 1997, PA 90-473 was passed after four legislative attempts. It amended the Psychology License Act to permit hypnotism to be practiced by unlicensed persons.

It's still the law and has worked fine. The only hypnotists who have gotten into trouble are those who thought they could ignore it.

With everything the Scot Giles had learned about legislation, it seemed only logical that he should head up the Guild's political efforts and once he agreed to "volunteer" he became the expert on hypnotism legislation, fighting state-by-state, getting Psychology Boards to back down. After Illinois, our next victory was in New Jersey (with Tony DeMarco, John Gatto and NFH #104), then Florida, New York, California, and the list kept getting longer. Finally we had enough momentum and enough victories under our belt that the Psychology Boards gave up ... at least for now.

1990 Florida laws on the use of hypnotism required intervention and personal legislative contact by NGH members Charles Francis and Gerald Kein. Meanwhile, in testing the local laws I had been denied a business license in Sarasota, but eventually after some positive action, I received the first hypnotism business license issued there. Based on this success, Charles Francis obtained a previously denied business license in Ft. Myers and Elsom Eldridge did the same in Tampa.

1993 was busy legislatively for Scot Giles and his legislative committee members as an effort began to amend the Illinois Clinical Psychologist License Act, which had been transformed into a practice protection act restricting the practice of hypnotism to licensed health care professionals. With the assistance of NFH 104 OPEIU, AFL/CIO, CLC, bills were introduced in several states to obtain registration or licensing and adverse bills introduced to put hypnotists out of business were fought ... always with *all* hypnotists' best interests in mind.

After the 1994 New Jersey Hypnocounselor Law was enacted, NGH/NFH 104 made other efforts to introduce hypnotist registration bills in MA, NH, ME, and Vermont without success, yet there were many positive legislative forays by NGH committee members. Most common objections of various state legislative committees were: 1.You can already do what you want. 2.The state doesn't want any more Boards to maintain. 3.The license fees for practitioners would have to be very high to pay for maintaining a board secretary, office, etc.

In 1996, the renewal of Florida's hypnotist exemption in Mental Health and Psychology License Laws passed. The bill renewing the exemption was the final bill passed on the last day of the legislative session, after intense union and NGH lobbying.

In 1997, a California group's attempted legislation unfairly restricting the practice of hypnotism in a way that benefitted only certain organizations was defeated. Dr Lisa Halpin and Fred Schiavo became the point persons, in conjunction with Legislative Liaison Officer Scot Giles. Lisa Halpin attended all the hearings in Sacramento with Fred Schiavo accompanying her to many of them. Reverend Julian Wick, Trent Davis, Gil Boyne (ACHE), George Kappas (HMI), Attorney Robert Strauss (ABH) and occasionally other California school owners became involved. NGH/NFH legislative liaison officer Scot Giles once again proved invaluable to the NGH group with advice and planning.

1998 was busy legislatively, with an exemption for hypnotists inserted in pending restrictive psychology legislation in Iowa; the states of Mississippi and Nebraska agreed not to consider hypnotism a regulated psychological practice; and failed legislative efforts by other organizations in Tennessee and Georgia were studied by teams in those states.

1999 saw action blocking hostile legislation in New York and Iowa that would have restricted the practice of hypnotism to licensed professionals. Intervention that year in Indiana was instituted to halt abuse by the state Hypnotist Committee, which oversaw the certification of hypnotists. Previously during 1995 - 1997 Scot Giles, George Baranowski, Michael Redell, and others fought an uphill battle to prevent the enactment of a registration act that favored graduates of only one school and member organization.

There was much underhandedness and intrigue involved. For example, as NGH president I was invited by Gil Boyne to be a guest speaker at a banquet in Indiana. However, I was warned by insiders that it was a set-up to personally embarrass me and the NGH. Actually, this had been quite evident to me from the time I received the invitation, so I "regretfully" turned it down.

The law was passed and the late Jack Mason, its author, was named as chairman of the Hypnotism Board. Coincidentally, the committee approved a school operated by Mason's wife. The committee also appeared to favor licensing members of a West Coast organization (ACHE).

Eventually, two lawsuits were filed against the committee, one jointly with the American Civil Liberties Union both of which were won. These legal victories resulted in a restructuring of the committee, with several members replaced and rules rewritten. In 2010 the committee was disbanded, and the law was taken off the books in July of that year.

In 1999, an experimental license law for hypnotists passed the Illinois Senate before being blocked in the House by the medical society. Meanwhile, a Georgia NGH legislative team headed by George Skillas blocked a restrictive license law for counselors that would have limited the practice of hypnotism to only state licensed professionals.

2000 saw defeat of a restrictive regulatory law (HB285) that would have prevented hypnotists from practicing in Iowa; a restrictive Georgia counselor license law (HB271) that would have limited the practice of hypnotism to persons licensed under that law, and a Kentucky certification law (SB 283) that would have allowed only graduates of specific schools to practice. Finally, a meeting was arranged with the Illinois Medical Association to explore ways hypnotists and physicians could work cooperatively.

2001 brought more legislative action as a veto of a restrictive law (SB 119) that would have limited the practice of hypnotism to persons licensed to practice mental health care was negotiated in Georgia. An Illinois bill (SB 79) that would require all hypnotists to practice in accordance with NGH Standards of Practice. In Louisiana a license law for hypnotists that would have allowed the local Chapter of the NGH to appoint the regulatory body were opposed by NGH as self-serving legislation, at the expense of other organizations.

A restrictive 2001 New York license law (AB 9214) that would have limited the practice of hypnotism to physicians, psychologists, counselors, and social workers was blocked and, in Ohio, negotiations were initiated with the Psychology Board for an understanding that hypnotists practicing within NGH Standards of Practice would not be considered to be in violation of that state's Psychology License Law. NGH also supported a 2001 Rhode Island Complementary and Alternative Medicine Freedom of Access Law.

2002 required retaining a local lobbyist in Texas and assembling a legislative committee that was successful in blocking enforcement of Cease and Desist Orders against some hypnotists in that state who were on a list on the Internet of members of the International Medical and Dental Hypnotherapy Association. Also in 2002, in Florida, the attorney general ruled that hypnotists who practiced within NGH Standards did not violate Florida Law, and used that ruling to issue a Cease and Desist Order against the State of Florida demanding it not enforce Cease and Desist Orders it issued to some hypnotists. The government agreed, and negotiations were made with the Psychology Board to clarify the nature of the hypnotists' exemption.

NGH gave financial support to groups seeking to pass Complementary and Alternative Medicine Freedom of Access Laws in Florida, California, Georgia, and Iowa.

2003 required the blocking of a proposed change in Indiana legislation that would have restricted hypnotism to physicians, counselors, psychologists and social workers and banned further credentialing of hypnotists. Work began to attempt to control the interpretation of provisions of a recently-passed mental health license law, resulting in negotiating an agreement that hypnotists practicing within NGH Standards and Terminology would not be deemed in violation of a new license law for counselors.

In 2004, hypnotists defeated a bill in Hawaii (HCR 22) that would have restricted the practice of hypnotism to psychologists, physicians, social workers and counselors; negotiated protective legislation (Ch. 146a) in Minnesota, to protect the right of hypnotists to practice after the repeal of the Unlicensed Mental Health Provider laws; reorganized a Texas legislative team to prepare to launch exemption legislation in the next legislative session.

Because it boasted more hypnosis professionals than any other state (as well as hypnosis schools), California was chosen as the test state for this new legislation. Although the bill gained preliminary acceptance, a major setback occurred on the very last day for amendments. George Kappas inserted a requirement that the hypnotherapist be "approved by the US Department of Education." This would have limited the practice of hypnotherapy to only graduates of HMI (outside of the APA and AMA), effectively eliminating most of the competition.

According to hypnotists who were in attendance, Gil Boyne and George Kappas arguing in front of the lawmakers had a direct bearing on the resulting death of the bill. All the king's horses and men couldn't put it together again; not even COPHO could revive it. NGH Legislative Liaison Officer Giles gave credit to Lisa Halpin and Fred Schiavo, who invested many hours and days working on the situation in California on behalf of all California hypnotists.

In 2006, after the trial and subsequent deportation of a convicted professional hypnotist in Connecticut, the attorney general of the state campaigned to have us put out of business legislatively. He wanted a registration or licensing law which was definitely slanted against our people. NGH/NFH and OPIEU AFL/CIO officers conferred.

The profession had just survived the negative publicity of newspaper headlines proclaiming "HYPNO-SEX" relating to the trial, and we faced a truly dire situation. Gil Boyne blamed it all on the NGH in a newspaper interview and, of course, on me personally, because the hypnotist in question had been an NGH member.

OPEIU President Michael Goodwin contacted the state of Connecticut AFL/CIO president, John Olson, who came on board as our lobbyist. Thanks to President Goodwin's request on our behalf, a fair registration law was enacted. I was proud to be one of the first hypnotists to be registered to show my solidarity with hypnotists in that state.

In 2007, practitioners in Ontario, Canada, asked for help regarding a legislative bill which was already in committee, and which would negatively affect all practicing hypnotists in that province. NGH Legislative Liaison Officer Scot Giles found that the Mental Health Practitioners Bill (171) definitely threatened to impact their practices, and could put them out of business. With the assistance of NFH #104, OPEIU, AFL/CIO, CLC a lobbyist was secured in Ontario and a positive outcome resulted regarding the impact of the bill on practicing hypnotists in that province. Ontario's newly appointed College of Psychotherapy director was charged with setting up rules and regulations, and it appears that practitioners will be protected when final guidelines are enacted.

With $18,000.00 from OPEIU, NFH 104 was able to hire a well-established lobbyist who represented professional hypnotists, and the bill was modified.

Most recently, in February of 2011, the exemption that allowed hypnotists to practice in Florida was jeopardized by a fledgling representative, and immediate action was called for by NFH local 104 Legislative Officer, Scot Giles, and OPEIU lobbyist, attorney Robert Levy. With the union action and support from professional hypnotists in Florida and across the US, the situation was quickly taken care of.

# Hypnotic Aids Through The Years

The BRAIN WAVE SYNCHRONIZER

PROFESSIONAL MODEL

TECHNICIAN MODEL

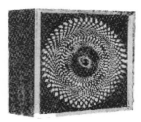

Brain Wave Synchronizer

Hypno-optiscope

Thomas Metronome

Radiometer

HypnoScope

Biofeedback Set-up

Hypno-Disk

Biofeedback Light Goggles

GSR2

*Through the years various electric and mechanical devices were utilized in the hypnotic induction.*

# Chapter 16
## COPHO
## Council of Professional Hypnosis Organizations

Many organizations have been started with very impressive names, often using "International" in their title although they have been very parochial in nature, sometimes with less than 100 members. However, on September 23, 1989 the Council of Professional Hypnosis Organizations (COPHO) was founded at the ABH convention in Irvine, California. The idea of a national coalition had been suggested by Roy Cage of Fort Worth, Texas, president of NSH, as a means to unify the profession of hypnotism by providing leadership and the promotion of standards for its practice. The purpose was "to unify the profession of hypnosis by uniting all hypnosis organizations and to monitor and support or contest legislation in North America pertaining to the practice of hypnotism, as well as to provide legislative information to its member organizations for dissemination to their members to promote and maintain the practice of hypnosis in accordance with rules, regulations, laws, and statutes of the respective states and provinces." Other purposes were to set professional educational and ethical standards for the practice of hypnosis and to continuously educate the public.

The magic number in order for organizations to join the Council of Professional Hypnosis Organizations (COPHO) was 100 active members. All subsequent organizations had to be voted on for acceptance by active COPHO member organizations. Soon, there were 13 charter member organizations united to present a consistent and positive image of hypnosis to the public. Initial tasks were to standardize titling and to create a National Certification, put together by all COPHO members. The members were to collectively set standards and structures for themselves as a group to influence legislation for the benefit of all, and to create licensing in 50 states.

Reverend Dr C. Scot Giles served as Chairman of COPHO from 1996-1998 and was involved with an eventual resolution for California. In the early 1990s, COPHO created what they called the "Model Legislation Bill" as a prospective piece of legislation to make hypnotherapy legally recognized in each state. Giles was directly involved when this was written. A copy of that model bill appeared in *The Journal of Hypnotism* in Vol. 7, No. 1, dated March,1992, and is included in the Appendix to this book.

COPHO was limited in its effectiveness because of lack of unity of purpose among the member associations. In the mid '80s, a number of larger and more active member organizations withdrew their support and dropped out of COPHO, indicating "nothing other than holding two meetings a year was going to happen no matter how hard they tried." Several of the groups that withdrew were charter members, had given financial support, and were active in supporting the original concepts of COPHO's purpose.

COPHO continues to meet several times a year and new organizations are accepted, but many observers feel it no longer lives up to the purposes for which it was originally formed. Current chairman for the past 14 years is Anthony DeMarco, PhD, LLB, DNGH, well-known teacher and columnist, who, with his experience as a lawyer, hypnocounselor, and teacher, has done a masterful job of keeping COPHO alive.

# Chapter 17
## The Cycles of Negative and Positive Press

*Liberty* magazine, in the September 1943 issue, ran an article entitled "HYPNOTISM Comes of Age," by Lois Mattox Miller. The very positive article was condensed the next month in *Reader's Digest,* with such positive statements as, "Through hypnosis, alcoholics are left with an abiding distaste for liquor, amnesia victims are being lifted out of their mental fog. Somnambulists who risked their necks almost nightly now stay safely in bed." The article also mentioned that at the University of Chicago's Sprague Memorial Institute and Department of Pathology, their age regression study of hypnotism had found that "a person under hypnosis can readily recall from his past life incidents and attitudes which have been entirely lost to conscious recollection."

*Look* magazine in the July 10, 1956 issue ran "The Facts About Hypnotism" by Ralph Daigh, which included photos of Chicago's Edwin Baron and also West Coast stage hypnotist Pat Collins. The article concluded that, "Hypnotism is no parlor game to be played by amateurs 'just for kicks.' It is a useful and serious science that should be left in the hands of experts who understand its usefulness as well as its limitations."

*Life* magazine of Nov 1, 1958 featured an article entitled "Hypnosis - Old 'Black Art' Is Now Accepted Medical Tool," which started out by stating, "Hypnosis has finally gone medically legitimate. Because it traditionally has been the secret of the stage magician, the public usually has looked on hypnosis as black magic ... in the past 10 years some 900 US doctors, dentists and psychologists have quietly employed hypnosis to help their patients. Their success has so impressed the American Medical Association that it has now endorsed hypnosis as a therapeutic aid for doctors and dentists properly trained in its use" The article presented photos and text about childbirth, pain relief in burn cases and cancer.

The final subtitle in the article is: "Humbug in the Past. Dangers in the Present ... The widest use of hypnosis in modern times has been for entertainment, and the medical profession views with considerable alarm the stage magician who puts members of his audience into trance. Both physical and mental harm can come from his act."

From the late '50s into the mid '80s there seemed to be less interest by the medical profession in attempting to get rid of stage hypnotists. However, in 1957, in Buffalo, NY, the entertainment industry beat down an attempt by medical doctors to have the city council enact a proposal banning hypnotism as entertainment in that city. A few state licensing attempts by hypnotists' groups around the country were also opposed when they were initiated.

It may be coincidental, but once the NGH was reborn and started to initiate more training classes, a convention and printed publications a great deal of "Hypno-Bashing" started up. Of course, it was also an era of blatant tabloid publications and TV show's in addition to the fact that there was suddenly a lot more interest by individuals in learning to hypnotize themselves and others.

Accordingly, the decade from 1986 - 1996, can be described as being filled with continuous hypno-bashing by the tabloid media. Story after story, in print and on television, seemed to materialize demeaning the practice of hypnotism by what the "establishment" (licensed health professionals) had mis-labeled as "lay hypnotists."

Surely there were some unprincipled practitioners and fly-by-night operators out to make a fast dollar from the public, but the same kind of fast-buck artists and unprincipled individuals can always be found in other professions or businesses. It just seems that the long-established skewed perception of the world of hypnotism offers more of an opportunity to sensationalize. And, of course, there were those who developed the "hypnotist's disease" that we discussed previously.

One example, was the tabloid article about a California psychologist's "Remote-Control-Wife," in which a Sacramento psychologist claimed to have hypnotized his wife so he could turn her on or off with a television remote. Then there was the convenience store clerk who said he was hypnotized by two men who took all of the money out of the cash register and left him in a trance … well, that's what the tabloids reported! We also had a tabloid TV show which interviewed several hypnotists, such as the pizza maker who shared the knowledge with viewers that, yes, cancer could be cured with hypnosis … and there were others. It almost seemed as if fledging hypnotists were trying to think of ways to gain notoriety, whether good or bad. Of course there would always be the sexual cases as happens in a lot of fields when a so-called professional betrays the trust of a client or patient, but the sensationalism really escalates when sex and hypnosis are both involved.

Licensed professions promoting hypnotism throughout the years have managed to get some good stories in the media, usually with a caveat warning the reader to seek out only licensed health professionals and members of groups such as ASCH (American Society of Clinical Hypnosis).

In recent years there have been attention-getting newspaper headlines such as, "HYPNO SEX" in Connecticut when a very unethical and unprincipled practitioner ended up in court in 2005-06. He was convicted of the charges and deported back to his country of origin, but that particular case was responsible for a law being passed in Connecticut for the annual registration of hypnotists.Thanks to the NGH/NFH legislative committee, OPEIU, and the state president of the AFL/CIO, who acted as a lobbyist for all hypnotists when the bill was being written, and very active members, it was a fair bill for practitioners as well as for the protection of consumers in that state.

Many times I've been contacted by a practicing hypnotist who was misquoted, or who had an interview that provoked a reader into writing a negative letter to the editor. I've found that, generally speaking, it does no good to respond and keep things in the news. This same principle applies on the Internet.

When hypnotism is portrayed in a negative way in magazines or on TV shows our organization is often asked by hypnotists to contact the source. We do follow through in a non-adversarial way, but in the media business the old saying that there is nothing as old as yesterday's news is really true. Negative things about your profession will bother you, but the casual reader will read it, get an impression, whether true or false, pro or con, good or bad, and then move on to some other sensational item that might have more of a personal interest.

Occasionally we can all be misquoted in a news article or interview with something we never said. Let's face it, when I speak to a reporter I am truthful, factual and positive. I have to assume the reporter is legitimate and wants to be truthful, factual and honest in what he or she will submit to the editor, and that the editor will also be factual and honest in editing the interview.

However, this doesn't always happen, and it's not necessarily with any ulterior motive to change statements of the subject, but because of sloppy note taking, or poor recall or comprehension by the reporter. Possibly a reporter or editor could be prejudiced about hypnotists/hypnotism, or even the person they are interviewing. He or she might just not like the looks or personality of the person being interviewed.

We never know, but we saw it happen at a convention a few years ago. The photographer did those of us being interviewed shooting from the floor up into our faces. This made for some rather weird pictures accompanying the slanted article which ran the next day in the Sunday edition of a local newspaper.

We all know that when you are interviewed by the media they are not going to let you look at the article before it is printed, so their interpretation and editing of what you said is what they use. Some misguided hypnotists still say, "It doesn't matter what they say about me as long as they spell my name correctly." However, we have gained so much ground as a separate and distinct profession that it *does* matter, so we professional hypnotists have to be very careful when being interviewed not to say something that will cast a negative light on us or our profession.

Although earlier years had been overrun with hypno-bashing by the media, things started to change. A partial list of media which featured more recent positive hypnotism articles includes *Reader's Digest Family Guide to Natural Medicine - Grolier Book of Knowledge - Bottom Line Personal - Business Week - Consumer Reports - Redbook - Women's Week - Woman's Health - Newsweek - O - The New Republic - Pressé (Canada) - Astra Opua* (Greece) - *NY Times* - PBS TV - TV's "20/20" - "Dateline" - British Royal Free & University College Medical School Library.

An NGH national P.R. program reached a readership of 1,426,652 several years ago, and in 2008, *The Wall Street Journal*® personal finance page featured an article and interview with Jacob Bimblich, "A Hypnotic Answer to Financial Angst." This resulted in many more articles and interviews about the profession spreading around the world in other publications and other languages.

The past few years we also have been receiving more positive publicity for hypnotism, thanks to progressive TV hosts such as the very popular Dr Mehmet Oz. Dr Oz who says that he first learned of the profound powers of hypnosis in medical school, states such things as, "Hypnosis unlocks your subconscious power to control the demons that make you overeat."

Dr Daniel Amen, physician, psychiatrist, brain imaging specialist and best-selling author who is all over public TV reaching millions of viewers, uses hypnosis in his medical programs and says, "It is very powerful, and brain imaging studies show it enhances brain function."

Brian Weiss, MD, Chairman Emeritus of Psychiatry at the Mount Sinai Medical Center in Miami is a leading proponent of hypnosis and past-lives, and another popular guest for TV shows.

Dr Bernie Siegel, in his book *Love, Medicine and Miracles*, wrote about the mind and body relationship, and he has been friendly to our profession in his writing and lecturing.

Another prolific and very popular researcher/author, Dr Andrew Weil, is also widely quoted as saying that he believes "that no condition is out of bounds for trying hypnotherapy on." Unfortunately it appears that he also believes that only members of ASCH should be consulted for these services.

It has been my observation that most well-grounded professionals such as these men don't have time to demean those of us who are non-licensed, but practicing ethically, professionally, and within the scope of what we are trained to do. Our day will come as we keep building our profession.

Oprah Winfrey, TV talk show legend, has often had guests on her show demonstrating and speaking about the many benefits of hypnotism.

In 2004, January 4 each year officially became known as "World Hypnotism Day" through the initiative of a very active consulting hypnotist, Thomas Nicoli, Jr, with the support of NGH. Now the annual day is a recognized and well established world event: Worldhypnotismday.com is the website which serves as a resource site for professionals year-round.

Many of the busiest hypnotists spread the word about the profession as well as their private practices through local or cable TV appearances, and also on the networks. Ones that readily come to mind are Jacob Bimblich, doing a successful smoking cessation with a volunteer on a TV broadcast of Fox's "Good Day New York", in Times Square; Tom Nicoli, who helped a participant lose weight on TV's "Dateline," Jerry Valley, in his segment on "20/20," Paul McKenna on the "Dr Oz Show." All of these positive appearances directly and indirectly help us to move forward as a profession, and help to shape the public perception of hypnotism.

*TV "Doctor" shows, "Talk" shows, and even "Reality" soap operas have all invited professional hypnotists as guests in this era.*

# Weird & Wacky Hypno-Headlines

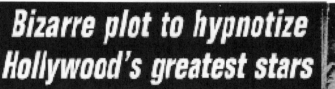

## Bizarre plot to hypnotize Hollywood's greatest stars

MONEY-MAD Holly-
wood moguls once
hypnotized actor Bela
Lugosi and considered
using the same stunt to
turn other top stars into
mindless robots.

Greta Garbo, Tyrone
Power, Paul Muni and Oli-
via de Havilland were all
mentioned by the New
York Times as performers
who might benefit from sitting studio bosses turn
them into hypnotized zom-
bies.

Lugosi, best known for
his frightening screen por-
trayal of Count Dracula,
was playing an evil mob
boss in the 1940 film Black
Friday which co-starred
Boris Karloff.

As a publicity stunt, studio bosses had Lugosi hypnotized for a scene in which
Karloff locked him in a clo-
et, where Lugosi suffo-
cated.

An astrologist and occult
worker named Manley
Hall put the actor in a
trance, report-
ed the Times
on January
28, 1940.
"Hypno-

**BELA LUGOSI** as the frightening Count Dracula

tists. Finally,
he slumped to
the floor. A doc-
tor who was in
attendance took the
actor's pulse, which
had soared from
normal to 160 —
seemingly, the
pulse a suffocating
victim would have.

"They carried Lu-
gosi to a chair,
where Hall awak-
ened him," noted
the Times. "Examin-
ation showed that
the phrase's pulse
was again normal."

Nobody was more
delighted than di-
rector Arthur Lubin —
who marveled that the
scene was more better
than a previous take without hypnosis.

Universal Studios was
very pleased with the ex-
periment, reported the
Times.

The effect on Lugosi
was so amazing that the
studio's exploitation engineers believe that hypno-
sis can be practiced on
writers to make them fin-
ish scripts, not most of all
on actors," the paper
noted.

It mentioned Garbo,
Muni, Power, and de Hav-
illand as performers who
might benefit from hypno-

**They were almost turned into robots**

### THE SCREEN WORLD
#### HERE WE GO, FOLKS?
Hollywood Discovers the Mesmeric
Powers of Hypnotism—Other News

Eaton engineers believe that hypnosis can be practiced on writers
to make them finish scripts, on
press agents (although one member of the department doubted
there would be any difference), on
actors to ensure good acting, but
most of all on actors—Garbo would
be made to talk. Tyrone Power
could really the Havilland de Los
Paul M...

**GRETA GARBO**

**OLIVIA DE HAVILLAND**

sis. But insofar as is known
by Hollywood historians,
none of them was ever ac-
tually hypnotized while
making a movie.
—LEONARD SANDLER

**AP Photo**

CHICKEN FUN — Harvey Hunt of Templeton, Calif., front waits for his chicken to go into a trance as others raise their hands indicating their chickens are already in a trance during an attempt to set a world's record for the fastest time to hypnotize chickens. Hypnotherapist Shelley Stockwell, Ph.D., of Rancho Palos, Calif., far left, who put the chickens into their hypnotic state claimed that a new world's record was set at the event.

# Chapter 18
## Movie, TV & Sports Personalities

The motion picture industry has had a powerful influence on the general public, perhaps even more than most people realize. Hollywood has influenced public opinion in many ways over the decades and shares responsibility for creating interest in hypnotism, but also has been guilty of dispersing an abundance of fictitious information regarding it.

Yet, many well-known celebrities of the era publically acknowledged obtaining benefit from hypnosis: Tony Curtis conquered his fear of flying, Cary Grant cured his insomnia, and Johnny Mathis overcame stage fright, according to hypnotist Arthur Ellen in his 1968 book, *"The Intimate Casebook of a Hypnotist."*

Movie stars were involved with hypnotism in many ways. During World War II Orson Welles became well-known for his magic and hypnotism talents as he presented his stage shows at West Coast military bases. His shows with his wife, Rita Hayworth, were an important part of morale building for our servicemen. In 1949, Welles also starred in *Black Magic*, as Joseph Balsamo (aka 18th century hypnotist, magician and scam artist Count Cagliostro).

John Calvert (the Falcon) was another movie star who became equally famous with the colorful magic and hypnotism productions which he presented around the world once the war years were over.

Ventriloquist Paul Winchell became an icon on American television during the 1950s and 1960s. Millions of dedicated fans watched the "Paul Winchell - Jerry Mahoney Show" each week. Very few people know that Winchell also had pursued several educational avenues that inspired him to be an inventor, acupuncture practitioner, and hypnotist.

Winchell worked at the Gibbs Institute in Hollywood as a medical hypnotist, creating new innovations in the field of hypnotherapy. His greatest claim to fame was his invention and patent of the artificial heart, built in 1963. He donated the invention and patent to the University of Utah and was given an honorary doctorate by the National Christian University.

TV's "Brady Bunch" star Florence Henderson handled her stress through the use of hypnosis. After being a client she studied at the Hypnosis Motivation Institute (HMI) in California, and graduated as a certified hypnotherapist. After her marriage to HMI owner Dr John Kappas, she also became involved in the operation of the school.

Popular celebrities such as Ben Affleck, Drew Barrymore, Kevin Costner,

Matt Damon, and Samuel Jackson have reportedly used hypnosis for smoking cessation. TV's Jane Pauly was hypnotized on her network show and explained the benefits of hypnosis. Hypnotism is now getting a lot of positive but unofficial endorsements by well-known personalities.

Terry Fator, million dollar winner on TV's "America's Got Talent," is currently headlining in his own show at the Mirage casino/hotel in Las Vegas. In his book, subtitled *Who's The Dummy Now?*, Terry mentions several times that he learned and used hypnosis for himself and his family.

In the early '50s, as TV first became popular, networks followed rules reputedly made by the FCC that hypnosis (hypnotic induction) was not to be broadcast on the air. The rule was meant to protect those listening at home from going into a trance. Whether it was an actual FCC rule or not, in the days when we were doing "window sleeps" or other on-the-air demonstrations, we simply used pre-conditioned subjects to re-enter the hypnotic state on cue.

With the advent of TV post-hypnosis was still the answer, simply hypnotizing volunteers off camera or microphone and giving them a post-hypnotic "cue" to return to the hypnotic state later. Dr Franz Polgar, who kept busy doing sponsored dates for civic groups, used a little key chain viewer which was a novelty of the time. His pre-conditioned hypnotized volunteers on TV appearances such as Arthur Godfrey's show simply looked into the small viewer and returned to hypnosis. People were so familiar with having seem Polgar do this on TV that he often used it on his volunteers when he did his live shows on stage around the country.

Throughout the 20th century some professional hypnotists and hypnotherapists have been critical of stage hypnosis and the use of hypnotism for entertainment purposes, but for many years before the Internet stage hypnotism was what was most visible to the public. The hypnotism profession might not have survived to the 21st century without the contributions of the stage hypnotists, so, regardless of a negative few, it is a statement of fact that the use of hypnosis for entertainment served a very important role in the development of our profession.

# Chapter 19
## Forensic Hypnosis

Forensic hypnosis was first used in US Courts in 1898, surfaced again in 1960, and was used often throughout the 1970s.

The public's interest was piqued in 1976 when in Chowchilla, CA, a small farming community, a school bus loaded with 26 children heading home after school was hijacked by three hooded individuals and held for ransom. It was a fascinating event; the children were herded into two windowless vans, driven about 100 miles to an abandoned stone quarry, and buried six feet underground in a sunken semi truck trailer. This became a headline story of the year, as the FBI was called in. Hourly reports were fed directly into the White House. Chowchilla's population tripled overnight with investigators and reporters. Sixteen hours later, the bus driver and the children were able to dig their way out and were safe.

The use of hypnosis became a crucial factor in the identification and subsequent apprehension of the kidnappers. Dr William S. Kroger was called upon to hypnotize the bus driver, Frank Edward Ray, to help recall the license plate number of the vans that had stopped the bus on the country road. With the use of hypnosis, the plate numbers were recalled, which led to the apprehension and later conviction of the three kidnappers.

Not surprisingly, due to this case, specialized hypnotism units were developed within the New York Police Department and in other major cities. On the West Coast, Dr Martin Reiser established a formalized early forensic hypnosis program for the Los Angeles Police Department. Reiser also founded the Society for Investigative and Forensic Hypnosis (SIFH) in 1978.

It was at that time that several men who later specialized in forensic hypnosis started their careers. These men were already in police work and interested in hypnotism, according to Inspector Marx Howell (ret.), formerly with the Texas State Police. He personally became interested, trained with Reiser, and recalls that in 1983 a group of lawmen met in Arlington, Texas to form an association primarily for police hypnotists; the Texas Association of Investigative Hypnosis (TAIH) was established.

Because some states were ruling against the admissibility of hypnotically refreshed recall with witnesses and victims of crime, strict rules are the standard of TAIH regarding training requirements and the actual practice of hypnosis in forensic cases, which has brought great respect to the group. In fact, Texas Senate Bill 929 specifically addresses and is limited to police officers who use hypnosis for investigative purposes. This bill does not, however, impose restrictions on individuals in the private sector who use hypnosis for any other purpose.

The US Supreme Court ruled (Rock vs. Arkansas), That hypnotically refreshed recall is admissible in all 50 states when used with defendants in preparation for his defense. However, hypnosis is admissible in only a few states (including Texas) when used by police with victims and witness of crimes.

To quote the US Supreme Court's decision in Rock vs. Arkansas, "The State would be well within its power if it established guidelines to aid in the evaluation of post hypnosis testimony." The Texas Court of Criminal Appeals followed the US Supreme Court's suggestion and established ten procedural safeguards in Zanie vs. Texas as a prerequisite to admissibility.

Inspector Marx Howell currently writes a *Journal of Hypnotism* forensic hypnosis column and does training on many specialized topics, such as criminal profiling and child molesters, for police groups around the country. He has also developed a personal safety seminar for hypnotism professionals with Patricia MacIsaac and myself.

George Baranowski of Michigan City, Indiana, also started his career in forensic hypnosis shortly after the Chowchilla case, while working in law-enforcement as a police detective and later as chief investigator in the La-Porte County Prosecuting Attorney's Office. George and his wife Paula operated Mindsight Consultants, a post-secondary state licensed hypnotism school in Michigan City, in conjunction with their hypnotism practice, for a number of years in the mid '90s. He was also very active in NFH union activities and on the NGH Board of Examiners. The Baranowskis, who are both certified polygraph examiners, currently specialize in court mandated examinations of sexual offenders in Michigan City, and are also called in for forensic hypnosis cases in that area of the country.

Don Mottin of St. Louis, Missouri, went from the Marines into police work with the Pagedale, Missouri police department in 1974. He first became interested in forensic hypnosis as a policeman, receiving further extensive training and on-the-job practice. In 1980 he left the Clark County Sheriff's Department with the rank of chief deputy and went into full time hypnotism practice. Mottin established five separate offices in the St. Louis area, gained additional personal experience, and developed workshops to train others. Having established a background in law-enforcement, he developed forensic workshops for practicing hypnotists, and emergency hypnosis workshops for law enforcement officers, ambulance personnel, certified hypnotists, and first-responder groups, in addition to many continuing-education seminars for the NGH.

Don Mottin's book, *Raising Your Children With Hypnosis*, was published by NGH in 2005. Don is currently vice president of the National Guild of Hypnotists. He is in charge of professional development and travels extensively to conduct continuing-education workshops for professional hypnotists across the US and in Canada.

Patrick Brady has been practicing hypnotism for over a quarter century. He was on the teaching faculty of Northeastern University in Boston, Massachusetts, and from 1980–1990 was the director of the Boston Police Hypnosis Unit. He has been an expert witness in forensic hypnosis and conducted hypnosis sessions for memory recall for federal, state and municipal law enforcement agencies throughout the country. He maintains a professional practice in Quincy, Massachusetts.

Charles Diggett was the NYPD's first staff hypnotist in the mid '70s when the technique was new to police departments. He stated that he never used hypnosis on a suspect, "lest it violate constitutional their protection against self-incrimination." Although he had studied and trained in New York, New Jersey and California, Diggett still had a hard time convincing the department on the usefulness of hypnosis. In the mid-seventies it was finally approved and he helped to develop new evidence in 62 percent of the cases in which he used hypnosis.

The hypnotism community has contributed a number of books on forensic hypnosis such as:
*Legal Aspects of Hypnosis* (Bryan, William J. - 1962)
*Hypnosis In Criminal Investigation* (Arons, Harry -1967)
*Handbook of Investigative Hypnosis* (Reiser, Martin - 1980)
*Hypnosis and The Law* (Kuhn, Bradley - 1981)
*Forensic Hypnosis Clinical Tactics in the Courtroom* (Kline, Milton V. - 1983)
*Forensic Hypnosis: Psychological & Legal Aspects* (Udolf, Roy - 1983)
*Trance on Trial* (Sceflin, Alan & Shapiro, Jerrold -1989)
*Hypnosis, Memory, and Behavior in Criminal Investigation* - (McConky & Sheehan - 1995)
*Clinical Hypnosis & Memory: Guidelines for Clinical &Forensic Hypnosis* (Hammond - 1995)
*Forensic Hypnosis:The Practical Application of Hypnosis in Criminal Investigating* (Hibbard -Worring - Falcon - King -1996)
*Investigative Forensic Hypnosis* (Niehaus - 1998)

*Look what Bridey Murphy started . . .*

# Chapter 20
## Past Lives and Hypnosis

In 1956, Morey Bernstein's controversial book, *The Search for Bridey Murphy,* was published amid a lot of press coverage and public interest. The book, which became a best seller and movie, was based on transcripts that Bernstein recorded during hypnotic sessions with Virgina Tighe.

Bernstein, a businessman and amateur hypnotist, put housewife Virginia Tighe in a trance at a house party they were attending and a sensation was created when she related information about a supposed past life in Ireland in the 19th century, as Bridey Murphy. This exploration with past-life hypnotic regression to a supposed previous life had a vivid impact on the minds of millions of Americans who read the book or some of the many articles in publications such as *LIFE* magazine.

Many believed it was a hoax, including the prestigious *Chicago SUN,* which attempted to debunk it with a series of exposé articles. The Bridey Murphy event, book, and movie made a long-lasting public impression regarding hypnotism. However, to this day, the belief in past-life hypnotic regression is still questionable. Many positive results have been reported in the offices of licensed health professionals when past lives have been involved with hypnosis and therapeutic methods.

When I was seeing clients, I wasn't eager to delve into past lives because I didn't wish to spend the time that was often consumed with just that one client. My associate, Dorothy Stratton, a lovely vocalist, teacher, TV/movie actress, and hypnotist didn't feel that way at all. One evening, after a client left the office, I kiddingly said to Dorothy that I hoped she charged for two consecutive sessions, since she had spent that much time with just that one client. She shrugged her shoulders and said, "She was a past-life client and it was sooo interesting." Personally, I prefer reading a book or going to the movies to listening to someone else's past life. However, a few names come to mind of those who have made their mark in the world of hypnotism writing, lecturing or teaching others about past lives during the past quarter of a century...

In 1997, while our NFH #104 crew was manning the "Most Popular" booth at the national OPEIU Union Label trade show in Phoenix, Arizona, George Baranowski introduced us to his brother Frank, a well-known figure in past-life circles.

Frank Baranowski had a successful call-in radio show that featured past-life issues. He received a lot of national tabloid press attention regarding a very detailed account by a female guest recounting a past life as a seaman on board ship during the December 7, 1941 Pearl Harbor attack.

Although Frank had little formal training in hypnosis, he did have determination and the outgoing personality to enthusiastically promote his beliefs. He and his callers/guests enthralled radio audiences with extraordinary stories of *Mysteries Around Us* on Newsradio 620 KTAR for nearly 13 years. He also did a mini version of *Mysteries Around Us* short stories for OnAirPeople.com. Frank passed on January 19, 2002.

Dick Sutphen, president of Valley of the Sun Publishing in Malibu, California, is also a practicing hypnotist in Westlake, California. Dick has created over 350 mind-programming CDs/NLPs, has appeared as a guest on over 400 radio and television shows, and is known worldwide for his presentations on past lives and similar topics. Among the many new-age and past-life books he has authored are the best seller, *You Were Born Again To Be Together* (1976), *Past Lives, Future Loves* (1978), *Past-Life Therapy In Action* (1983), and *Predestined Love* (1996). Dick Sutphen has also contributed much to the hypnotism profession as a speaker and instructor at the leading conventions and conferences.

Another of the most prolific writers, speakers, and teachers in the study of hypnosis and past lives is Henry Bolduc, widely known in the US and other countries where he has lectured and taught extensively on past lives, is known for his calm, friendly, sharing, and always positive personality. One of the features of his workshops has been group past-life sessions for the entire class. Henry has always shared so much of his work, often giving open permission to anyone to download and copy his books and other material without cost.

Although a native New Englander, Henry lived with his wife Joan in the Blue Ridge Mountains of Virginia, where he was very active with the Edgar Cayce Foundation and other organizations such as the Association for Research and Enlightenment (ARE). Like another pal, Ormond McGill, Henry Bolduc can also be described as a gentleman and a gentle man, who could always be counted on to put a positive spin on sometimes negative situations.

Dr Edith Fiore, a licensed psychologist practicing in California, was using hypnosis with a client in her office in the '70s when he spontaneously started describing what sounded like a previous life. This incident started a new career direction for Dr Fiore, who would gain international fame for her two best-selling books, *You Have Been Here Before* and *The Unquiet Dead*. She was soon in great demand as a speaker, writer, and teacher on hypnosis and past lives. She was brought to my attention by Ormond McGill, who suggested that I interview her for the *Journal of Hypnotism.*

When the magazine with the interview was printed and Ormond received his copy, he called me. We did our usual greeting—his, "Hello pal," and my reply, "What do you think, McGill?"—from the1963 movie, *Please Don't Touch Me*, in which he appeared with western star Lash LaRue. I was amazed when he asked why I used someone else's photo on the cover. He and I had no idea that he had sent me a picture of a California hypnotist look-alike by mistake. I called Dr Fiore to apologize and told her we were going to reprint that issue (in those days we had a much smaller circulation). She very graciously said it didn't matter, but I wanted to have the correct picture, so that now, years later, it would be historically correct … and it is. Currently Dr Fiore enjoys an active retirement in Florida.

Dr Garrett Oppenheim was a licensed psychotherapist in Westchester County, New York, with a sterling international reputation as a journalist and editor. He was well known for his hypnosis work with trans-gender clients, but after many years of almost repetitive work with numerous clients, he developed a new interest in past lives, and made that his new specialty. Dr Oppenheim was the editor of the *Journal of Regression Therapy,* a feature columnist of the *Journal of Hypnotism*, and author of the popular book, "*Who Were You Before You Were You?*" Dr Oppenheim died in 1995.

Georgina Cannon, a practitioner and certified instructor in Toronto, Canada, is the author of *RETURN – Past Life Regression and You.* She was asked by Shirley MacLaine to host her chatroom on the website www.shirley-maclaine.com every month to talk about hypnosis, relationship issues, past life, and the interlife. Georgina is also a popular monthly guest on Talk Radio Europe's Hannah Murray Show.

Don Mottin, National Guild of Hypnotists vice president and continuing-education director, sometimes asks in a workshop how many attendees believe in past lives. When those attendees raise their hands he says happily, "Nice to see you again!"

You see, we are both neutral on the subject, and I agree when Don also says, "I've taken hundreds of people back to what they say are past lives… whether or not it is fact or fiction I leave it up to each individual to decide for themselves."

*"Svengali"*
*Above—The film "Svengali" was based on "Trilby," the 1894 novel by*
*George du Maurier*

*Left—Gil Boyne was hired as technical*
*director regarding hypnosis for the movie*
***"Hypnotic Eye"***

*Right—Ormond McGill appeared in*
*the movie,*
***"Please Don't Touch Me"***

# Chapter 21
## Hypnosis in the Movies
## A Source for Many Myths About Hypnosis

We live in a very media oriented society, in which television and the movies often help to mold public opinion. Unfortunately, when Hollywood misrepresents a subject, this viewpoint is frequently accepted as fact by the general public. This certainly appears to be the case in the way that hypnotism and those who practice it are portrayed in motion pictures.

Hypnotism, hypnotist, mesmerist … they are all common words in our English language. Take, for example, the well known holiday classic movie, *It's a Wonderful Life*. This 1946 RKO film is almost continuously on one TV channel or another between Thanksgiving and the New Year. In this story about a despondent man who wishes that he had never been born, his guardian angel is showing him what the world would have been like without him. As George Bailey (Jimmy Stewart) makes his way through the world without his presence he asks the guardian angel, "You a hypnotist?"

Is the implication that if something strange or weird is going on a hypnotist is the likely culprit?

Here is a filmography recollected and compiled for us by hypnotist/movie buff, Curtis Drake Morley, of Chicago, Illinois:

*The Cabinet of Dr Caligari*, 1919, Germany; US rights, MGM. Silent film.
*The Bells,* 1927. Silent film. Boris Karloff.
*Rasputin and the Empress,* 1932, MGM. Lionel Barrymore.
*13 Women*, 1932, RKO, Myrna Loy.
*Hypnotized,* 1932, Mack Sennett Studios. Moran & Mack.
*Carefree*, 1938, RKO, Fred Astaire and Ginger Rogers.
*Mark of the Vampire,* 1935, Universal Studios, Bela Lugosi, Lionel Barrymore.
A remake of a 1927 silent movie called *London After Midnight.*
*Black Friday,* 1940, Universal Studios, Boris Karloff, Bela Lugosi.
As part of a publicity stunt, Lugosi was placed into hypnosis on the set for his death scene.
*Calling Dr Death,* 1943, Universal Studios, Lon Chaney, Jr.
*Lost In a Harem,* 1944, Universal, Abbot and Costello.
*The Climax,* 1944, Universal, Boris Karloff.
*The Frozen Ghost,* 1945, Universal Studios, Lon Chaney, Jr.

*The Woman in Green,* 1945, Universal Studios, Basil Rathbone as Sherlock Holmes.

*The Mask of Dijon,* 1946, PRC Productions.

*Scared to Death,* 1947, Monogram, Bela Lugosi.

*The Road to Rio,* 1947, Paramount, Bob Hope and Bing Crosby.

*Abbott and Costello Meet the Killer,* 1949, Universal, Boris Karloff.

*Black Magic,* 1949, RKO, Orson Wells as Cagliostro.

—Also released as *Caliostro.*

*Whirlpool,* 1950, 20th Century Fox. Mel Ferrer.

*Invasion USA.,* 1953, 20th Century Fox.

The mid to late 1950s brought forth a virtual deluge of movies that featured hypnosis as a plot device. The Bridey Murphy case was selling newspapers throughout the country, and the film industry wasted no time cashing in on the public's newfound interest in hypnotism.

*How To Be Very, Very Popular,* 1955, 20th Century Fox.

*The Court Jester,* 1955, Dena Enterprises. Danny Kaye.

*The Three Faces Of Eve,* 1957, Paramount. Joanne Woodward, Lee J. Cobb.

*The Search for Bridey Murphy,* 1957, Paramount.

*Blood of Dracula,* 1957, American International.

*Daughter of Dr Jekyll,* 1957, Allied Artists.

*The She Creature,* 1956, American International Pictures.

—Remade into an even worse version in 1967 as *Creature of Destruction.*

*Spell of the Hypnotist,* 1956, Exploitation Productions.

*The Undead,* 1956, American International Pictures.

*Hold That Hypnotist,* 1956, Allied Artists, Bowery Boys.

*The Bride and the Beast,* 1958, Allied Artists.

*Curse of the Demon,* 1958, Columbia Pictures. Dana Andrews.

*Tales of Terror,* 1959, American International Pictures. Edgar Allen Poe. Edgar Allen Poe stories include "The Facts in the Case of M. Valdemer."

*Please Don't Touch Me,* 1959, Ormond Films. Ormond McGill and western film star Alfred "Lash" LaRue.

*The Manchurian Candidate,* 1962, United Artists.

*The Hypnotic Eye,* 1960, Allied Artists. Filmed in "Hypnomagic."

*The Devil Doll,* 1963, Associated Film Distributors.

*Those Incredibly Strange Creatures Who Stopped Living and Became Mixed-Up Zombies,* 1964, Fairway International. Made in "Halucogenic Hypnovision."

*Rasputin: The Mad Monk,* 1966 Hammer Films. Christopher Lee.

*Eye of The Devil,* 1967, MGM, David Niven.

*Divorce American Style,* 1967, Columbia Pictures.

—Concludes in a nightclub with a first-rate stage hypnosis act by Pat Collins.

*The Crimson Cult,* 1968, British Tigon Film Productions, Boris Karloff.

*The Stranger Within,* 1971, Universal.

*The Devil and Miss Sarah,* 1971, Universal, Gene Barry.

*The UFO Incident,* 1975, Made for TV, James Earl Ray.

*JD's Revenge,* 1976, American International.

*On a Clear Day You Can See Forever,* 1970, Paramount, Barbara Streisand.

*The Exorcist,* 1973, Warner Bros. During one of the early scenes in the film a hypnotist attempts to work with the possessed girl and is promptly physically attacked by her.

*Let's Do It Again,* 1975, Warner Bros.

*The Reincarnation of Peter Proud,* 1975, Avco Embassy Pictures.

*Audrey Rose,* 1977, United Artists, Anthony Hopkins.

*Exorcist II, the Heretic,* 1977, Warner Bros.

—Once more, hypnosis is ineffectively employed to combat this supernatural menace.

*The Natural,* 1984, Tri-Star Pictures, Robert Redford.

*Jack's Back,* 1988, Paramount.

*Two Evil Eyes,* 1991, 20th Century Fox. Video release.

*Dead Again,* 1992, Paramount.

*The Search For Grace,* 1994, CBS-TV.

*Stir of Echoes,* 1997, Kevin Bacon.

*A Nightmare On Elm Street 3–The Dream Warriors,* 1988, New Line.

*Ripper Man,* 1998, Turner Home Entertainment.

*No Dessert Dad, Until You Mow the Lawn,* 1994, Disney.

*Holy Man,* 1998, Touchstone, Eddie Murphy.

*Office Space,* 1999, 20th Century Fox, Ron Livingston, Jennifer Aniston.

*Curse of the Jade Scorpion,* 2001, Paramount, Woody Allen.

*Horror,* 2001, Lion's Gate, The Amazing Kreskin.

*Shallow Hal,* 2001, Fox, Tony Robbins.

*K-PAX 2001,* Universal, Kevin Spacey.

*Just Close Your Eyes,* 2004, Lion's Gate.


Hollywood's depiction of hypnosis and hypnotism, with a few exceptions, is negative. Hypnotism is portrayed as something macabre and mysterious, tinged with the supernatural. Its practitioners are frequently pictured as dark and malevolent manipulators of the human mind, controlling their subjects like puppets and moving them to acts of murder and self-destruction. The films that dealt with reincarnation usually had subjects who sought to find out about their past life experiences, and were thrown into perilous, life-threatening situations. Overall, the film industry would have the public believe that any contact with a hypnotist is potentially dangerous and that hypnotism is something to be feared and avoided or mocked and ridiculed.

Many of the films in this filmography are old and obscure, and seldom trouble the TV airwaves with their appearance. Even when they were first released (or in most cases escaped) these were the kind of movies that would have been the third feature of a double bill or shown at a drive-in during a blizzard. The more recent releases are another matter. These films are shown on cable TV on a fairly regular basis. It is truly sad that some people base their opinion of hypnosis on how it is portrayed in the movies or on TV.

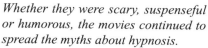

*Whether they were scary, suspenseful or humorous, the movies continued to spread the myths about hypnosis.*

# Chapter 22
## Stage Hypnotism

Looking at who the players were in the establishment of a separate and distinct profession for hypnotists after WWII (1945), we see there has always been in-fighting, professional jealousy, back-stabbing, and general unfriendliness among stage performers.

One well-known Vegas nightclub hypnotist, Ronald Pellar, performed under the stage names Ron Dante and/or Dr Dante, and was briefly married to actress Lana Turner. Having seen him in person as an entertainer, and also in promoting his "Certified Hypnotherapy" classes, I can attest to the fact that he had an abundance of stage presence and professional charisma.

In 1974 he went to prison when he tried to put out a contract for the murder of another nightclub competitor, hypnotist Dr Michael Dean … very unfriendly competitors!

During his career, Pellar was charged with a number of criminal offenses, including mail fraud in connection with his operation of the diploma mill Columbia State University.

Stage hypnotists of the '40s and '50s, mentioned earlier in this book, such as Harry Arons, Melvin Powers, Gil Boyne, John Calvert, Tex Morton, Rexford North, Franz Polgar, and Ormond McGill, as well those who followed, such as Peter Reveen, Jerry Valley, Sam Vine and others, presented outstanding stage shows which treated volunteers with respect and courtesy during their participation on stage.

Thankfully most stage hypnotists don't fit into any narrow mold, or exhibit criminal tendencies, but are just good showmen who have found their star quality in entertaining with hypnotism, and helping good-sport volunteers have their seconds of glory in the spotlight.

As was reported in earlier chapters, the major member organizations for hypnotists were started by stage hypnotists in the late '40s and early '50s. That was also the era when Joan Brandon on the East Coast and Pat Collins on the West Coast made names for themselves as female stage hypnotists. This was a new concept and garnered a lot of publicity for those two performers, particularly Collins, who ran her own nightclub. They both either had a talent for publicity and self-promotion or excellent publicists working for them, as you can see by the publicity material included in this book.

Stage hypnotists continue to be busy in the 21st century, although it seems that, because of the large number of newcomers to the field, R-Rated hypnotists have become popular in the club scene and particularly venues such as Las Vegas.

When a group of former stage performers start to "jackpot," or tell stories about the good old days, it is always fun to hear about their experiences. I have many "war stories" to match most of theirs.

Larry Garrett was typical. He was new at hypnosis, having recently finished classes with Fred Schiavo and he was eager to do hypnotism professionally. Larry had a strong ego, and says, "I was too naïve to know what I didn't know." He had seen a hypnotist perform in one of the Chicago nightclubs and had asked the bouncer how much the performer got paid. The hypnotist was getting $60, and Larry figured he could do it for less. He had done many of the same things in class and why couldn't he do them in an act and get paid. He only needed to find someone to hire him. He went into a place called Lucifer's Den, where the owner looked like the bouncer and even a little like Lucifer himself. Rocky, the owner, was a big guy and said, "If you can hypnotize me, you got the job."

Anxious to become a stage hypnotist, Larry said, "'Of course I can hypnotize you," and proceeded to do what he had learned in class and it worked. Larry was even amazed, so he had the bouncer and bartender lay the owner across two chairs, somebody grabbed a Polaroid, took a photo, and then they took Rocky off the chairs and brought him out of hypnosis. Larry used selective amnesia as it seemed to be more fun when the person didn't recall the suggestion or experience. When Rocky opened his eyes, he said, "See I told you couldn't hypnotize me!" Larry showed him the photo and immediately got the job at $25 per show and $35 for two-show nights.

In his first show he did a nice routine for a beginner and at the end of the show suggested selective amnesia as he had learned in class. He said to the group on stage, "On the count of three open your eyes —stuck to the chair—remembering nothing." They opened their eyes and they all stood up. Larry was horrified and red faced—his first show and he had failed—nobody was stuck. Of course, thinking about it later he realized an important lesson, that the last suggestion is the strongest. His was, "stuck to the chair—remembering nothing" instead of, "remembering nothing—stuck to the chair."

Fred Schiavo, a bit miffed asked him,."What do you think makes *you* a professional?" Larry told him the dictionary says if you get paid for your skills you are considered a professional.

That was the beginning of what turned out to be a prestigious lifetime career in hypnotism and what today is *the* outstanding hypnotism center in Chicago.

I've spent my adult life multi-tasking and in the mid '90s our theatrical agency had a client who insisted he wanted a hypnotist for the annual banquet of their Fair associations members. I was closely connected to the Fair as their Entertainment Superintendent and had been with them for 44 years, so I knew their members quite well. I advised against it because of the makeup of those who attended the function annually, but the Fair president insisted, so I booked the best in the area at that time—Jerry Valley.

As members, my wife and I were also attending the banquet, and when Jerry could only entice three women and one man to volunteer I knew he was in trouble. Two of the females were very active church ladies and, I think, wanted to let him know what he was doing was really the work of the devil or something—they weren't about to succumb. They were thanked and dismissed early on. The younger lady. I knew was going to be a "seat warmer." She would be there, but really wasn't going a great participant.

I had known the male volunteer for many years. He was a nice, easy going guy who worked hard at the Fair, but never got any recognition, so I knew he would be good. I wiped the sweat off my brow and watched Jerry do a completely entertaining show with this one fellow and the "seat warmer." After the banquet we were standing out in the hall when the Fair President came over to give me the check, exclaiming, "That was the funniest entertainment we've ever had, maybe we can do it again next year." Jerry and I just exchanged looks, smiled, said thanks, and made our exit.

I ran into a similar incident in Wilton Junction, Iowa, at a High School Banquet. The Senior Class of about 20 members voted on a hypnotist, but also had decided since they all wanted to *see* the show, nobody would volunteer. They figured this way their *teachers* would have to volunteer. I remember that their banquet was pot roast, but I when I started my act with my usual group handclasp test and *nobody* clasped their hands I had a feeling *I* was about to be cooked with no volunteers for the show.

Fortunately we always carried a second act with us, and Lois passed the briefcase to me. I had recently received a lot of publicity with a sightless boat drive up the Mississippi River to LeClaire, and another, through the downtown streets of Davenport. I had no trouble getting volunteers on stage to put gauze pads, adhesive tape, an aluminum shield (contributed for the boat trip by Alcoa in Bettendorf, Iowa) plus two double blindfolds and an opaque hood. Those high school seniors really wanted to make sure I couldn't see … anything. However, after I performed my "Sightless Vision" and "Miracles of the Mind" act they became mine!

After that act concluded successfully, and all the bandages etc. were removed, they all wanted me to hypnotize them, and their class advisor went to my wife and asked if they paid me double would I do the hypnotism act also? You know the old saying,"money talks"? Of course I would! After all, we depended on the shows and hypnotism classes for our income while I was in college, and now those wonderful high school seniors were primed for what turned out to be a fun-filled and successful hypnosis show.

Everybody was happy. They gave us a check and a couple of pot roast sandwiches to enjoy on our way back home ... a show was booked a day later for another school and we also had more money than we expected that week for groceries, gas and rent on our mobile home lot. That's show biz!

Now, in the 21st century there is a lot of discussion about whether hypnotism shows are good or bad for our profession as we continue our path of helping ordinary, everyday people with ordinary, everyday problems. A lot of successful people in the profession would like to see the images created by hypnotism as an entertainment disappear because they feel it demeans what they do in their offices, and perpetuates the myths we've been trying to live down, such as having power over someone's mind and so forth.

There has been a recent movement underway to encourage professional member organizations to disavow connections to hypnotism as an entertainment, particularly when occasional negative situations have arisen from participants after a show. Most of the problems, aside from receiving a bit of bad publicity, usually turn out to be handled adequately on a local level. Many times it is simply an attempt of a teen participant to get a lot of personal attention after a show, or parents wanting to impose their beliefs on others before a post-prom show.

A second group of successful practitioners have found that well presented, ethical, and entertaining hypnotism shows are often a reason that people decide to come their offices for professional services, such as smoking cessation, weight management, etc. They've seen people do rather silly things under the direction of a hypnotist, so maybe there is something to it that might help them. When I was seeing clients I had several clients who came in because of seeing one popular hypnotist at local venues who was R-Rated. They usually said his language and his show was "gross," but it still aroused their interest in hypnotism for serious subjects.

A third group of successful performers figure they are entertaining people with their shows, and see no reason to want to do away with a well-established type of entertainment. Many of these performers mention professional hypnotists who are available to help with many problems and often advise  their audiences to check for someone in their area.

The National Guild of Hypnotists, as I stated earlier, was started by stage hypnotists, hypno-hobbyists and just a few clinical and licensed hypnotists. Because of this heritage the organization has never disavowed or disowned that segment of the profession, and always features one evening with several professional stage hypnotists performing to packed houses.

Although there were laws against performing hypnotists enacted many years before, in the 20th century the situation started to change. The prohibitive law in England after the Slater trial and outdated laws in several states in the US prohibiting stage hypnotism were rarely enforced or were dropped entirely.

Curiously, attempts to ban stage hypnotists were made in a few cities in the US by a few AAEH members licensed in other health fields such as medicine, dentistry and psychology, but these efforts failed when AGVA (American Guild of Variety Artists) and other unions interceded. Right now you can see dozens of hypnosis shows in Las Vegas and other entertainment cities, on cruise ships, and later many high school after-prom lockdown parties.

Although there are some parents who object to this type of entertainment at the after-prom parties they still flourish because that age group really like the shows. Of course, the real professional stage hypnotist is covered by liability insurance, and it is only rarely that there is a complaint, which in most cases, turns out to be frivolous.

Will we eventually see the complete disappearance of hypnotism as an entertainment? I doubt it, because, let's face it, anyone can learn to be a demonstrational hypnotist. They can perform impromptu shows wherever they go. People will participate and will enjoy seeing these demonstrations. Unfortunately many people will still believe the old myths, because stage hypnotists are apt to get the "hypnotist disease" mentioned early in the book and perpetuate the myths to make themselves appear more mysterious and powerful than normal folks.

# OFFICE & PROFESSIONAL EMPLOYEES
## INTERNATIONAL UNION

*Doth grant this*

# LOCAL UNION CHARTER

*to:*

DWIGHT F. DAMON, DC   ELSOM ELDRIDGE, JR, EDM   GEORGE BARANOWSKI   PAULA BARANOWSKI
DON MOTTIN   CHARLES FRANCIS, MA   C. SCOT GILES, DD   EDWARD MORRIS, BA
JOHN C. HUGHES, DC   EDWARD HIGHTOWER   LARRY GARRETT   RICHARD HARTE, PHD
C. ROY HUNTER   MARX HOWELL   SOL LEWIS   THOMAS LITTLE
ROYE FRASER   GERALD KEIN   SHIRLEY L. KEIN   MASUD ANSARI, PHD
JERRY VALLEY, MA   LAWRENCE BERRY   PATRICIA MACISAAC   GEORGE BIEN, PHD
LARRY TILLMAN   SIDNEY WALKER, MSC   PATRICIA TROWBRIDGE, RN

to any other named applicants, and to their successors, legally qualified, to constitute this local union, which shall be known as

**NATIONAL FEDERATION OF HYPNOTISTS**
**OFFICE AND PROFESSIONAL EMPLOYEES INTERNATIONAL UNION, AFL-CIO, LOCAL NO. 104**
**Located in Merrimack, New Hampshire**

*This Local Union Charter* is hereby granted as of March 1, 1994 in accordance with and subject to the constitution and laws of this International Union.

*This Local Union* shall be devoted and dedicated to promoting, protecting and championing the legitimate struggles of professional, office and clerical employees toward achieving economic well-being, their general welfare and rights as workers and citizens.

*In Witness Whereof,* we have subscribed our names and affixed the seal of the Office & Professional Employees International Union

*National Federation of Hypnotists Local 104 OPEIU AFL/CIO, CLC officially became a powerful partner of our profession in 1994.*

# Chapter 23
## Hypnotists' Unions

The union movement in the world of hypnotism had never really gotten off the ground since the first four locals were established in 1971. Only two still existed in 1990, one in Pennsylvania and one in California.

These hypnotist union locals had been in existence, but as stated elsewhere, there was no sharing of information with other interested organizations or leaders who wanted to organize in other areas of the country. Here in a nutshell is the story of how the union movement began in the profession of hypnotism, and how it has helped us in so many instances.

In 1971 a charter had been granted to the Hypnotist Union, Local # 467 in Pennsylvania, when it looked as if hypnotism was about to be declared legal only for licensed health professionals such as physicians, dentists, etc. The situation indeed seemed bleak and hopeless for hypnotists who were in practice in that state.

According to Pennsylvania's Norbert Bakas, the Hypnotism Society of Pennsylvania was intent on not letting these other professions take the practice of hypnosis for their own. Dewey Deavers, who practiced in Pittsburgh, went all out to back the society's efforts to protect members. However, according to Harry Arons and AAEH, who were adamantly against most of the Pennsylvania legislative attempts, they were mostly misguided. Bills such as H.B. No. 94 in 1970, and Senate Bill No. 638 in 1972, had proposals for as much as 1100 hours of study in a school or college approved by the Department of Education and the proposed Board. Arons was also very critical of the proposed "grandfather clause," which he pointed out would only be a problem if it was included.

Historically, in 1968 the Pennsylvania group was able to get HB 2265 introduced to license hypnotists, but the bill died in committee. Submitted again in 1971, SB 638 was passed by the senate and the governor indicated his approval, but on the last day of the session Governor Shapp held a news conference and vetoed the bill. Bakas reports that the governor also remarked to the press that he would not only veto it, but would do all within his power to see that hypnotism would be banned forever in Pennsylvania.

Then, even with opposition to the group who introduced HB 1040 (to limit the use of hypnosis), the Pennsylvania hypnotists didn't have the financial resources to fight that legal action.

Edward Hayes, who was a part-time hypnotist, a full time union plumber and a union steward at work, presented the idea for Pennsylvania hypnotists to unionize. The president of the AFL/CIO-CLU suggested that the group affiliate with OPEIU (Office and Professional Employees International Union), a branch of the AFL-CIO, and in November 1971 a charter was granted to The Hypnotist Union, Local #467, for the state of Pennsylvania.

Edward Hayes was elected president and Dewey Deavers became union organizer, hoping to develop hypnotist locals throughout the United States. His contact with John Kappas resulted in a California charter, Local #472; Frank Genco in Philadelphia was instrumental in Hypnotist Union #476; and Walter Sichort in New Jersey for Hypnotist Union Local #474. OPEIU president Howard Coughlin sent word to union lobbyists in Harrisburg, who, in turn, contacted the state representatives. One of the key questions he asked them was, "Do you want to go on record as being a legislator who deprived a union worker of a livelihood?" Since Pennsylvania was a very strong union state with the steel mills, etc., the union prevailed and the bill was defeated. In 2002, Local #469, the original union local in Pennsylvania, merged with the National Federation of Hypnotists Local #104. Except for Local #472, which is associated with John Kappas' Hypnosis Motivation Institute in California, the other locals did not survive.

According to one disgruntled hypnotherapy student, Jeffery Higley, in Case No. BC 209228, filed against HMI et al. in the spring of 1999 in Los Angeles Superior Court, "HMI unfairly required students to join defendants' AHA, Local #472 and, in turn, OPEIU, in order to take a clinical course at HMI." This was only a small portion of the lawsuit and not the main thrust of the legal action.

### A Union "Local" That Is International In Scope

NGH had been searching for information about establishing one large union local, but met only roadblocks from a key figure in the profession, who could provide it. However, in spring 1993 a meeting was set up in Daytona Beach, Florida, with officials of OPEIU AFL/CIO, CLC. Representatives of other hypnotism member organizations had been invited to participate and all the various groups took part in the day-long summit.

Another small meeting was held at the annual NGH convention in August in New Hampshire, but there was no official outcome until March of 1994 when NGH moved ahead and received authorization to organize the National Federation of Hypnotists Local #104 OPEIU AFL-CIO CLC. The union charter encompasses all of the US and Canada, and has proven to be beneficial when legislative clout has been needed to help protect our profession.

NFH #104 legislative officials are unpaid volunteers who work for the benefit of the profession with the help of OPEIU, which has been there for the profession wherever they were needed to provide lobbyists and financial aid.

NFH 104 has been the legislative branch of the National Guild of Hypnotists for the past 17 years under the direction of legislative liaison officer C. Scot Giles. Dr Giles is an ordained Unitarian minister, licensed counselor, and recognized authority on medical/hypnosis cancer programs. He is a tireless advocate for the high standards and code of ethics provided by the NGH and has accepted the responsibility to insure that any legislative efforts are to be for *all* practicing hypnotists.

Previous Convention Held in Las Vegas, Nevada
June 18-21, 2007

*Recognized by the public and union members as being a union hypnotist.*

## Union Hypnotists? Yes, It's True!

What if someone told you that you can lose weight, stop smoking, eliminate anxieties, and maintain a better quality of life?

All these positive results can be accomplished through hypnotism, according to Dr. Dwight F. Damon, President of the National Federation of Hypnotists, OPEIU Local 104. Damon is also the president of the National Guild of Hypnotists, the oldest and largest organization of its kind in the field of hypnotism.

Local 104 Secretary-Treasurer Sharon Morris has nothing but high praise for their affiliation with OPEIU. "Since we received our union charter in 1994, we have had the backing of OPEIU and state AFL-CIO federations in our legislative endeavors as we became a separate and distinct profession," said Morris. "When we have been faced with restrictive legislation that favored other professions' attempts at putting our members out of business, we have been able to count on the union's strength and experience to help us in our battles. OPEIU has always come through for us in the U.S. and Canada."

"This relationship has allowed Local Unions wellbeing programs to use union hypnotists to provide group sessions in smoking cessation, stress and weight management for their members," said President Michael Goodwin. "We encourage OPEIU members to always ask about practitioners' union affiliation when looking for a well-qualified consulting hypnotist, including Local 104 and Hypnotherapist's Local 472."

*The centuries-old practice of hypnotism was a male-dominated field until the 1950s. Pictured above is a very small sampling of books authored by female hypnotists during the profession's past quarter century.*

# Chapter 24
## Women as Professional Hypnotists
## Credit Where Credit Is Due

If we wonder why it took so long for women to become active as hypnotists, we have to look at the pre-World War II years when most women were homemakers. Outside the home, there were specific jobs which were filled by women, such as nursing, teaching, telephone operators, and eventually replacing males in executive secretary positions.

When the war took a majority of able-bodied males into the service of their country, it was the women who moved out of their customary roles and became welders and defense plant workers, as well as filling non-combat positions in the military. Times were changing around us at a rapid pace and, after the war, women's roles in the US were also changing.

Previously, in our field, the predominate hypnotic approach was strictly what we now call paternal, or dominating the subject in our induction process. By nature, this was really not suitable for a woman to use as a hypnotist, although through the years that followed there would always be paternal and maternal approaches.

If we stop and think about how the use of hypnosis on a "helping" basis has evolved, doesn't it make sense that females, with their God-given abilities to nurture, understand, relate to, and even "heal" their loved ones, could be considered "naturals" to have a starring role in the art, science, and philosophy of hypnotism?

At first, it started with stage hypnotists such as Joan Brandon and Pat Collins, who are discussed in our chapter on stage hypnotism. Soon, having seen what performers such as these two ladies were able to do as hypnotists, inquisitive women searched out courses and schools so they, too, could learn. It wasn't an instant change, but rather a slow integration of the women into what traditionally had been strictly a male dominated profession.

With every successful step along the way we find that women established practices and schools, developed courses, and wrote books. The ratio of female to male membership in organizations and attendance at conventions increased. My big problem in writing about this metamorphosis of the profession is that not enough historical data exists outside my memory about those women who were pioneers, acting not only for their counterparts, but also for their profession.

Nevertheless, I am going to present a few names from the era that we are discussing:

Helen Baucum opened her first office on Las Vegas Boulevard in Las Vegas, Nevada in 1965. She was a major figure in the city, introducing the benefits of hypnosis, not as an entertainment attraction, but for personal well-being. She was known locally as "Hypnotist to the Stars," through her work with many Vegas headliners, and was inducted into Penny Dutton Raffa's Hypnosis Hall of Fame as "Woman of the Century."

Baucum established a school in the '70s, and also held offices in the National Society of Hypnotherapists for many years. She is known for her book, *Self Hypnosis in Action*, co-written with daughter Kimberly in the early '90s. The book contains many case histories and helps to explain her "pinpoint" method of hypnotherapy, according to her student and associate Layne Keck, who continues her work with clients and training in Las Vegas.

Josie Hadley in Palo Alto, California (1944 -1997) helped many people as a teacher, author, and hypnotherapist. Her book, *Hypnosis For Change,* was published by New Harbinger Publications, and translated into 13 languages. She founded the Palo Alto School of Hypnotherapy in 1979, the American Association of Professional Hypnotherapists in 1980, and was well known in her community for her civic activities and pioneering public relations work in bringing hypnosis into hospitals and medical centers in that area of California.

Dr Irene Hickman was born May 21, 1915 in Iowa, received a BA degree from Simpson College in 1938 and graduated in 1949 as a Doctor of Osteopathy from the College of Osteopathic Physicians and Surgeons in Los Angeles. In addition to using hypnosis in her practice, she also became a teacher/lecturer at conventions across the US She was the author of *Mind Probe-Hypnosis* and *Remote Depossession,* and a member of the National Society of Hypnotherapists.

Other notable California female hypnotists include Livona Stillman, and Dr Freda Morris, founder of the Hypnosis Clearing House in Lafayette, California.

Anne H. Spencer, PhD, was a teacher accomplished in the Montessori educational methods when she graduated from AIH with her doctorate. She began her practice in 1980 in Detroit, Michigan, establishing Infinity Institute, a state licensed school to teach hypnotherapy.

Spencer founded the International Medical and Dental Hypnotherapy Association (IMDHA) in 1986. After years of teaching, writing and presenting at conventions and selling both the school and the organization, she is now semi-retired and continues to publish *Subconsciously Speaking* online.

It has been a major project to gather the brief information I've included in this chapter about the women I've mentioned. Probably because, with the exception of the female stage hypnotists, they did not have the male-ego factor of needing and seeking recognition and/or personal publicity.

In more contemporary years there have been so many women who have made their mark on the profession that it would almost warrant a book by itself. For me to list all our current outstanding female colleagues would be a personal and political impossibility. Although I am tempted to compile a list I would never finish this book by my established deadline if I attempted it.

As I stated previously, women have definitely become an integral part of this profession as seen at the most recent NGH convention when 63% of attendees were female and 37% were male. Whether this same percentage can be applied generally to those who are actually in practice I really don't know, but I do know that it is a good possibility. Since we need more people practicing professionally, it really doesn't matter whether they are male or female.

It certainly has been shown that a woman can set up an office, network, and establish a practice. She can became an excellent certified instructor, write a book, and best of all can help ordinary, everyday people with ordinary, everyday problems as well as some male practitioners.

It would be a monumental task to list all of the contemporary women in our profession and I would not want to remiss in leaving out even one name, so I have opted not to list them individually. However, from what I have written, it should be obvious to the reader that I hold all of our female hypnotists in high regard and give them a great deal of credit for their participation in helping move our profession to where it is today.

I hope that more women will come into our profession, go into practice, teach, write books, and perhaps by their example inspire their male counterparts to do the same.

PERFORMANCE

# For Athletes, Better Focus With Hypnosis

Moments before the gun sounded to start his World Cup 400m race, Iwan Thomas gently tugged on his left ear lobe. This subtle movement helped him block out the noise of the crowd and the runners on either side of him. Like a number of other top athletes, Mr. Thomas has been using hypnosis to enhance his performance. The action of pulling his ear lobe is known as an associative post-hypnotic command, which brought him into a heightened state of concentration. He won the race that day, capping off his best season ever.

Associated Press

Iwan Thomas of Wales, triumphant at the finish line.

Mr. Thomas, 24, of Wales, described how he came to work with a hypnotist: "I met Robert Farago in 1995 when the BBC was looking for a guinea pig for one of their morning breakfast programs. Then last year things weren't going well for me, and my parents said 'Why don't you give that hypnotist a try?' I think it helped to keep me calm and focused."

Professional athletes and their weekend counterparts are turning to hypnosis to help correct everything from a poor golf swing to precompetition jitters. Dr. Dwight Damon, president of the National Guild of Hypnotists in Merrimeck, N.H., said he believed more and more of the guild's 7,000 members are using hypnosis to help athletes improve performance.

"What hypnosis does is it takes the champion's best performance, makes it available 100 percent of the time," said Mr. Farago, who works with athletes at his hypnosis clinic in Windsor, England. "Sports people know it as going 'into the zone.' "

Mr. Farago works this way: He brings out a pocket watch and asks the subject to focus on it as he swings it to and fro, which results in a trance. For the next hour, Mr. Farago commands the required change, either something specific like "You will hit the ball straight down the fairway" or more general as in "You will win!" These commands might be tied to a gesture like tugging on the ear lobe.

Bob Reese, former head trainer for the New York Jets, also uses hypnotherapy with both professional and recreational athletes. He said he believed that the only drawback of the practice was its image problem. "One of the things I learned early on about hypnosis is to quit calling it that," said Mr. Reese, who runs a company called Train Your Brain in North Port, N.Y., and charges between $65 and $150 a session. "There was a built-in fear — they didn't want to give up their minds. Instead, I started telling athletes we were going to do some high powered visualization techniques."

*PAUL GAINS*

# Chapter 25
## Sports and Hypnosis

Sports hypnotists seem to have found that Coué's "Laws of Autosuggestion" are invaluable. Examples are—*when there is a conflict between the will and imagination, the imagination always wins*—the law of concentrated attention—the law of auxiliary emotion—the law of reversed effort, and the law of subconscious teleology.

I wrote earlier about Dr David Tracy and baseball's St. Louis Browns, which was well publicized in print. Stories that were told about Jimmy Grippo and World Light Heavyweight Melio Bettina, John Halpin and Heavyweight Champion Mike Tyson, whether substantiated or not, are all believeable. Along the way, through the years, other hypnotists have worked independently and quietly with athletes of all types.

In reality there isn't any sport in which a player wouldn't benefit from the use of hypnosis and self-hypnosis. Hypnosis can be used widely to enhance performance and encourage optimum results with individuals and teams. There have been hundreds of golfers, wrestlers, bowlers, hockey and baseball players—sports participants of all kinds—who have experienced hypnotic enhancement and encouragement, but are the fans and public ready to accept it?

In the early '50s a group of hypnotists worked with bowlers in New Jersey, reporting their results only in our own publications. Publicly, the first widespread publicity on the use of hypnosis in sports was in the '60s with stories about Russian Olympic athletes and mental programming. Due to misconceptions of what hypnosis really is, the American people have been apprehensive about this type of training as being "brain washing," which makes them uncomfortable and very wary.

Although even high school athletes could benefit from group hypnosis, one can imagine the uproar from parents if it was ever suggested for their youngsters, yet these young people are constantly being programmed through TV and advertising to buy certain things. For that matter, part of a parent's job is to program their offspring in a positive way to become successful adults. Isn't this really a matter of conversational hypnosis, direct and indirect suggestions?

*Journal of Hypnotism* columnist Emanuel Orlick grew up in a family that practiced Couéism, and as a young adult of 16 he organized the Hamilton Hypnotic Research Society in Canada. As a writer/editor he reputedly had more than 10 million words published, many of them on hypnosis, self-hypnosis, and mind/body unity. His son, sports psychologist Terry Orlick, followed in his father's footsteps and has authored over 20 books as well as working with some of the world's top athletes.

In recent years we have seen more certified consulting hypnotists becoming involved in athletic training. In a recent survey, 5% of the respondents specialize in the use of hypnosis with amateur and professional athletes.

Bob Reese, former New York Jets trainer for 20 years, is the author of *Develop the Winner's Mentality: Integrating 5 Easy Mental Skills for Enduring Success,* and has worked with US Olympic athletes and professionals in the NFL, PGA, USTA and CART as well as with amateur college, high school and recreational athletes.

After establishing a successful practice in Pittsburgh, John Weir relocated to Florida and currently travels extensively working with golfers and teaching other hypnotists the intricacies of working in this field. John Weir, Jerry Valley, Wil Horton, William Smith, and other leading hypnotists have also participated in video programs for golfers produced by and for golf pros.

Pennsylvania's Dan Vitchoff acted as a mental training and performance coach at the 2008 Summer Olympics in Beijing, China, where he used hypnosis methods and techniques along with NLP and some deep breathing exercises to help Walton Glenn Eller and Vincent Hancock bring home the gold.

Drake Eastburn from Colorado started working with cyclists in the *Tour de California* and which led to the Tour de France and several riders in the Olympics who came out very well up in the overall competition.

There has been an increasing interest by school athletes in the potential positive effects of hypnosis and self-hypnosis to enhance and improve their natural abilities in all sorts of sports.

In 1997 I worked with my grandson, Jereme Bachand, a high school senior at the time, to improve his performance on the wrestling team. When we started he was low man on the totem pole, but after a couple of sessions the improvements came. While competing at the state championships he felt in need of a hypno-fix, but I was vacationing in Sarasota, Florida. Since he was already well conditioned as a subject we did a brief re-enforcement over the phone from the sunny beach to the snowy gymnasium, and he won all three of his matches and finished fifth in NH state high school wrestling.

After graduation Jay trained as a certified hypnotist and now is communications director for NGH, as well as coach of two school wrestling teams. His reaction to a recent press release about a NJ high school wrestling team utilizing hypnosis was a knowing smile.

Around the world hypnotists are finding eager clients for their services since any athletic activity you can think of can benefit from the use of hetero-hypnosis and self-hypnosis. Amateur or professional, school or olympic athletes, can all improve their performance when they are guided by a hypnotist who also can teach them the use of self-hypnosis, so if we start working with youngsters in high school using the principles of what we do, we will be preparing them for future success, not just in athletics, but in whatever they do in life.

At this point in time the biggest problem with this is that many parents still believe the old myths about hypnotism and would never give permission for their children to be hypnotized, because they mistakingly think it is like brainwashing. On the other hand, too often parents are guilty of unthinkingly brainwashing their children in negative ways which sets up blocks for the rest of their lives.

It is pretty well accepted that by using positive hypnotic principles it is relatively easy to promote improvement for any sports endeavor even when the hypnotists doesn't know that much about the sport. Actually, a thorough interview with the client in advance, combined with a bit of research into proper terminology of the sport, leads to the best overall results.

# READER'S DIGEST FAMILY GUIDE TO NATURAL MEDICINE

## How to Stay Healthy the Natural Way

## Which is another name for hypnosis?

1 Asphyxiation
2 Mesmerism
3 Somnambulism

**Hypnosis**

Mesmerism was named for Franz Mesmer of Vienna, who introduced the technique of hypnosis in the late 1700s.

Mesmer was more showman than medical man. He claimed to have supernatural powers which he used to put subjects into a trance. This, he said, cured disease. Physicians thought Mesmer was a phony, but some saw value in inducing a relaxed, trancelike state. They continued research and renamed the technique hypnosis, after Hypnos, the Greek god of sleep.

**Call It Sleep**

Hypnosis actually isn't a form of sleep. It's intense concentration—so intense that the subject is able to block out all distractions. This helps a person achieve a state of complete relaxation. A hypnotized person may become so relaxed he doesn't even feel pain.

**Medical Uses**

Before the invention of anesthetics, surgeons sometimes used hypnosis to relax patients for surgery. Today, dentists and physicians use hypnosis as an anesthetic or to relieve anxiety. Hypnotherapists use it to enhance memory, help patients overcome fears, or alter behavior.

**Hypnosis was once known as mesmerism.**

Hypnotherapist Dr. Dwight Damon works with a client.

*"Readers Digest Family Guide to Natural Medicine" and "Grolier Book of Knowledge Flash Cards for Children" both requested information for their chapters about hypnosis. The National Guild of Hypnotists provided the information and photo for these publications.*

128

# Chapter 26
## It's a Litigious World

In the early years of stage hypnotism in the US, although there was a lot of mysticism connected with hypnosis, there didn't seem to be any serious lawsuits against the showmen/hypnotists worth reporting. Perhaps it was the nature of the general public to accept any somewhat aberrant behavior of post-show volunteers as normal for that particular person. Generally speaking, the public was less litigious and perhaps more naive in those days.

During the heyday of vaudeville, one popular headlined stage hypnotist was said to employ a cast of twenty to present his one-man hypnotic act. With that many "stooges" in the audience at various performances, he was able to produce some spectacular performances without worry, since the best of his audience volunteers who responded to his more spectacular suggestions on stage were actually "plants"—sort of a do-it-yourself insurance!

Probably the first litigation that had widespread publicity involved hypnotist Ralph Slater (born Joseph Bolsky) in England in 1952. Although this trial did not occur in the US, it is included, since he was referred to as the "American" hypnotist by the media, although he claimed in his book, *Hypnotism and Self Hypnosis,* to be a child of well-to-do parents in a suburb of London. Of course, we also know that showmen and movie actors, particularly in the days before the Internet, could make a lot of claims that could be considered as puffery, embellishment of the facts, or just plain hype, to glamorize their professional biographies.

The lawsuit of Diana Grace Rains Bath against hypnotist Ralph Slater, according to the media, was a claim that Slater not only hypnotized her in his act, but sent her home in a psychological depression that lasted for almost three years. It took, she said, 23 visits to Australian-born Dr Sidney VanPelt, president of the British Society of Medical Hypnotists and an avid foe of stage hypnotism, to dehypnotize her. According to media reports, Slater took over his own representation when his lawyer quit the case. He spent the trial boasting of the fact that he had hypnotized over 25,000 people and often earned up to $15,000.00 a week. After 62 minutes of deliberation, Slater was fined $8,490 for the claimed damages, and the "Hypnotism Act" was subsequently placed into law with regulations pertaining to licensing of public hypnotism as entertainment in England.

Slater, who claimed to have previously set a record by appearing at Carnegie Hall seven times in one year (1948), came back to the US and appeared just off Broadway with his "four-walled" hypnotism show in 1951-52.

Four-wall booking of Carnegie Hall and other theaters was not difficult if you were able to pay the rent, services, and any union charges that were incurred. It is still often done today by hypnotists, magicians, and other entertainers in prestigious locations such as Las Vegas. The bottom line in these booking arrangements is for the star (renter) to be able to promote enough in ticket sales to return the rental and other costs and make a profit, not just to be able to state that they had starred on the Las Vegas Strip, or in some well-known Las Vegas venue.

Regarding insurance for hypnotists ... in the late 1980s in the US, it was not actually a hypnotism show, but a high school classroom demonstration that prompted litigation against Joseph Scott in Pennsylvania. Joe Scott, a police officer who had specialized in forensic work, had been medically retired and operated a professional hypnotism practice.

Scott had been invited on occasion to speak to psychology classes about hypnosis at a local high school, and once again accepted an invitation for September 27, 1986. He did his usual program—the history of hypnotism, a general explanation of what hypnotism is—questions and answers—and a group induction. It was pretty basic stuff that had always been well received by the students and their teachers, and he and his assistant left the school feeling that the lecture-demonstration had been a successful student learning experience and a goodwill gesture on his part to the educational system.

However, within a short time he was served legally with papers from two sets of parents who had teenagers, each in one of the two separate class presentations. The two students, a boy and a girl, were not related or connected other than being students in the same school.

Joe Scott and the school district were being sued because the students in question reported ill-effects after simply being present at the programs. They reportedly had trouble sleeping, bad dreams, etc., and wanted to be compensated for their discomfort. Newspaper headlines appeared, depositions were taken and this simple school program was headed for court. Kits of the depositions were prepared by NGH and sold to help member Joe Scott with his legal expenses.

Monday morning hypnotism quarterbacks pointed out that Scott shouldn't have worn all black when doing the program (mentioned by one of the complainants) and wondered such things as, "Why didn't he require permission slips from parents of the class students?" He probably didn't think it was necessary since he hadn't bothered the year before, and students who didn't want to participate were allowed to just watch the demonstration. And the

*Philadelphia Inquirer* reporter asked me, "When the case first emerged he was just Joe Scott, but as it progressed how did he suddenly became, *Dr* Joe Scott?" Actually, he received his DCH (Doctor of Clinical Hypnotherapy) from AIH in California, having completed his distance-learning classes while this litigation was underway.

Dr Martin T. Orne, well-known "hired gun" in cases involving hypnosis, was brought in by the prosecution for this case. A little known fact, appearing in any deposition regarding Orne's qualifications, was that as a graduate student at Harvard and medical student at Tufts he had training from Dr Rexford L. North, a stage hypnotist. It is alluded to in the following excerpt from official court documents of the direct examination of Dr Orne as a witness for the prosecution.

"*Q. Are you familiar with laybodies and organizations that involve themselves in the practice of hypnosis?*

*A. Yes.*

*Q. And have you been involved in any way in your work over the years with laypersons who conduct hypnosis?*

*A. Yes, sir, some of the better known people. LeCrong (sic), who was a lay individual in a sense, had a bachelor's degree only and yet was a very competent person.*

Mr. Friedman: *Excuse me, your Honor, I must interrupt at this time, I believe the questions called for him to indicate yes or no and then not to start going into other sidetracks here.*

The Court: *That's overruled, go ahead.*

*Q. (By Mr. Kelly) You may continue, Dr Orne.*

*A. Well, Mr. LeCrong has published a major book in the area and was a very useful contributor. I've also — I also knew Rexford North, who was a stage hypnotist and who founded a hypnosis group and put out a journal, a quarterly journal.*

*Q. These are lay hypnotists, is that right?*"

*Editor's note: Dr Martin T. Orne became a shining light and acknowledged authority in the world of the licensed practitioners who use hypnosis, but there is still no escaping the fact that, as many others did, he learned from a stage hypnotist. He spent a great deal of time at the Hypnotism Center while a grad student in Boston. Also, please note that "LeCrong" mentioned in the previous exact transcript is, in all probability, hypnotist/author Leslie LeCron, whose name could have been misunderstood by the court stenographer/reporter since electronic recording hadn't yet come in common use in courts.

Needless to say, the Joseph Scott litigation raised a lot of media attention, but finally went nowhere and the school district and Joe Scott were off the hook. Scott had serious heart problems before entering the hypnotism world, retiring from the police force on a medical disability. His friends say that due to all the stress involved in the lawsuit, his health declined drastically and he died a short time after the conclusion of the trial.

Although this was just a classroom demonstration of hypnosis, it brings up some present day situations. One of the more popular entertainments for post-prom "lockdown" parties is hypnotism shows. They are usually a lot of fun since high school age volunteers generally respond well to suggestions. Often there are parents who, due to their beliefs, or misbeliefs, object to having hypnotism shows at these functions. These are parents who also object to certain books in schools, and usually are publicly very vocal with their opinions.

Because of this, and other factors such as "R" rated hypnotists, there has been a recent movement underway to encourage professional member organizations to disavow connections to hypnotism as an entertainment, particularly when occasional negative situations have arisen from participants after a show. Most of the problems, aside from receiving a bit of bad publicity, usually turn out to be handled adequately on a local level. Many times it is simply an attempt of a teen participant to get a lot of personal attention after a show, or parents wanting to impose their beliefs on others before a show.

### A Most Recent School Situation
EXCLUSIVE TO THE JOURNAL OF HYPNOTISM®
The George Kenney Wrap-Up
By Elaine Allen-Emrich

The international headlines were far reaching -"Florida Principal George Kenney Hypnotizes Students; 3 Dead."

As news of North Port High School principal George Kenney's use of hypnosis on students — two who later committed suicide and one who died in a car crash — has been reported nationally, some, including Kenney's attorney Mark Zimmerman, say the facts are skewed.

Kenney's story was reported online in the Huffington Post, on "Good Morning America," MSNBC and CNN, as well as in the San Francisco Chronicle.

The news spread again on Jan. 31, shortly after a judge sentenced the former NPHS principal to one year of probation, 50 community service hours and court costs Tuesday after he pleaded no contest to two criminal misdemeanor charges of unlawful practice of hypnosis on students.

Sarasota Twelfth Circuit Judge Phyllis Galen also ordered Kenney, 52, not to unlawfully practice therapeutic hypnosis for the duration of his probation. He must also pay court costs and $50 to the North Port Police Department for the cost of a four-month investigation, which is standard in misdemeanor cases. Kenney originally faced up to 120 days in jail and $1,000 in fines.

"Dr. Kenney was not accused of any wrongdoing associated with students who committed suicide," Kenney's Attorney Mark Zimmerman said. "When you mix a high school principal, hypnotism and suicide, it makes for interesting headlines. While the timing of these deaths is extremely unfortunate, they are not connected with hypnosis."

16-year-old Wesley McKinley's parents asked the principal to stop doing hypnosis on students. They believed there might be a correlation between the hypnosis sessions (one which was the day before) and their son's suicide in April.

For years, Kenney, who is a nontherapeutic hypnotist, used "relaxation techniques" on students, with parental permission, to help them with test-taking skills, anger management and sports performance. In a 134-page investigative report, which cost $12,258.55 and was launched by Sarasota County School Superintendent Lori White, Kenney said Wesley was interested in hypnosis and psychology. Wesley asked Kenney if he could be hypnotized to help become a better guitar player and to be more outgoing. Others were with Wesley each of the three times he was hypnotized.

A family member said Wesley became withdrawn in late February and stopped doing some of the things he routinely enjoyed. The other student, Brittany Palumbo, 17, who committed suicide was hypnotized in November 2010. The honors student wanted to be hypnotized to be able to focus better while taking the SAT test. Her mother accompanied her to the session. After Wesley's death, Brittany expressed grief on her Facebook page. Her family was working with school counselors to help Brittany. She committed suicide in May.

Zimmerman said Kenney also disputes claims that he ignored directives to stop using hypnosis.

"Anyone who knows George Kenney understands he is not defiant," Zimmerman said last year. "He believed in the benefits of hypnosis as a tool for helping students focus on test taking and athletic performance, but he didn't push it and he was not a zealot. If he were given a clear directive, he would have followed it. It was so common that Dr. Kenney was doing hypnosis on campus that it was almost a part of the school culture. The fact that his boss never told (him) to stop using hypnosis in writing is interesting to me." From the beginning, Zimmerman said the case was "blown out of proportion by the media."

After the district investigation, a complaint was waged with the state in June. The North Port Police spent four months investigating. Then the State Attorney's Office reviewed the investigation and did one of its own. Kenney originally entered a written plea of not guilty in Sarasota County court. However, in court last month Zimmerman, said his client acknowledges the state has factual evidence to prove its case in court.

Assistant State Attorney Art Jackman said it wasn't necessary, according to state statute, to name victims at the hearing, but he would have produced witnesses who were impacted by Kenney's use of hypnosis if the case had gone to trial.

Jackman said the State Attorney's Office took into consideration Kenney's lack of criminal history, as well as his "well-meaning intentions" when offering the plea agreement."He (Kenney) is trained to be an educator, not a hypnotist,"

Jackman said. "He should have referred his students and staff to trained professionals. Due to the circumstances, we felt it necessary to bring the charges against Mr. Kenney. In our opinion, the case is over."

Court records show Kenney hypnotized about 75 students over a year period. Jackman said no lawsuit has been filed yet on behalf of any of the deceased students' families.

"During the time Dr. Kenney was hypnotizing students, FCAT and ACT scores rose, (and) jump shots and foul shooting improved in athletes," Zimmerman said.

While Zimmerman said Tuesday's outcome wasn't what he wanted, it was what was best for Kenney, who was relieved the case is over. He said expert witnesses would have been called in to do battle if the case had gone to trial.

Kenney, who stood silently for most of the TV reporters' questions, spoke up when asked if he had a message for students and colleagues at NPHS. "I've already thanked them for the tremendous support," he said. "I also apologized for the media controversy and negative publicity brought to the school. Now my family and I can move on."

Kenney will retire June 30. Zimmerman said Kenney plans to do his community service at a nonprofit organization, likely a church.

**Herald Tribune**　　Herald Tribune

Police investigate North Port High principal

**Hypnosis prosecution unlikely for George Kenney, experts say**

By Halle Stockton

North Port High principal on leave over hypnosis

By Saskia Austin Stuff

**Herald Tribune**

Agency to investigate North Port High student hypnosis

Herald Tribune

North Port principal hypnotized player 30-40 times

**Police investigate North Port High principal**

**abcNEWS**

**Florida High School Principal Lied About Hypnotizing Students Who Later Died**

**Mail**Online

Police probe school principal over deaths of THREE students after he hypnotised them to improve their performance

**Support for suspended principal**

Published. Wednesday May 8, 2011 at 10.10 p.m.

## Professional Liability - Malpractice Insurance for Practitioners

Consulting hypnotists working on a one-to-one basis with clients were uninsurable before 1990 unless they were also in a licensed health profession and degreed. So counselors, psychotherapists, psychologists and so forth were insurable, but unlicensed hypnotists without at least a master's degree could just forget about it.

On behalf of NGH members, it became a priority to secure a well-rated agency that would cover all certified members of that particular organization who also met other basic criteria. Once insurance became available for NGH members in 1993, other organizations followed the lead and were able to offer liability insurance to their members through the same company. The fact that professional hypnotists could be insured for personal liability along with psychotherapists and other similarly licensed health professionals was certainly noteworthy as one more step toward the establishment of hypnosis as a separate and distinct profession.

Because US insurance underwriters couldn't cover Canadian members, NGH went on the hunt again and in 2007 announced at their convention that Canadian members could apply for reasonably priced, top-rated personal liability (malpractice) coverage from an agency in Canada. In the spirit of solidarity, Martin Kiely, NGH Ambassador for Ireland, also located an insurance source for members on that side of the Atlantic.

However, the professional liability insurance for office practitioners did not cover performance hypnotists, and as the US became a more litigious society stage hypnotists had to find insurance coverage. At first the only insurance coverage that would include hypnosis shows came by joining a group called the Clown Club of America, which must have made some agents and venues a little nervous when they saw the insurance certificate. Other more appropriately-named insurance underwriters soon approved coverage for current performers of stage hypnotism.

# Hypnotism Proves Helpful for Many Health Problems

NewsUSA

(NU) - What if someone told you this; you can lose weight; stop smoking, eliminate anxieties, and maintain better quality of life?

It's not done with a new "wonder pill." Actually, these positive results can all e accomplished with the use of hypnotism, according to Dr. Dwight F. Damon, president of the National Guild of Hypnotists, the oldest organization of its kind in the field of hypnotism and hypnotherapy.

The relationship between the mind and the body has come to the forefront of health news reporting in recent years. Since authorities say that all hypnosis is self-hypnosis, or hypnotizing oneself. We all have the opportunity to benefit according to our personal involvement in developing this innate ability.

Self-hypnosis is best learned by being hypnotized and then trained to duplicate the state on your own. NGH certified hypnotists are trained to help their clients develop individual mind and body resources for vocational and avocational improvement, such as dealing with the small but important personal changes we all encounter in everyday living. Medical or psychoneurological health problems, which hypnosis can help, are routinely handled by hypnotherapists through referral by licensed physicians and other health practitioners.

This year, the prime time TV show "Dateline" conducted a series of weight loss programs in which leading diet regimens, including hypnotism, were used with the hypnotic participant faring well in results under the guidance of NGH certified hypnotist Dr. Thomas Nicoli.

Has the day finally arrived for hypnosis in the emergency room, the birthing rooms, and the oncology wing of a hospital? It is already a reality. Although it's not in every hospital, it is used often enough to verify its usefulness, according to NGH. Actually, the practice of hypnotism has been officially sanctioned by the American Medical Association since 1958.

The NGH was founded in 1950 by a small group of Boston hypnotists and hypnotherapists with a mutual interest in hypnotism. In the ensuing years, the organization has become incorporated as a not-for-profit educational association and has almost 8,000 members in 45 countries.

Hypnotherapy training based on the group's core curriculum is being taught across the United States and in numerous other countries. Continuing education workshops, annual educational conference and professional publications help members attain required continuing education credits, while keeping them informed as to advancements in the field.

With the goal of informing the general public about hypnotism, NGH maintains a Web site at www.ngh.net, published a consumer-oriented magazine Hypnosis Today and has a client referral line at 1-603-429-9438.

# Chapter 27
## The AMA Made a Statement
## and Took It Back Years Later

The first *AAEH Bulletin* was published in October of 1958, and it included an announcement of the AMA approving hypnosis: *"The American Medical Association at its 107th annual meeting gave hypnosis official status as a medical tool,"* although that decision is now controversial.

Originally the statement, which was included in its entirety in a report that endorsed a 1955 British Medical Association study, concluded, *"The use of hypnosis has a recognized place in the medical armamentarium and is a useful technique in the treatment of certain illnesses when employed by qualified medical and dental personnel."* ("Medical use of hypnosis," *JAMA*, 1958). However, according to the AMA, *"In June 1987, the AMA's policy-making body rescinded all AMA policies from 1881-1958 (other than two not relating to hypnosis)."*

Many hypnotists cite the initial 1958 endorsement by the AMA, but not with the full explanation as just stated. One could also cite the 1892 report that there is a *"genuineness of the hypnotic state"* (*British Medical Journal*, 1892) or the 1955 BMA report stating:

> The subcommittee is satisfied after consideration of the available evidence that hypnotism is of value and may be the treatment of choice in some case of so-called psychosomatic disorder and it may also be of value for revealing unrecognized motives and conflicts in such conditions. As a treatment, in the opinion of the Subcommittee, it has proved its ability to remove symptoms and to alter morbid habits of thought and behavior [...] ... there is a place for hypnotism in the production of anesthesia or analgesia for surgical and dental operations, and in suitable subjects it is an effective method of relieving pain in childbirth without altering the normal course of labor.

Furthermore, hypnotists could even cite the following approval by the Catholic church:

> The late Pope Pius gave his approval to the use of hypnosis on several occasions. He stated that the use of hypnosis by physicians and dentists for diagnosis and treatment was permitted, but that it was not permitted for Catholics to enter into hypnosis for entertainment purposes. In an article entitled, "Hypnosis as Anesthesia" by Reverend Gerald Kelly, S.J. ( Hospital Progress,

December, 1957), *he listed the following quotations: The first quotation from the Vatican is from an address given to an audience of physicians on January 8, 1956, on the use of hypnosis in childbirth. Reverend Kelly summarized the Pope's three cardinal points as follows: (1) Hypnotism is a serious scientific matter, and not something to be dabbled in. (2) In its scientific use the precautions dictated by both science and morality are to be heeded. (3) Under the aspect of anesthesia, it is governed by the same principle as any other from of anesthesia. This is to say that the rules of good medicine apply to the use of hypnotism; and in so far as its use conforms to these rules, it is in conformity with good morality.*

It would be unusual that prospective hypnosis clients are going to say to themselves, "Wow, the AMA approved of the use of hypnotism in 1958, so I guess I can call a consulting hypnotist and make an appointment."

I'm not too sure the powers that be in the Vatican would really appreciate having us use the Pope's statement regarding the use of hypnosis as an endorsement of what we do and, frankly, I don't think it would really motivate a person to become a client, no matter how devout he or she might be.

Frankly, I would say that for a hypnotist to advertise that he or she is a union member would have more of an impact on attracting other union members as clients. Of course, the key to readily attracting clients is being the best we can be as we help ordinary, everyday people with their ordinary, everyday problems of life—and getting results. After all, money is the by-product of services rendered.

Successful hypnotists have established their profession, their practices, their publications, and trainings on one thing—RESULTS—so, as long as they keep helping ordinary, everyday people with ordinary, everyday problems they will not only build their reputations and practices, but will also contribute to the growth of their profession.

The following letter from the AMA Media Outreach Coordinator was widely circulated in 2008:

*"Hypnotherapists commonly refer to a 1958 report published by an AMA advisory committee on hypnosis, which stated: 'The use of hypnosis has a recognized place in the medical armamentarium that is a useful technique in the treatment of certain illnesses when employed by qualified medical and dental personnel.'*

*Unfortunately, hypnotherapists will omit the fact that the 1958 hypnosis report is no longer included in current AMA policy. In June 1987, the AMA's policy-making body rescinded all AMA policies from 1881–1958 (other than two not relating to hypnosis)."*

However, according to Alfred A. Barrios, PhD, in Vol 7, No. 1 of the magazine *Psychotherapy*, "In 1961 the AMA recommended that medical professionals receive 144 hours of training in hypnotherapy." However, every year the AMA issues the CPT publication, which includes all recognized and approved procedures and their codes. Current Procedural Terminology lists all these recognized procedures, along with a five-digit code that is used to report the procedure on an insurance form, and hypnotism is included.

Yes, it is true that there was approval of hypnotism by the AMA "when employed by qualified medical and dental personnel," so, in my opinion, the 1987 action really doesn't alter the original intent and actions that were taken in 1958 and 1961, but it should not be used as a printed endorsement of hypnotism in any of our literature . . . simply as an historical fact.

Many instructors cite the initial 1958 endorsement by the AMA when speaking to a class, with the full explanation as just explained. They could also cite the 1892 report that there is a "genuineness of the hypnotic state" (*British Medical Journal*, 1892), or the 1955 BMA report.

HYPNOSIS
OLD 'BLACK ART' IS
NOW ACCEPTED
MEDICAL TOOL
1958

THE USE OF HYPNOSIS
TO CURE MENTAL ILLS
1960

Hypnotism Comes
of Age
1943

HYPNOSIS AND YOU
Quick Medical Therapy
That Makes Your Life Easier
1969

# Chapter 28
## Letting the Cat Out of the Bag

I'm going to talk about an incident that happened to us a few years ago, and some hypnotists find it embarrassing, only because they don't stop and analyze who the scammer was, and who the victim was. According to *Webster's New College Dictionary*, a scam is a "fraudulent scheme," which is what occurred when an application for membership was received for certified membership in the National Guild of Hypnotists a few years ago.

You see, Steve K D Eichel, PhD, scammed several professional groups to make a point. There was a psychotherapy association he belonged to and three professional hypnotism organizations, including NGH.

Eichel created a false identity and credentials for Zoe D Katze, his cat, and applied for professional memberships. Since the Guild is the largest of the professional hypnotism organizations, we have been cited on the Internet and in print many times because of his publishing the details of this scam. All the Guild did was honor the membership reciprocity it has had for many years with other professional hypnotism organizations. NGH accepted credentials that they believed to belong to an applicant who also was a member of ABH and IMDHA, and granted membership.

In a subsequent magazine article, Eichel discussed "lay hypnotists," which is what the ASCH (American Society of Clinical Hypnosis) calls unlicensed hypnotists. However, ASCH clinical hypnotist status is earned, as we understand it, with their approved 20-hour course, if their members possess at least a master's degree from a regionally-accredited program in the healing arts that matches the guidelines set forth in *Standards of Training in Clinical Hypnosis* (Hammond and Elkins, 1994), or through ASCH training.

In the same article, Eichel speaks about how *"lay hypnotists have (wrongly, according to organized clinical hypnosis) cut into practices (and incomes) of clinical hypnotists."* Eichel further comments, *"Clearly, one hears far more anecdotal complaints against physicians and psychologists than against lay hypnotists. Where is the hard evidence that lay hypnotists are harming people? Or is this battle merely part of a larger turf war, waged to protect practitioners (as opposed to consumers) in an era of shrinking health dollars?"*

Also mentioned in the article is the fact that *"among the larger (or most vocal) organizations is the National Guild of Hypnotists"* … and, of course, Eichel had noticed the activity of the National Federation of Hypnotists, Local 104, OPEIU, AFL-CIO, CLC.

His final solution, or suggestion, in yet another article, is that *they* (psychologists) should somehow *"regulate lay hypnotists"* by engaging in their training and supervision. In his words, it presents *"a unique economic opportunity"* for them (licensed clinical hypnotists). We really liked one of his final statements, though ... *"If we* (licensed clinical hypnotists) *miss the boat—if lay hypnosis achieves some form of legitimization without input from clinical hypnosis–it is unlikely that we will gain much of anything. Lay hypnotists will continue to capture a slice of our 'pie' as they continue to train and supervise their own with little or no input from us."*

OK! So where does that leave us? It is my opinion that we know *our* boat *has* sailed and they already missed it ... we *are* a separate and distinct profession and will continue to build on what we have achieved. So, in answer to those who never heard or read the real cat story before—in the words of a famous radio commentator —"Now you know the rest of the story."

All this non-event really proves is that it's easy to get a credit card or mail-order degree and create a phony persona if you want to—just check the media archives and find out about government employees, politicians, famous authors, law-enforcement personnel, and so many others who have done this. And then there was a cat, not Zoe I hope, who, according to the news media, became a registered voter not too long ago.

# Chapter 29
## Licensed vs. Unlicensed

Unfortunately some practitioners on the licensed side of hypnotism still have a problem with unlicensed but certified hypnotists, as can be seen in the following excerpt from an article written by the perpetrator of the Zoe D. Katz scam you just read about, Steve K. D. Eichel, PhD. It has also previously appeared in several professional (clinical) publications and on the Internet:

Eichel writes: *"Lay hypnotists have (wrongly, according to organized clinical hypnosis) cut into practices (and incomes) of clinical hypnotists."* Eichel further comments, *"Clearly, one hears far more anecdotal complaints against physicians and psychologists than against lay hypnotists. Where is the hard evidence that lay hypnotists are harming people? Or is this battle merely part of a larger turf war, waged to protect practitioners (as opposed to consumers) in an era of shrinking health dollars?"*

Also mentioned in the article is the fact that *"among the larger (or most vocal) organizations is the National Guild of Hypnotists"* … and, of course, Eichel had noticed the activity of *the National Federation of Hypnotists, Local 104, OPEIU, AFL-CIO, CLC.*

His final solution, or suggestion, in another article, is that they (*licensed clinical hypnotists*) somehow *"regulate"* the so-called *"lay"* hypnotists by engaging in their training and supervision, since in his words, it presents *"a unique economic opportunity"* for them (the elitists). Significant though are his final statements, *"If we (licensed clinical hypnotists) miss the boat—if lay hypnosis achieves some form of legitimization without input from clinical hypnosis–it is unlikely that we will gain much of anything. Lay hypnotists will continue to capture a slice of our 'pie' as they continue to train and supervise their own with little or no input from us."*

### We Probably Really *Could* Co-exist

As a profession, are we making inroads? Definitely! At the 2004 NGH convention, James Council, PhD, the chair of a university psychology department who is a past president of the Board of Psychological Hypnosis, a division of the American Society of Clinical Hypnotism (APA Chapter 30), was an NGH adjunct faculty member. Dr Council also sat down for a round-table discussion with leaders of NGH and other organizations, so some progress had finally been made, and the door is still open for a future of mutual respect and perhaps even cooperation.

In a post-convention letter to the me, Dr Council said, "We truly enjoyed our visit and your wonderful hospitality. The convention itself was very impressive for its organization and quality. Speaking for myself, I think you and your board are doing a great job of increasing the stature and credibility of the Guild. Establishing hypnotism as a profession is a lofty goal, but I'm convinced you have the motivation, commitment, and resources to accomplish it."

It is really "better to light one candle than to curse the darkness," so we need to keep on helping ordinary, everyday people with ordinary, everyday problems and every success will build on the previous one. Remember that if you can conceive it and believe it . . . you can also achieve it. Imagine if we all could conceive and believe the same "it," how much sooner we would achieve what we want to accomplish. We conceived the idea of being recognized as a separate and distinct profession and we have achieved that recognition, for the most part. Now we need to make our profession bigger, better, and more professional without the old, outdated "branding" that some hypnotists still help to perpetuate in the public's perception. Will we be able to do this? A handful of us conceived and believed in a separate and distinct profession—and we have achieved it thus far. Now, if *all* hypnotists join us, we can take the next big step, and it's easy—just conceive, believe, and we *will* achieve.

Hypnosis is a short-term, non-invasive, non-addictive, approach utilizing the innate ability of the client's mind/body connection to make personal changes of a positive nature for his or her benefit. *Helping ordinary, everyday people with ordinary, everyday problems of living* is truly a worthwhile goal and a boon to humanity.

As consulting hypnotists we need to be professional in what we do. Just think of how many stressed-out people can be helped to get through rough times they may be experiencing; how many dollars smokers can save in tight economic times as they become non-smokers through hypnosis. This is not even counting the many lives that can be actually saved through hypnotic smoking cessation.

The profession has a substantial number of our members who participate in educational programs and have spoken before medical, psychological, academic, health, and professional groups, and it is becoming more common all the time. I have been invited to speak to these types of groups many times, and others such as Cal Banyan, Fiona Biddle, Jacob Bimblich, Shaun Brookhouse, Georgina Cannon, Tony DeMarco, Michael Ellner, Ron Eslinger, Larry Garrett, Scot Giles, Richard Harte, John Hughes, Jerry Kein, Maurice Kershaw, Arnold Levison, Patricia MacIsaac, Marie Mongan, Don Mottin, Tom Nicoli, Debbie Papadakis, and John Weir readily come to mind, and there are many more I'm sure.

Media opportunities, such as the *Wall St. Journal* article on the financial page in November 2008 prompted other media writers to contact NGH, and, whenever possible, they were put in touch with hypnotists around the world. Months later, the interest was still there and inquiries still came in when the Zoe article showed up on the Internet—talk about "spreading the light" concerning hypnotism!

In April of 2011 the *New York Times* ran an article titled, "Using Hypnosis to Gain More Control over Your Illness," which featured Dr David Speigel, director of the Center on Stress and Health at the Stanford University School of Medicine who was quoted as saying that hypnosis is "an effective and inexpensive way to manage medical care." It was a fine article and very positive, with mentions of a number of prestigious medical institutions now achieving good results when using hypnosis. Of course it did mention that because there is no licensing a person "should look for a licensed health professional—for instance, a psychologist, medical doctor or social worker—who has been trained in hypnosis."

Does that bother me? No, not really, because I know that as we continue our efforts to be a separate and distinct profession we are also building a solid background of dedicated and knowledgeable practitioners.

I believe that professional consulting hypnotists need to be loud and proud as we tell as many people as we can about how hypnotism can help ordinary, everyday people with ordinary, everyday problems. It may seem strange that after all my years as a hypnotist I still get enthused when I talk to people about hypnotism, but most people are intrigued with the subject and that really gets me warmed up. I love to see the reactions I get, and rarely is there a negative one, because people in this age of mind/body advances are interested to learn more about their own well-being.

# Wise & Wonderful Hypno-Headlines

*More*

A QUARTERLY NEWSLETTER
FROM THE GARVEY GROUP

Please direct comments and suggestions to:
Fellow & Register
The Garvey Group
P.O. Box 1680, Suite 202
Nolan, LA 01970-1680
847-593-1900

Editor-in-Chief: Edward J. Garvey Jr.
ed.garvey@thegarveygroup.com

Art Director: Jim Dulanski
Staff Writer: Debora's Lash

© 2008 The Garvey Group

• W W W . G A R V E Y I M R E G I S T E R . C O M

## HYPNOTIC HELP

The global financial meltdown is driving more and more Americans to enlist the aid of professional hypnotists, according to National Guild of Hypnotists president Dwight F. Damon. Calming tones or music are...

AARP Bulletin article on Hypnosis

January 10, 2009

**AARP Bulletin today**

Hypnotic Help

# NEW USES OF HYPNOSIS ENTRANCING DOCTORS, DENTISTS—AND POLICE

...e and more Americans to enlist the aid of professional hypnotists president Dwight F. Damon. Calming tones or ...at hypnotists call a wakeful state of focused attention, ...t to achieve a desired behavioral result. People are also ...um debt by curbing their spending habits, Damon says.

## ERNEST R. HILGARD

by Paul Katzeff

Brookline police used it to nab a Brighton rapist. When the female victim tried it, she was able to recall key clues, like the peculiar green stripe on her assailant's underpants and the exact threatening words he had said
Thea Gaudette of Georgetown, Mass., used it during dental surgery. She wa

THE MAINICHI DAILY NEWS, TUESDAY, MARCH 3, 1970

# Hypnotism Not Cure-All But Therapy Aid: Expert

## A Study in Hypnosis

DIRECTOR OF STANFORD'S LABORATORY OF HYPNOSIS RESEARCH FOR MORE THAN 30 YEARS, HILGARD PAVED THE WAY FOR THE GROWING RESPECTABILITY OF HYPNOSIS.

Two hundred years ago, pioneering hypnotist Franz Anton Mesmer was hounded out of use unsympathetic scientific communities in Vienna and Paris for his experiments in animal magnetism. Today, hypnosis is solidly established in medical schools and research universities throughout the United States and Europe. Much of the present respectability of hypnosis, as well as much of the new knowledge in the field, can be credited to Ernest R. Hilgard, Stanford University professor emeritus of psychology. The past quarter-century of research in hypnosis has been strongly influenced by work done at Stanford's Laboratory of Hypnosis Research, which Hilgard founded in 1957 and directed until 1979.
Two years after he opened the laboratory, Hilgard

## LIFESTYLES

### THE STRAITS TIMES

Tuesday    SINGAPORE EDITION    Jan. 4, 2005

Hypnosis helps turn lives around

Interview with Barbara Davison - NY

## Hypnosis

"You diet, you try this, you try that. It really comes down to believing in yourself. Food used to be on my mind all the time. It's not any more."

TOM STARK

### DESPERATE MUM SENDS HIM FOR HYPNOSIS TO GET BETTER MARKS

EXTRA! EXTRA!

...e on hypnosis

...E. Brody published an article on hypnosis in *The New York Times*: "The Po ...t Has the Power." Here's an excerpt:

...s the epitome of mind-body medicine. It can enable the mind to tell the body...

THE WALL STREET JOURNAL

## PERSONAL HEALTH

### Doctors, Hospitals Use Hypnosis

World Hypnotism Day
January 4th, 2005
Unleash The Power Of Hypnosis!

Attend a FREE HYPNOSIS SEMINAR near you!

California Chapter Members Co-op

## NATIONAL POST

You are getting very sleepy...

Interview with Debbie Papadakis - Toronto, Ontario

# Chapter 30
## Psychologists' Master Plan Against "Lay" Hypnotists

In 1993, D. Corydon Hammond, president of the American Society of Clinical Hypnosis (ASCH), Chapter 30, of the American Psychology Association, presented a master plan to eliminate so-called "lay" hypnotists. ASCH, founded in 1952 by Dr Milton Erickson, is the organization of physicians and psychologists who believe that only their members should be able to practice hypnotism. In fact, their Code of Ethics forbids the membership of that organization from doing anything to encourage the practice of hypnotism by someone who is not a licensed health care professional.

According to their rules most of our hypnotists are not eligible to become members (even if they wanted to), and, of course, their members are not allowed to be members of an organization like any of ours ("lay hypnotists"), which is not to say that some of theirs wouldn't also like to be some of ours.

At the conference there was a program entitled "The Problem of Lay-hypnosis" and in it they laid out their plan for our destruction. We went to work within 48 hours of the New Orleans presentation, thanks to insiders who made sure we knew what was in the works. Although all major unlicensed hypnotism organizations were asked by us to participate in taking action, it turned out to be an NGH campaign, mostly because of the way other groups operated with committee members scattered around the country, and no one person who could make a commitment to act without taking a vote.

Now we will share the story with you and put it in print for future generations to read about. In the following introductory paragraph, D. Corydon Hammond, PhD offers the free use of the material, and so, with thanks to D. Corydon Hammond, PhD, we hereby take advantage of his printed offer and reproduce the original material here. We are including the first few paragraphs with italicizing added to call your attention to their intent:

### American Society of Clinical Hypnosis Public Information Packet
### D. Corydon Hammond, PhD, ABPH President
**Intro**

As the Executive committee has surveyed what our members want, one of the most consistent requests has been for more widespread public education and work in the legislative arena. In response to this, I have generated the following packet of materials. It will assist you in feeling more prepared for being interviewed on radio, television, or by newspapers. It will also prepare you for writing your own "Common Carrier Editorials" in your local papers. In this regard, please do not be concerned about plagiarizing portions of this information pack. It is being supplied for your use in educating the public, and you may feel free to use verbatim material from it (without referencing this publication) in anything you write for the newspaper or in educating local or state government officials.

*We are now faced with thousands of quacks and unethical lay hypnotists who seek to practice medicine, psychotherapy, and dentistry without a license. It is tragic that in local areas, more public education about hypnosis is sometimes done by lay hypnotists than by legitimate professionals. It is time that we began providing more accurate information to the public. At the same time, it is imperative that we educate the public about the danger of unethical lay hypnotists and how to select a qualified hypnotherapist.*

What I have learned first hand is that when you get into the media and educate the public, you not only perform an important public service, but it is the most responsible kind of advertising.

In the pages ahead, I will provide you with practical and brief information to guide you in your media contacts. In a television or radio interview or call-in program, you have a relatively brief period of time to present your message. Accordingly, a brief interview is not ordinarily the time to be discussing intricacies and scholarly debates about the theories of hypnosis. Therefore, in the pages ahead I will provide you with brief, suggested dialogue in each of the following areas: (1) What is hypnosis? (2) Myths and misconceptions of Hypnosis. (3) Areas of application of hypnosis. (How hypnosis may help listeners or viewers). *(4) How to select a qualified hypnotherapist. Given the buyer beware marketplace today, I personally feel that the most vitally important of these four areas that must be mentioned is number four.* A more substantial amount of information will be provided for you under this topic. This information may also prove useful for some of you in working in the future with legislators, boards of education, PTA's, departments of consumer protection, and state agencies.

**Targeted Media Resources**

I want to request that over the next two or three months that you seek to do each of the following.

1. Call all your local newspapers. Seek to be interviewed, and inquire, if you don't already know, about whether they have a special editorial column where members of the general public may contribute editorial messages for consideration. Please seek to be interviewed by each local newspaper, and even ones in nearby cities.

2. Call several different local radio and television stations. State your professional qualifications, and inquire who the persons are that you should talk or write to in order to be considered for an interview about hypnosis. Instead of talking about being interviewed about the dangers of lay hypnotists, which is a narrow and more controversial focus that is less likely to meet with enthusiasm, simply indicate your desire to educate the public about the nature of hypnosis and the many exciting areas in which it is being applied in medicine, psychology, and dentistry.

3. Write "Common Carrier Editorials" for local newspapers about the dangers of lay hypnotists. For each of your local newspapers that have this type of column, prepare a common carrier type of editorial specifically on the dangers of lay hypnotists. There will be space limitations for such editorials. Therefore, *I recommend that your contribution focus exclusively on the dangers of lay hypnotists and how to select a qualified hypnotherapist.* I have provided an example of a column that I authored about eight years ago, and a large amount of material and analogies that may be used in educating the public about hypnotists.

4. *Educate your state medical association. In Utah I was successful in having the UMA House of Delegates unanimously pass a resolution recommending that physicians not refer patients to people calling themselves hypnotists, but only refer for hypnosis services to licensed professionals. The Unprove Health Practices Committee of the state medical association then sent this along with a strong letter of support to all MDs in the state. This is important public education. Particularly emphasize that if they refer patients to unlicensed lay hypnotists, they significantly increase their liability. Also educate them that some lay hypnotists now use mail order PhDs and call themselves "doctor." Therefore it is vitally important to be sure a referral source is licensed.*

Full Reprint of additional documents is in the Appendix on page 161

*Above - Virgil Hayes teaching*

*Left - A young Virgil Hayes*

*Below - Hayes and guest Ormond McGill*

# Chapter 31
## A True Defender of the Profession

There is one person I wanted to be *sure* to include in these recollections, a hypnotist by the name of Virgil Hayes. During all the years we're recollecting, I had spoken by phone with Virgil Hayes only once. At that time he was pretty well identified with Gil Boyne and there was that on-going antagonism from ACHE towards NGH and me, which made me wary.

As I recall, the conversation was civil and professionally friendly, but I can only assume it was concerning legislative problems in Utah. This was before we had the expertise and dedication of C. Scot Giles to be on top of these matters. I soon lost track of Virgil Hayes, and unfortunately, so did many others, including his students and associates in Salt Lake City.

I knew through the grapevine, that Virgil had worked and fought hard for our profession in Salt Lake City and had gone toe-to-toe fighting the profession's arch-enemy, D. Corydon Hammond, who was a tenured professor at the Utah State University. Hammond was the architect of the "Master Plan" to eliminate all "lay hypnotists." It was a plan that we successfully shot down before it had a chance to grow as you will see in another chapter.

Because he had fought Hammond on his home ground, I knew that Virgil Hayes' story definitely belonged in this book. When I started working on this book I called hypnotists in Utah and along the West Coast down into California trying to locate him, but to no avail. Yet, there were a few clues … "He moved away"… "He died" … "He moved to Arizona" … "He's on a witness protection program" … WAIT, "He moved to Arizona. "He's in a witness protection program"? It was time to contact Arizona's busy hypnotist, Don Rice, and his associate, Sandi Graves, to enlist their help.

The first hopeful break was when Don called to say that they found the witness protection program rumor was true, but his name hadn't been changed and he was retired to a small Southern town. Best of all, they had his telephone number! I called, but the phone had been disconnected. I checked with town offices, and so forth, and … "he moved away."

Nevertheless, Sandi kept digging for us and finally found and spoke to Virgil Hayes himself, explaining her mission and mine. Thankfully, he was happy to make contact with me so we could document his efforts. So, now, here is the rest of the story—

Virgil Hayes established himself with a state approved post secondary ACHE school in Salt Lake City, Utah in 1976, and soon became a name to be reckoned with. He developed a busy school and private practice. However, during the '80s he found himself battling tirelessly against D Corydon Hammond, the nemesis of our professional development and the man who tried to initiate a "master plan" for the licensed psychologists to use in order to wipe out "lay hypnotists."

We will have more about Hammond later when we discuss his master plan, formulated and presented to fellow members of the American Society of Clinical Hypnosis, Chapter 30, of the American Psychology Association, at their convention in New Orleans in 1993.

After over 17 years of spending three to six months in the Utah legislature as an unpaid lobbyist, at his own financial and emotional cost, and with all of the TV, newspaper, and radio debates, Virgil Hayes stopped Hammond's attacks on hypnotists in the state of Utah. Virgil Hayes will always be remembered for this above all else.

In the 1993/94 legislative sessions, Hayes completely stopped the rewriting of the Mental Health Therapists Practice Act, which was being forced onto the unknowing public (by D Corydon Hammond) as a so-called public service, to protect those who "were not competent and knowledgeable enough to decide which practitioner to seek out, and therefore that must be regulated by the Utah State Department of Occupational and Professional Licensing" (stated in legislative sub-committee and transcripts, by the division director Dave Robinson) and Dr D Corydon Hammond of the psychological association as a consultant.

I believe it would be best to let Virgil Hayes to personally tell the story as he experienced it:

*"The only way he (Hammond) would remove our concerns was for them to exclude any and all 'control' over the hypnotism profession and 'Stay the hell out of ours' and the public's business!' The Utah State Division of Occupational Licensing was finally ordered by the members of that particular sub-committee to include our concerns in the rewriting of the bill; The Utah State Mental Health Therapists' Act was dead in the water unless they could get our support. We had called and motivated every person we had ever worked with and asked them to notify their senators and representatives to kill this bill if we were not excluded. These very good people did that and better by calling everyone they knew, who also did the same! This bill was passed by both houses of the Utah legislature and signed into law by the Governor with total exclusions from the Dept. of Occupational and Professional Licensings' control to conform to Dr Cory Hammond's desires to destroy us as competition. He realized that competition weeds out incompetence!*

*At the same time, I was hit with a Social Security audit because of one part-time employee who was working as an independent contrac-*

*tor. At the end of an extensive time and financially consuming audit, I ended up owing the Government $2.34. This collector sat across from me at my desk and stated, "Mr. Hayes, if we could have got this bill down to $2.33 we could have waived this delinquent payment." I asked him, "How much did this cost me and the American taxpayers for your investigation?" He said, "We can't be concerned with that, Mr. Hayes as citizen protectors." I wrote a check to the government for the amount, threw it at him and said, "I have to be concerned as I am an American citizen and taxpayer, now get [the Hell] out of my office!"*

*I had not been done with Social Security a week when I was hit with an IRS audit of the same magnitude! Another three months of living hell while trying to fight The Utah State Division of Occupational Licensing, aka Dr Cory Hammond's manipulated groupies!*

*As it was exposed at that time, there was an Internal Revenue Service auditor in Utah who had, it appeared, flagged us to keep us entertained and misdirected instead of fighting in the legislative process! I still beat them.*

*I ended up writing the entire Behavioral Modification Practices Act, from a blank page to approximately six pages of exclusions, and differentiating between hypnotists and psychologists (inserted into the mental health practices act as exclusions) before we would release our considerations. They didn't like it, but I didn't care what they might like or not like as they had no right or reason to try to control us without any cause. To my knowledge, this exclusion from any control of the Utah State Mental Health Practices Act is still unchanged and in effect in the year 2011.*

*I have also kept every single student evaluation from every person [approx. 25,000] I taught to utilize hypnosis from federal/state/local law enforcement and the department of corrections both state and federal. I had the highest number of teachers of any of the American Council of Hypnotist Examiners' divisions anywhere in the United States at that time. I also got to teach coursework in every hospital in Salt Lake City, Utah.*

*Do you still wonder why Dr Cory Hammond was ticked off? He was a tenured professor, at the Utah State University and he was not offered these opportunities because of his own failures. I took every opportunity to bring that to his attention. If he had come to me for work in this area, maybe ..."*

Then there was the bank robbery, which was the breaking point and they couldn't stay any longer in Salt Lake City. The story continues …

On what seemed like just another day, Virgil Hayes and his wife, Connie, were in their office on a break between students and clients when Virgil noticed a young woman in jeans and a hooded sweatshirt and carrying a shoe box, who walked by the front of the office. Wondering why she could be on the backside of this strip mall as usually only vehicles came to that area, Virgil was drifting in and out of a mild hypnotic relaxing state when he heard what he thought was screaming. At the same time he heard footsteps running past the glass office door—it was the same young woman running in the opposite direction as she had previously traveled.

It turned out that Virgil had witnessed the approach and getaway of a solo bank robber attempting to qualify for membership in one of the toughest gangs in the area. The police, however, caught her and her getaway driver (boyfriend and gang member) within twenty blocks of the bank.

Virgil was called to identify her in a lineup, which was successful and the police obtained a full confession. He was very proud that he could assist in solving problems in this manner. They were told this armed robbery was perpetrated as a gangland initiation for membership, part of the decadence required to join this pack of deviants.

Virgil and Connie came under constant prolonged attack and their students' vehicles and office were broken into and vandalized. They were threatened with knives and guns, and harassed at every opportunity, but were not going to run, and stood their ground as long as they could. However, this all changed the day five separate law-enforcement agency reps came and told him they could no longer provide protection. The Hayes must find another way to make a living at something else, a long way away from there, quickly and quietly.

It became a matter of moving quite quickly from one location to another having to start over in each, and as soon as they thought they might get to settle, their location was exposed through Connie's maiden name. Standing up for what is right cost them everything, but they did what they had to do … and, by the way, they just moved again in 2011!

# Chapter 32
## What Does The Future Hold?

Earlier I stated that, "We are hypnotists, not prognosticators, so we can only wait and see what the next sixty-five years bring." However, I've been urged by friends and associates to include my thoughts about the future of our profession, so here they are—

I'm privileged to have been a founding member of the National Guild of Hypnotists sixty-five years ago, and its resurrector and president for the past twenty-five years, so my perspective comes from that life experience, or, as the popular saying goes, I've been there and done that.

People whose careers appear to be conducted mostly on Internet forums or chat rooms are eager to tell us what we've *done* wrong, what we're *doing* wrong, and what we *will do wrong* in the future, yet, they rarely have actually participated in what we've done *right* in the past or present.

Educational standards for our profession have been an ongoing process and the result of divergent philosophies based on: (1) Personal theories or methodologies, (2) Financial goals of the instructor or school, (3) Ego of the instructor.

*This will probably never change. Standardization at this point would level the playing field, but not necessarily enhance the ability of graduates.*

Those who want to see college education leading to a recognized academic degree for hypnotists are going to have a long wait. What they are thinking about (i.e. college curriculum leading to an accepted degree) is already in place leading to degrees for practitioners in psychotherapy, psychology and other licensed "talk" therapies; those professionals are not going to welcome us into the fold as a separate and distinct profession.

*We will see more ancillary studies becoming part of our profession's certification training in the near future. However, it will be a gradual process and should be only specific studies which apply to our work.*

There is nothing in their education that uniquely qualifies a licensed physician, dentist, osteopath, chiropractor, etc. to practice hypnotism. Usually hypnosis is only touched on briefly in college psychology classes. Also, a physician or dentist who sees a need for hypnosis for a patient rarely has the time or knowledge to provide this modality. Generally speaking, the individual licensed practitioner has no prejudice against us, even though licensed professionals are required to drop their membership in "lay" organizations such as NGH to join one of the "elitist" organizations such as ASCH, according to a letter which was forwarded to us recently..

*As the profession we've created builds in credibility and professionalism*

155

*we will see more and more professional referrals if we get results with those clients.*

Organizations such as ASCH and ASCEH definitely will continue their opposition to "lay" hypnotists. They will continue to oppose us and will pursue a way to control us, since we are a financial threat to their practices. It's happened before in the "therapeutic" world … physicians opposing the psychologists … psychologists opposing the psychotherapists … psychotherapists opposing the counselors … all the way down the line.

*We need to build our own professional reputation for results which will validate what we do.*

Our profession is made up of numerous schools and organizations which compete for students and professional members, and there is very little cooperation between these different organizations. Every year someone else starts another organization or holds another convention and that will probably never change.

*Many smaller groups and individuals will continue joining organizations such as NGH or NFH local 104 to work for the common good, protection, and advancement of its members.*

If we continue our short-term process which empowers clients and teaches them to use their innate resources to attain the results they want, we will continue to grow as a recognized "helping" profession. We don't have to add other methodologies or invent "new" hypnotic techniques—we just need to have confidence in what we already have.

*Our previous professional advances and client results which have anchored us so far will keep us growing.*

We need to realize the potential of what we have to offer the public—the fact that we really can be a "womb to tomb" profession—from "hypnosis for fertility" to "hypnosis in grief counseling." We can be there to help our ordinary, everyday clients in handling their ordinary, everyday problems of living for an entire lifetime.

*We have the veritable "Acres of Diamonds" that Russell H. Conwell wrote about many years ago; we just need to realize where they are … in our own backyard.*

I'm sure some hypnotist is going to read this and wonder why anybody would become a lifetime client if we are teaching them how to help themselves, and not performing some mystical, magical mojo with our hypnotic "power" that the old myths implied. I know from personal experience and observation of such successful consulting hypnotists as Cal Banyan, Jacob Bimblich, Tony DeMarco, Larry Garrett, Scot Giles, Pat MacIsaac, and Don Mottin, to name just a few, that you can build a practice of lifetime clients, their children, relatives and friends … when you get results.

*People see their physicians, chiropractors, dentists, and massage therapists regularly, year after year, because they want to feel good and want to be healthy. Why shouldn't they also want to see their consulting hypnotist for the same reasons?*

*We need to tell more people about hypnotism ... we need to get more positive results for clients, and we will become more firmly entrenched as a profession.*

*To those of us who work professionally with hypnotism, the era covered in this book has been one of trials and tribulations ... disappointments and accomplishments. We have come a long way in establishing ourselves as a profession, yet, there is still a long way to go. Will we ever be able to just rest on our laurels, or is it always going to be a case of having to "prove" ourselves?*

*Whatever the case may be, I am proud of these men and women who have devoted their time and energy to get us to where we are today. Not only have they become my colleagues, but also my friends.*

*I look forward to the upcoming generation continuing side by side with us until they are in our position of looking back at another 65 years of accomplishment for our profession.*

# January 4th
## Celebrating World Hypnotism Day

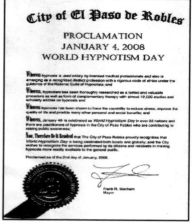

WORLD HYPNOTISM DAY

# Appendix

# Memorabilia

# Index

# *18 Years Ago . . .*

## 0280 Symposium VIII
## American Society of Clinical Hypnosis
## "Dealing with the problem of lay hypnosis"
## March 27-31, 1993, New Orleans, LA

(pages 161-170)
*(continued from 149)*

(Continued from page 149)
### American Society of Clinical Hypnosis Public Information Packet
### D. Corydon Hammond, PhD, ABPH President

**Presenting Yourself to the Public**

When you appear in the media, it is of utmost importance for you to present a very professional image. Therefore, may I suggest a few common sense guidelines for you to follow:

1. Dress in conservative and highly professional manner. For example, men should wear conservative sport coats or suits with ties.

2. Do not make exaggerated claims about hypnosis or its efficacy. Present it realistically as simply one more tool in medicine and psychology that is available and often beneficial, but not a cure-all with everything or for everyone.

3. Don't name specific lay hypnotists or lay hypnotist organizations. Talk in generalities so that you don't risk slander or libel suits.

When the newspaper, radio ro television station allows it, provide your telephone number and/or location of employment. This is not only facilitates referrals, but allows you to further answer questions or make referrals to other legitimate professionals if you cannot treat all the referrals.

5. State your professional credentials (e.g., physician, etc.; diplomate; professor; officer in a professional society) and mention that the only two legitimate national hypnosis societies are the American Society of Clinical Hypnosis and the Society of Clinical and Experimental Hypnosis. In some cases, they may allow you to provide the phone number of ASCH (708) 297-3317 for persons to call for referral to someone qualified. Also, it an interviewer refers to you as a "hypnotist," it is suggested that you correct him or her and indicate: "I'm not a hypnotist, but a physician/psychologist (etc.) who uses hypnosis as an important part of my work."

6. Remember that it is unethical to perform demonstrations of hypnosis for the general public or the media.

7. When you occasionally cite a brief research finding it increases your credibility and professional image. Particularly on radio and for newspaper interviews, don't be afraid to take relevant parts of this information pack with you.

**Definition of Hypnosis & Myths About Hypnosis**

On the radio or television, or in interview, we have a limited amount of time to make our major points. Therefore, it is best to say things "short and sweet." There is probably more detail in this section than you will usually have time to say. But, it is included in the event you have sufficient time and because something here may be useful in responding to a question.

Remember, however, you want to reserve enough time to also discuss problem areas where hypnosis is often useful, *and to allow sufficient time to address the qualifications in selecting a hypnotherapist.*

**Qualifications in Selecting a Hypnotherapist**

In this section, I have modeled what I actually tend to say in interviews, as well as in articles. Once again, bear in mind that you will often have a very limited amount of time to say everything you wish in an on-air interview. Therefore, I recommend that you keep track of your time and be sure to bring up the topic of "how you can select a qualified hypnotherapist" by the two-thirds point in the interview. I suggest that you make very effort to present the points listed below. Occasionally, phrases or sentences have been printed in bold and headings included to make it easier for you to pick out key points during interviews.

As a practical tip, I often pick up my pace of speaking when I discuss this information. In this way I can present more information on this final topic, and it becomes more difficult to interrupt me and change the topic if the interviewer is somewhat uncomfortable with the topic. On the infrequent occasions when an interviewer seems to want to move the topic away from "qualifications," I have found that along with talking faster, if I don't look directly into the interviewer's face I am also able to say more about what I think is important. It is more difficult for them to change the subject when you don't pick up their nonverbal cues or give them as much time to interrupt.

Also bear in mind that if the interviewer does try to change the topic before you are ready, you can always say, "Just let me add one more thing that I think is very important." Later on in the interview, or in response to a question that is called in, you can usually add an additional analogy or some of the other points about lay hypnotists contained in this section.

Some of the information that is included below under the heading of "Additional Material About Lay Hypnotists" can be included when you have time, and can be incorporated in articles for newspapers, or in lobbying or writing letters to public and state government agencies.

I recommend that you study the information below, as well as the earlier material in this packet, like you would speech or debate notes. Be thoroughly familiar with the concepts and analogies before going on radio, and especially before going on television. For radio or newspaper interviews, keep these notes with you.

## Selecting a Qualified Hypnotherapist

The public must be very careful in selecting someone qualified to provide hypnosis services. There are many quacks who hand out shingles as "hypnotists," because currently there are no state laws protecting the public from charlatans who practice hypnosis. Therefore, it is a buyer beware marketplace. In fact, a person stripped of his professional license one day for unethical behavior can open up shop the next day as a hypnotherapist.

For example, someone calling himself a hypnotherapist may have an eighth grade education, be a convicted sex offender and rapist, and have been employed as a dishwasher, but with no training at all they can open a practice and begin advertising as a hypnotherapist.

## Level of Lay Hypnotist Training

There are mail order programs and two-day seminars from fly-by-night groups who then give out impressive looking certificates saying someone is "certified" as a hypnotherapist. So the public must be very cautious! A listing in the yellow pages that says someone is "certified" may be meaningless. Now there are even diploma mills that grant meaningless PhD's and masters degrees in hypnotherapy.

Some lay hypnotists cite that they have received 100 or even 200 hours of training in hypnosis.

Barber Analogy: But, barbers are required to have more training than that to simply touch your hair. I hardly think that I would want to trust someone trying to do therapy on me with so little training. Even if a lay hypnotist has one or two hundred hours of training, this is paltry in comparison to legitimate health and mental health professionals. Psychologists, for example, typically have 9 years of total university coursework, and then have 2,000 hours of supervised internship and 2,000 hours of postdoctoral supervised work before they can even qualify for licensure. Their hypnosis training is an addition to these 9 years and 4,000 supervised hours of work.

Cab driver Analogy: Lots of cab drivers have delivered babies, but if your wife were going to deliver, would you call yellow cab, or would you prefer someone with many years of carefully supervised training?

Meat Cutter Analogy: Meat cutters, like lay hypnotists, are trained by trade schools in one skill—in this case, meat cutting. That's fine. But would you want your local supermarket butcher to start presenting himself to the public as qualified to be a brain surgeon? Training in one skill, whether it is hypnosis or meat cutting, doesn't prepare a person to work on someone's mind. To be a brain surgeon you have to know how to diagnose the problem, where to cut, what to take out and what to leave alone, and how to put someone back together again.

When you go to someone calling himself a hypnotist or hypnotherapist for work on medical or psychological problems there is a very genuine danger that it will be like allowing your local butcher to do surgery. It's easy to do hypnosis or wield a scapel, but what do they do once they are in there? The risk is that you may be seriously harmed, much like someone doing surgery without doing suturing afterwards, so that you may walk out all opened up, but not put back together again. A lay hypnotist may, for example uncover abuse or trauma in someone's past, and then they are not adequately trained or licensed to know how to help the person work through the trauma therapeutically.

Pharmacist Analogy: Anyone can play with a chemistry set. But do you we want someone who read a book or two, and then tinkered with a chemistry set to begin presenting themselves to the public as pharmacist? This is in essence what many lay hypnotists do, and a great deal of consumer deception, fraud, and danger may be involved. Fortunately, more unethical lay hypnotists are now beginning to be prosecuted across the country. In late 1991 and early 1992, there were convictions of lay hypnotists in Virginia, Ohio, Utah, and Montana for illegal activities.

Qualifications to Look For.

(1) Don't just look for a degree, because there are now phony, diploma-mill PhD's and masters degrees. Instead, ask, "Are you licensed (not certified) in the state as a psychologist, physician, social worker, marriage and family therapist, etc.? If they are not legitimately licensed, I recommend that you immediately avoid them.

(2) If they do have a PhD or MA degree listed, ask them "What is your degree in?" If it is in hypnotherapy instead of a legitimate area such as psychology, they are a lay hypnotist. Some lay hypnotists not only have diploma mill degrees, but occasionally they may call themselves "doctor" or list an MA degree, but the degree may be in music.

(3) Are they a member of the American Society of Clinical Hypnosis or the Society for Clinical and Experimental Hypnosis? These are the only nationally recognized organizations of legitimately licensed professionals.

Health Insurance.

The public should realize that they will usually pay no more, and that they often actually pay less, by seeking hypnosis from a legitimately licensed health care professional. Licensed professionals may charge a little more, but their services may be reimbursed by health insurance. Insurance companies do no recognize lay hypnotists as legitimate health care providers.

Danger Signs About Someone to Avoid.

(1) Avoid hypnotists without advanced degrees if you are seeking help for psychological or medical
problems.

(2) Be very cautious about someone trying to promote prefab, over-the-counter tapes.

(3) Beware of someone making exaggerated claims for hypnosis as a cure-all or who claims to have phenomenal success rates. They may be a snake oil salesman.

Consumer Disclaimer.

Lay hypnotists always try to claim that hypnosis is harmless. However, I have 56 references from the professional literature that document that someone may be harmed when they are treated with hypnosis from someone unqualified. Included among these articles are ones in such prestigious journals as the Journal of American Medical Association, American Journal of Psychiatry, American Psychologist, Journal of Nervous & Mental Disease, Psychiatric Quarterly, Journal of Abnormal Psychology, Psychotherapy and in prestigious hypnosis journals.

Not a Legitimate Profession.

Hypnosis is not an independent science, but only one modality of medical, psychological and dental treatment. Training in hypnosis alone does not make one a therapist.

Lay hypnotist groups try to make themselves sound legitimate and professional by claiming that the US Department of Labor recognizes them as a legitimate occupation, falsely implying governmental recognition. In reality, the terms hypnotist and hypnotherapist are simply listed in the Dictionary of Occupational Titles, along with virtually any work task that individuals perform. As a matter of fact, hypnotist is indexed under the category of the DOT that contains along side it such other highly qualified professions as a fortune teller, palm reader, weight guesser, psychic reader, crystal gazer, animal impersonator, and tea leaf reader. The DOT also includes such impressive professions as a human projectile and a carrot washer, and even illegal occupations such as a bookie are listed. I think this says something important about the degree of professionalism that the Department of Labor sees as associated with lay persons calling themselves hypnotists or hypnotherapists. (This paragraph is particularly powerful to use when a lay hypnotist calls in claiming that lay hypnosis is a legitimate profession recognized by the Department of Labor, or should you ever be in a debate with a lay hypnotist.)

Encouraging the Public to Report Harm.

Some of you who are listening (or reading) this may have been harmed or inappropriately treated for medical or psychological problems by someone calling him or herself a hypnotist or hypnotherapist. If this is the case, I recommend that you report this to the state department of consumer affairs or the medical or psychology licensure board in the state.

## Additional Material About Lay Hypnotists

Consumer Fraud

In the area of hypnosis there is a serious problem with consumer fraud. Some lay hypnotist groups have become diploma mills, granting meaningless PhD's and masters degrees in hypnotherapy. This is inherently deceptive to consumers who believe that they are legitimate, licensed health care professionals when they list themselves as "Dr" Even more widespread is the practice of calling themselves " hypnotherapists." The term "therapist" is deceptive and conveys the impression to the consumer that such an individual is skilled in counseling and psychotherapy and licensed, which lay hypnotists are not. Laws need to be passed restricting the use of the term "therapist" and the use of hypnosis to legitimate health care professionals.

Consumer Protection

The public must be aware that it is a buyer beware marketplace. Therefore, in the interests of consumer protection, let me state that because lay hypnotists are not legitimate professionals recognized by law (or by health insurance companies), there are no laws protecting confidentiality for someone using their services. Thus, there are instances of movie stars seeking their services, only to later have their names used without their permission in public advertising.

Particularly because they commonly use the term "therapist", there is consumer deception because the public may assume that someone working with a mental health technique must have a doctor-patient privilege, which they do not. When you go to a lay hypnotist, there is no guarantee of privileged communication or confidentiality.

Another concern in the area of consumer protection is with the standard of care provided. A consumer has no recourse if they feel that services provided by a lay hypnotist are inadequate. There are no definable standards of care among the dozens of lay groups, each of whom have different requirements to practice with their title. In medicine, psychology, psychiatry, social work, and marriage and family therapy, there are established standards of care below which it is defined as malpractice. But, with lay hypnotists there is no way to test if services have fallen below a nonexistent standard at which time it is defined as malpractice.

Ethical Standards

Another major area of concern is with ethical standards among lay hypnotists. Such standards exist with some lay schools or groups, but they are not binding. That is, a lay hypnotist who the ethical standards of a particular group can still continue to practice if they violate ethical codes. They may be dismissed from a lay group, but there is no legal or practical effects as there are with physicians, psychologists, etc..

Training

Another major problem with the practice of lay hypnosis is with standards of training. Licensed professionals must be trained in state and nationally approved and regulated programs and facilities, and then pass state and nationally approved examinations. This is not the case with hypnotists. Anyone can hang out a shingle as a "hypnotist," "master hypnotist," or "hypnotherapist." Even if such a person has gone to one of the lay schools, the content of the curriculum of such schools is not regulated, nor are there methods in place in such operations to screen for things like psychological disturbance or past criminal record.

Consumer Danger

(This module of information is provided primarily for use in working with legislators, investigators for consumer affairs of licensing agencies, boards of education, Parent Teacher Associations, or prosecuting attorneys rather than with the general public.)

A considerable body of literature indicates that hypnosis is a therapeutic modality that fosters and intensifies transference and countertransference in therapeutic relationships. In part, what this means is that hypnosis may appeal to power or seductive needs of an individual, whether a professional or lay person. However, with legitimate professionals, as already indicated above, there are ethical and legal protections for the clientele, as well as professional training in such matters which is lacking with aly hypnotists. Unethical behavior on the part of lay persons is particularly serious because clients who are hurt by them may subsequently be reluctant to seek legitimate professional help because of the increased distrust of mental health persons that may be engendered.

Lay hypnotists try to emphasize that hypnosis is benign, and sometimes quote old authorities in the field to the effect that hypnosis is not harmful. These quotes were typically made to increase the acceptance of hypnosis and they referred to its use by legitimately trained medical and psychological professionals.

Neutral hypnosis by itself is not usually harmful, although occasionally even it is associated with negative side effects. However, specific procedures in hypnosis, such as uncovering (unconscious exploration) techniques and age regression, wherein someone remembers traumatic events, can be extremely harmful in the hands of a novice, And, in fact, as time has gone on in the field of hypnosis, there has been a progressive shift toward a position of recognizing that hypnosis may produce harmful and destructive effects.

I have a list of 56 references in the professional literature attesting to the dangers in misusing hypnosis. These articles in respected and well established professional journals (such as the Journal of American Medical Association, American Journal of Psychiatry, American Psychologist, Journal of Nervous & Mental Disease, Psychiatric Quarterly, Journal of Abnormal Psychology, Psychotherapy and respected hypnosis journals) document that harmful effects have occurred, including among lay and stage hypnotists. Lay hypnotists would like to deceive the public in believing that hypnosis is utterly harmless, and, therefore, no one should object to them practicing. As you will see if you study this literature, this is a blatant and self-serving falsehood.

You should also be aware that currently (in 1992) in California and Pennsylvania there are lawsuits underway as a consequence of stage hypnotists causing harmful effects. I believe that the secondary schools, colleges and universities are irresponsible in allowing stage hypnotists to perform, and that by so doing they will open themselves up to the possibility of future lawsuits. Furthermore, there have been criminal convictions against lay hypnotists this past year in Virginia Beach, Virginia, Cincinnati, Ohio, Orem, Utah and in Montana.

In this regard, you should also be aware that the US Department of Health, Education, and Welfare has identified hypnosis as something that has risk of causing negative effects. Thus, in legitimate research on hypnosis, we must pass a human subjects committee review to demonstrate how any negative effects may be handled and what we are doing to minimize the likelihood of their occurrence.

Lay hypnotists say that they should at least be able to work with smoking and weight control because they are no different than Weight Watchers. This is not the case, however, because such programs do not use a psychotherapeutic technique (hypnosis) that creates an intense transference relationship. Furthermore, Weight Watchers and diet center employees do not hold themselves out as being "therapists." Such programs are more open and public, and not held behind closed doors.

Thus, popular diet center type programs create less public confusion about the qualifications of their personnel. Their focus is on nutrition and education concerning behavioral self-control principles, and not on working with the mind and intrapsychic matters. A patient coming to someone for hypnosis expects emotional counseling and therapy, especially from a "hypnotherapist." There is not such deceptiveness or the use of mentally and emotionally intrusive techniques in popular diet center programs. You should also be aware that there are specific case reports of serious complications deriving from the use of hypnosis with obesity patients (see Haber, Nitkin & Shenker, 1979, below).

Finally we should note to the public that we are not seeking to put lay hypnotists out of business. This is a good point to emphasize because lay hypnotists will say we are trying to deprive them of a livlihood, and this is not our intention. In every state, lay hypnosis, without certain confines, may be a legitimate business enterprise. We recognize this point and have no quarrel with it. However, we do speak out against two dangers. The first is the use of hypnosis by unqualified persons in the practice of psychology or medicine. The second point is consumer confusion over the terms "doctor," "therapist," or "hypnotherapist." These points have already been addressed, but it is useful to emphasize that we are not here to eliminate lay hypnosis, but rather to protect the public from those unqualified persons who might prey upon them.

References on Harmful Effects of Hypnosis
D. Corydon Hammond, PhD, ABPH
Research Associate Professor, University of Utah School of Medicine
President, American Society of Clinical Hypnosis
Diplomate, American Board of Psychological Hypnosis

Coe, W.C., & Ryken, K. (1979). Hypnosis and risks to human subjects. *American Psychologist,* 34, 673-681.

Crawford, H.J., Hilgard, J.R., & MacDonald, H. (1982). Transient experiences following hypnotic testing and special termination procedures. *International Journal of Clinical & Experimental Hypnosis,* 30(2), 117-126.

Crasilneck, H.B., Hall, J.A. (1985). *Clinical Hypnosis: Principles & Applications.* New York: Grune & Stratton.

Danto, B. L. (1967). Management of unresolved hypnotic trances as forms of acute psychiatric emergencies. *American Journal of Psychiatry,* 124, 134-137.

Deyoub, P.L. (1984). Hypnotic stimulation fo antisocial behavior: A case report. *International Journal of Clinical & Experimental Hypnosis,* 33, 301-306.

Duncan, B., & Perry, C. (1977). Uncancelled hypnotic suggestions: Initial case studies. *American Journal of Clinical & Experimental Hypnosis,* 19(3), 166-176.

Echterling, L.G., & Emmerling, D.A. (1987). Impact of stage hypnosis. *American Journal of Clinical Hypnosis*, 29, 149-154.

Erickson, M. H. (1962). Stage hypnosis back syndrome. *American Journal of Clinical Hypnosis*, 3, 141-142.

Faw, V., Sellers, D.J., & Wilcox, W.W. (1968). Psychopathological effects of hypnosis. *International Journal of Clinical & Experimental Hypnosis*, 16, 26-37.

Finkelstein, S. (1989). Adverse effects after exposure to lay hypnosis in a group setting: A case report. *American Journal of Clinical Hypnosis*, 32(2), 107-109.

Fromm, E. (1980). Values in hypnotherapy. *Psychotherapy: Theory, Research, & Practice, 17, 425-430.*

Haber, C.H., Nitkin, R., & Shenker, I.R. (1979). Adverse reactions to hypnotherapy in obese adolescents: A developmental viewpoint. *Psychiatric Quarterly*, 5, 55-63.

Haberman, MA (1987). Complications following hypnosis in a psychotic patient with sexual dysfunction treated by a lay hypnotist. *American Journal of Clinical Hypnosis*, 29(3), 166-170.

Harding, E.C. (1978). Complications arising from hypnosis for entertainment. Chapter in F.H. Frankel and H.S. Zamansky (Eds.), Hypnosis at its Bicentennial. New York: Plenum, pp 163-167.

Hilgard, E.R. (1965). The Experience of Hypnosis. New York: Hancourt, Brace, Jovanovich.

Hilgard, J.R. (1974). Sequelae to hypnosis. *International Journal of Clinical & Experimental Hypnosis*, 22, 281-298.

Hilgard, J.R., Hilgard, E.R., & Newman, M.R. (1961). Sequelae to hypnotic induction with special reference to earlier chemical anesthesia. *Journal of Nervous & Mental Disease*, 133, 461-478.

Hoencamp, E. (1990). Sexual abuse and the abuse of hypnosis in the therapeutic relationship. *International Journal of Clinical & Experimental Hypnosis*, 38(4), 283-297.

Joseph, E.D., Peck, S.N., & Kaufman, M.R. (1949). A psychological study of neurodermatitis with a case report. *Mt. Sinai Hospital Journal*, 15, 360-366.

Judd, F.K., Burrows, G.D., & Dennerstein, L. (1985). The dangers of hypnosis: A review. *Australian Journal of Clinical & Experimental Hypnosis*, 13, 1-15.

Judd, F.K., Burrows, G.D., & Dennerstein, L. (1986). Clinicians' perception of the adverse effects of hypnosis: A preliminary survey. *Australian Journal of Clinical & Experimental Hypnosis*, 14, 49-60.

Kleinhauz, M., & Beran, B. (1981). Misuses of hypnosis: A medical emergency and its treatment. *International Journal of Clinical Hypnosis*, 29, 148-161.

Kleinhauz, M., & Beran, B. (1984). Misuse of hypnosis: A factor in psychopathology. *American Journal of Clinical Hypnosis*, 26, 283-290.

Kleinhauz, M., Dreyfuss, D.A., Beran, B., Goldberg, T., & Azikri, D. (1979). Some after effects of stage hypnosis. *International Journal of Clinical & Experimental Hypnosis*, 27, 219-226.

Kleinhauz, M., & Eli, I. (1987). Potential deleterious effects of hypnosis in the clinical setting. *American Journal of Clinical Hypnosis*, 29(3), 155-159.

Kline, M.V. (1976). Dangerous aspects of the practice of hypnosis and the need for legislative regulation. *Clinical Psychologist*, 29, 3-6.

Kost, P.F. (1965). Dangers of hypnosis. *International Journal of Clinical & Experimental Hypnosis*, 13, 220-225.

Kroger, W. (1977). *Clinical & Experimental Hypnosis*. Philadelphia: Lippincott.

Laurence, J.R., & Perry, C. (1988). *Hypnosis, Will and Memory: A Psycho-Legal History*, New York: Guilford.

Levitt, E.E., & Hershman, S. (1962). The clinical practice of hypnosis in the United States: A preliminary survey. *International Journal of Clinical & Experimental Hypnosis*, 32, 55-65.

Kleinhauz, M., Dreyfuss, D.A., Beran, B., Goldberg, T., & Azikri, D. (1979). Some after effects of stage hypnosis. *International Journal of Clinical & Experimental Hypnosis*, 27, 219-226.

Kleinhauz, M., & Eli, I. (1987). Potential deleterious effects of hypnosis in the clinical setting. *American Journal of Clinical Hypnosis*, 29(3), 155-159.

Kline, M.V. (1976). Dangerous aspects of the practice of hypnosis and the need for legislative regulation. *Clinical Psychologist*, 29, 3-6.

Kost, P.F. (1965). Dangers of hypnosis. *International Journal of Clinical & Experimental Hypnosis*, 13, 220-225.

Kroger, W. (1977). *Clinical & Experimental Hypnosis*. Philadelphia: Lippincott.

Laurence, J.R., & Perry, C. (1988). *Hypnosis, Will and Memory: A Psycho-Legal History*, New York: Guilford.

Levitt, E.E., & Hershman, S. (1962). The clinical practice of hypnosis in the United States: A preliminary survey. *International Journal of Clinical & Experimental Hypnosis*, 32, 55-65.

Lindermann, H. (1973). *Relieve Tension the Autogenic Way*. New York: Peter Wyden.

MacHovec, F.J. (1987). *Hypnosis Complications: Prevention & Risk Management*. Springfield, IL: Charles C. Thomas.

MacHovec, F.J. (1987). Hypnosis complications: six cases. *American Journal of Clinical Hypnosis*, 29(3), 160-165.

Marcuse, F.L. (1964). *Hypnosis Throughout the World*. Springfield, IL, Charles C. Thomas.

Marcuse, F.L. (1969). *Hypnosis: Fact and Fiction*. Baltimore: Penguin Books, pp. 169-170.

McCartney, J.L. (1961). A half century of personal experience with hypnosis. *International Journal of Clinical & Experimental Hypnosis*, 9, 22-33.

Meares, A. (1960). *A System of Medical Hypnosis*. New York: Julian Press

Meares, A. (1961). An evaluation of the dangers of medical hypnosis. *American Journal of Clinical Hypnosis*, 4, 90-97.

Meldman, M.J. (1960). Personality decompensation after hypnosis symptom suppression. *Journal of the American Medical Association*, 173, 359-364.

Miller, M.M. (1979). *Therapeutic Hypnosis*. New York: Human Sciences Press.

Milne, G. (1986). Hypnotic compliance and other hazards. *Australian Journal of Clinical & Experimental Hypnosis*, 14, 15-29.

Orne, M.T. (1965). Undesirable effects of hypnosis: The determinants and management. *International Journal of Clinical & Experimental Hypnosis*, 13, 226-237.

Page, R.A., & Handley, G.W. (1990). Psychogenic and physiological sequelae to hypnosis: Two case reports. *American Journal of Clinical Hypnosis*, 32(4), 250-256.

Lindermann, H. (1973). *Relieve Tension the Autogenic Way*. New York: Peter Wyden.

MacHovec, F.J. (1987). *Hypnosis Complications: Prevention & Risk Management*. Springfield, IL: Charles C. Thomas.

MacHovec, F.J. (1987). Hypnosis complications: six cases. *American Journal of Clinical Hypnosis*, 29(3), 160-165.

Marcuse, F.L. (1964). *Hypnosis Throughout the World*. Springfield, IL, Charles C. Thomas.

Marcuse, F.L. (1969). *Hypnosis: Fact and Fiction*. Baltimore: Penguin Books, pp. 169-170.

McCartney, J.L. (1961). A half century of personal experience with hypnosis. *International Journal of Clinical & Experimental Hypnosis*, 9, 22-33.

Meares, A. (1960). *A System of Medical Hypnosis*. New York: Julian Press

Meares, A. (1961). An evaluation of the dangers of medical hypnosis. *American Journal of Clinical Hypnosis*, 4, 90-97.

Meldman, M.J. (1960). Personality decompensation after hypnosis symptom suppression. *Journal of the American Medical Association*, 173, 359-364.

Miller, M.M. (1979). *Therapeutic Hypnosis*. New York: Human Sciences Press.

Milne, G. (1986). Hypnotic compliance and other hazards. *Australian Journal of Clinical & Experimental Hypnosis*, 14, 15-29.

Orne, M.T. (1965). Undesirable effects of hypnosis: The determinants and management. *International Journal of Clinical & Experimental Hypnosis*, 13, 226-237.

Page, R.A., & Handley, G.W. (1990). Psychogenic and physiological sequelae to hypnosis: Two case reports. *American Journal of Clinical Hypnosis*, 32(4), 250-256.

Perry, C. (1977). Uncancelled hypnotic suggestions: The effect of hypnosis depth and hypnotic skill on posthypnotic persistence. *Journal of Abnormal Psychology*, 86, 570-574.

Perry, C. (1979). Hypnotic coercion and compliance to act: A review of evidence presented in a legal case. *International Journal of Clinical & Experimental Hypnosis*, 36, 187-218.

Rosen, H. (1959). Hypnosis in medical practice: Uses and abuses. *Chicago Medical Society Bulletin*, 62, 482-436.

Rosen, H. (1960). Hypnosis: Applications and misapplications. *Journal of the American Medical Association*, 172, 683-687.

Sakata, K.I. (1968). Report of a case failure to dehypnotize and subsequent reputed after effects. *International Journal of Clinical & Experimental Hypnosis*, 16, 221-228.

Starker, S. (1974). Persistence of a hypnotic dissociative reaction. *International Journal of Clinical & Experimental Hypnosis*, 22(2), 131-137.

Venn, J. (1988). Misuse of hypnosis in sexual contexts: Two case reports. *International Journal of Clinical & Experimental Hypnosis*, 36(1), 12-18.

Watkins, J.G. (1972). Antisocial behavior under hypnosis: Possible or impossible? *International Journal of Clinical & Experimental Hypnosis*, 20, 95-100.

Watkins, J.G. (1987). *Hypnotherapeutic Techniques*. New York: Irvington.

Weitzenhoffer, A.M. (1989). *The Practice of Hypnotism, Volumes I & II*. New York: Wiley.

West, L.J., & Deckert, G.H. (1965). Dangers of hypnosis. *Journal of the American Medical Association*, 192, 9-12.

Wineburg, E.N., & Straker, N. (1973). An episode of acute, self-limiting depersonalization following a first session of hypnosis. *American Journal of Psychiatry*, 130, 98-100.

Williams, G.W. (1953). Difficulties in dehypnotizing. *Journal of Clinical & Experimental Hypnosis*, 1, 3-12.

# Comments By Key Figures of the Era

In August of 1986 I attended a Learning Annex class, "How to be a Hypnotist: A Lucrative New Income Opportunity," hosted by Richard Harte. I was always interested in hypnosis since I hypnotized my mother from a book at the age of twelve. I attended the class and was "hooked." After a basic and advanced class, I joined the AAEH and became certified in October, 1987. In August of 1989 I attended the NGH second annual conference in NYC. What a conference! I was like the Energizer bunny. I kept going and going ... never took a lunch break. I loved every minute and still do.

Joann Abrahamsen, CI, OB (New York)

This has been an amazing time, where knowledge of ancient hypnotic techniques mixed with the unique techniques of stage hypnotists and trickled down to members of the new emerging profession of hypnotism. These new professionals have carved out a place for themselves in the history of hypnotism in an environment filled with both challenges and promise. Challenges came from physicians and psychologists wanting to shut them down and paradoxically, at the same time the new concepts of "alternative medicine" and "complementary medicine" offered hope for an alliance in the future. Individuals like Dr Dwight Damon, and the National Guild of Hypnotists played a large part in making the future look so bright for the profession of hypnotism.

Cal Banyan, MA, BCH, CI, DNGH (California)

In my fifty plus years as a practicing hypnotist I have been privileged to have had many other health professionals become clients, students, and also colleagues. I am proud that my status as a consulting hypnotist carries with it the respect and prestige that brought me to officially be asked to participate in such programs as the New York City Medical Reserve Corps and the medical department of the Amtrack Police Department. Most of the changes in our professional image have been in the past 25 years, thanks to the ethics and professionalism of NGH, the oldest and largest hypnotism member organization, and its leadership.

Jacob Bimblich, CH, CI, OB (Brooklyn, New York)

The profession of hypnotism is a field which undoubtably attracts younger people because of the myths, not the reality. Because of their vast potential, we could use a wave of excitement from our younger graduates who become active and enthused about our work. The groundwork has been provided by those who came before and the opportunity is there. The question is—will the work be continued?

Henry Bolduc, CH, OB (Virginia)

Today, we teach hypnosis to members of the medical and complimentary communities. At least 50% of our clinic clients are referrals, and there is much less fear or apprehension about the process of hypnotism. It is an honor and privilege to do this work – to be allowed into the client's and student's vulnerable space, and to be trusted to help them find their resilience and magnificence. Because once they understand their own power, it's as if a light goes on and they realize anything is possible. And I couldn't be more grateful for the past 16 years!

Georgina Cannon, CI, CMI,OB (Toronto, Ontario)

In the 80's the power of hypnosis was not fully recognized by the world until its persevering proponents began teaching laymen how to use it, albeit in a helter-skelter fashion. With the advent of the HMO's in the 90's, the psychologists brought much attention to hypnosis in their unsuccessful maneuvering to usurp hypnosis exclusively in their scope of practice. State licensed schools of hypnosis started to spring up with registered curricula offering a minimum of 100 hours of in-class instruction. Our right to practice hypnosis was championed by several individuals and a few organizations, with the result that our legislators recognized that hypnosis was being re-born as an independent profession and that society was entitled to benefit from the aforementioned power of hypnotic experience.

Anthony DeMarco, LLB, FNGH, OB (New Jersey)

The pioneering and creative spirit that has historically enriched so much in America successfully infused the acceptance and subsequent growth of the hypnotism profession in the United States ... especially during the last six decades or so. Studying many of the best masters herein will inspire how the possibilities for the use of hypnosis have such a phenomenal future ahead for improving the health of so many throughout the world.   Elsom Eldridge, Jr OB (Florida)

In 1968 I had the great fortune to train with one of the best instructors, Fred Schiavo. My wife at that time told my mother, "Look what he is wasting his money on, hypnosis classes." My life was filled with anxiety related symptoms. I smoked, I stuttered, had constant headaches and experienced tremors when under stress, and I was heavily medicated for about eight years. Today, none of those exist. After three months of seeing my improvements, my mother also joined the classes and as a nurse she uses hypnosis regularly. In 1970 I was beginning to see clients and needed to make a decision, leave my regular job and do hypnosis or stop doing hypnosis, as it was affecting my regular profession. I feel I have become a great consulting hypnotist because I have been there and have learned how to get out. I now teach my clients how to get out and learn to feel better.                          Larry Garrett, CH, OB (Illinois)

I began doing hypnosis professionally in the 80s. At that time, hypnosis was something that was perceived as a "fringe" method, and very few people understood what it was about. More people knew about "guided visualization" or "deep relaxation," but to some, the word hypnosis conjured up the image of the caped charlatan entrancing people with a pendulum and hypnotic gaze. Now it's a completely different world and hypnosis is known in the mainstream as a time-honored, profound practice that helps people overcome all the difficulties of their lives. When I found out that the work I'd been doing with guided visualization since the 70s was hypnosis and I could become a certified practitioner, I truly jumped for joy. I knew it was a great profession, and it was the answer to all the questions I'd been asking about what I'd come to this earth to do.                          Marilyn Gordon. CH, CI, OB (California)

There has been a major change in the dynamics of hypnotism from 1960-1985 and then from 1985 to the present. As someone who studied with several of the "old masters" of hypnosis and personally witnessed how they kept their brand of hypnosis a big, mysterious secret, I experienced a breath of fresh air when Dr Dwight Damon and NGH came along in the late 1980s and offered an eclectic association. The open sharing of information, training, and research under the auspices of NGH finally came to the fore and has made hypnotism the profession it is today.

Richard Harte, PhD, CMI, FNGH, OB (Florida)

Early in the era covered in this book very few people turned to hypnosis, even as a last resort, in dealing with life's problems. The police seldom used hypnosis to solve crimes until the kidnapping of 26 school students and their bus driver on July 15, 1976 in Chowchilla, California. That was the catalyst case that moved the police into considering hypnosis as a viable investigative tool. The US Supreme Court ruled (Rock vs. Arkansas) that hypnotically refreshed recall is admissible in all 50 states when used by the defense in a criminal case. Bit by bit, the mainstream use of hypnosis has been popularized by the establishment of professional standards and training as we've become a separate and distinct profession.

Insp. Marx Howell (ret.), CH, OB (Texas)

When I entered this fascinating field, the use of hypnosis as a therapeutic modality was virtually nonexistent. Back then only a small number of maverick doctors used hypnosis openly in their practices. Milton Erickson, William Kroger, Louis Wolberg, and a few other brave souls had the courage to use hypnosis and advocate its use by other practitioners. At that time hypnotherapy, as we know it today, did not exist; and none of the medical or dental schools then provided postgraduate training in hypnosis.   John C. Hughes, DC, DNGH, OB (Nevada)

I have witnessed the profession of hypnotism grow from the late 1940's through today. We have gained an enormous amount of knowledge and understanding of the power of hypnotism to help the human condition in all areas of life. Today we see hypnotism being used by medical physicians, psychologists, psychiatrists, mental health counselors, and professional hypnotists as a beneficial and accepted clinical intervention for various issues mental, physical, and spiritual affecting man's quality of life.

Even as there has been much progress over the years, I believe we have only scratched the surface of hypnotism's potential. Future progress will be gained through knowledge of new hypnotists entering the profession today and will greatly benefit mankind for generations to come.

Gerald Kein, CH, FNGH, OB (Florida)

It's really like asking whether the music of Tchaikovsky, Chopin, and Mozart have changed over the years. Has the literary genius of Shakespeare, Dickens, and Keats been altered since their creative periods? Was the hypnotic magic of Ormond McGill dulled or varied from his early skills to his recent passing?

Nothing that was genius and great in history has in essence changed our world today. The exception is, of course, our modes and speed of communication, and the hypnosis profession has certainly jumped aboard that bandwagon.

As the lyrics of that old song go ...

"It ain't what you do, it's the way you do it!
It ain't what you say, it's the way you say it!"

Maurice Kershaw, CH, DNGH (Montreal, Canada)

Now that I am 87 years old many memories return, such as grad school and the frequent visits to the office of Dr Rexford L. North, with whom I became friendly as a result of my interest and work in hypnotism developed while in high school. I read every book, pamphlet, or article in order to get educated.

My knowledge grew as a result and I used to help Dr North publish the *Journal of Hypnotism* in the office of the Boston Hypnotism Center.

He gave weekly demonstrations at his St. Botolph Street office in Boston. Being stone deaf, he spoke in a variable pitch voice but made himself understood quite easily. Through these demonstrations he developed a rather significant following.

We formed a group so we could advance our interest and knowledge as the National Guild of Hypnotists. I was the first treasurer and we met monthly. We also had the pleasure of having Harry Arons come to a couple of meetings. Later, some of us chartered another organization named the American Society of Research and Clinical Hypnotism after Dr North disappeared, as if by magic. No one knew where he went or when ... no one could find him ... and rumors abounded with sightings of him all over various parts of the country, but none were validated.

Life went on and I opened my office in a medical building and began to accept referrals of patients from physicians in the building. I lost touch with the Guild members and, after many years, started a search and was successful in finding that it not only was strong and healthy but with a fast growing membership. Once again I became happily active in it and with my old friend, Dr Dwight Damon. I'm so happy that I did. I continue my practice but only see a few patients a week. However, I attend every NGH convention without fail.

Arnold Levison, PhD, CH, OB (Massachusetts)

During my early years as a full-time professional hypnotist I entered a pharmacy, owned by a friend, to pick up a prescription. The young lady behind the counter began to stare at me. I asked if I could help her. She continued to stare. Again I asked if I could help her. She replied, "I just wanted to see what a hypnotist looked like!"

Many years ago I was asked to speak to the Orange County (Florida) Medical Association's meeting. I was invited when the scheduled speaker cancelled suddenly. I gave a short history of hypnosis and its many uses in the field of medicine. Halfway through my talk one of the doctors called out critically, "You are only treating symptoms." Immediately, another doctor stated loudly, "What *we* do every day?" After the audience applauded I finished with a question and answer period. I received numerous referrals following the program during the next several months.

Joe B. McCawley, Ethical Hypnotist (Florida)

What an honor and a privilege to be given the tools that took my work as a hypnotist from Hingham, Massachusetts to Botswana, Africa. Working as a missionary but using the principles of hypnosis, I taught staff members at a local hospice in Botswana how to empower themselves and others as well as teaching AIDS patients that they are not dying with AIDS, but living life with AIDS.

I wish to thank Dr Dwight Damon and the National Guild of Hypnotists for enriching my life's journey in helping me to make a difference in the world.

Patricia MacIsaac, LPN, CMI, FNGH, OB (Massachusetts)

I'm amazed that we have survived as a profession with the many obstacles we've faced through the past half-century. We've not only hung on, but we've grown, especially during the past 25 years. I've lived through some of the drama recounted in *Hypnotic Recollections*, but not as much as I had thought. Since reading some excerpts it has given me a new respect for our profession and appreciation for our heritage. What we practice may be thousands of years old, but is very new in professional and public recognition.

Edward Morris, BS, MEd, CI (New Hampshire)

Back in 1968 there was a television commercial for Virginia Slims cigarettes. Their slogan was, "You've come a long way, baby." Hypnosis in this country has definitely come a long way. Forty years ago, the only way to learn more about hypnosis was to try to find a hypnotist who would be willing to train you. Back then there was no way of knowing if this training was good, bad, or up to date. Training in hypnosis today seems to be light years ahead of what took place in the sixties. Now, it is possible to train with professionals who are not only hypnotists, but who are also certified nationally as instructors. These people make sure that the training constantly be evaluated and updated as new techniques are developed.

Don Mottin, CMI, DNGH, OB (Missouri)

Becoming an NGH Certified Consulting Hypnotist in 2003 has taken me on a path of positivity, clarity, awareness, and focus. My very first client was my mother. Her long history of chronic pain led me on my journey in becoming a part of this wonderful profession. The results my mom achieved learning self-hypnosis was the icing on the cake and I knew my nursing career was taking a new path in helping individuals be the best they could be.

Wendy Packer, RN, CH, CI (New York)

As a medical professional and clinical hypnotherapist, I have come to respect how much the mind is connected with the body. With the use of hypnosis and its many powerful tools, one can change the thoughts that change our body. How does this happen? Our mind responds to external events. How we respond is based upon our internal thoughts. These internal thoughts instruct our body how to respond via chemical language. Change our thoughts ... change our body. Hypnosis is a tool to change thoughts, reframe thoughts, and release those toxic thoughts that are speaking internally to our body.

Seth-Deborah Roth, CRNA, CCHt, CI (California)

# A Few of the Many "Pioneers"

Row 1 - Harry Arons - Norbert Bakas - Calvin Banyan - Maureen Banyan - George Baranowski - Edwin Baron

Row 2 - George Bien - Jacob Bimblich - H. Leo Bolduc - Walter Brackelmanns- Shaun Brookhouse - William Bryan

Row 3 - Dwight Damon - Anthony DeMarco - Elsom Eldridge, Jr - Michael Ellner- Dave Elman - M. Ron Eslinger

Row 4 - Edith Fiore - Charles Francis - Arnold Furst - Bruno Furst - Larry Garrett - John Gatto

Row 5 - C. Scot Giles - Marilyn Gordon - Sandi Graves - Lisa Halpin - Richard Harte - Virgil Hayes

Row 6 - Edward Hightower - William Horton - Marx Howell - John C Hughes - C. Roy Hunter - George Kappas

Row 6 - John Kappas - Gerald Kein - Maurice Kershaw - Al Krasner - Steve LaVelle -
Arthur Leidecker
Row 7 - Arnold Levison - Patricia MacIsaac - Joe McCawley - Ormond McGill -
Marie Mongan - Edward Morris
Row 8 - Donald Mottin - Thomas Nicoli - Rexford L North - Garrett Oppenheim -
Emanuel Orlick - Robert Otto
Row 9 - Melvin Powers - Sydney Schneider - Walter Sichort - Anne Spencer -
Charles Tebbetts - Dave Tracy
Row 10 - Jerry Valley - Tommy Vee - A L Ward

# Wise & Wonderful Hypno-Headlines

## Self-hypnosis course to combat phobias

SOME weeks ago the fears of flying were highlighted in this column as a result of a call to me by a young man who is getting married this year and hopes to fly off to warm climes for his

other fears or phobias.

"Due to this response," he says "I will be conducting a self-hypnosis course for those who wish to overcome their fears - whatever they may

the imagination and positive thinking.

"Bolstering of personality resources, such as self-confidence, assertiveness, motivation, goal determination and achievement.

## Health and Happiness with Hypnotherapy

By Nigel SOMERSET

Y ou can conquer phobias, lower anxiety, banish panic, build confidence,

Far too many people, being in hypnosis doesn't feel much different to how they usually feel. "But most likely, you'll feel relaxed, possibly more relaxed than ever before." says Dr.

not ideologically involved the way a priest or minister is, but nevertheless 'loves' the client and thereby works on his or her own resources to get better. The love liberates the client to trust, but hypnosis is the

## Hypnosis: Toward A Better Image

By RICH BARLOW
Valley News Staff Writer
NASHUA — "Close your eyes. Take a deep breath and exhale. So

## HYPNOSIS FOR BETTER PERFORMANCE

*Where greater strength and conditioning was once the athlete's edge, today it's the mind. Are you getting the most out of your's?*

**MSNBC.com**

Altered States
Hypnosis can help with problems from anxiety to pain. How it works, and what it does in the brain.

By David Noonan
Newsweek

## Dieters get boost from hypnosis

**Health** | Americans hoping alternative treatment will break food's spell over them.

And as wai bulge, hyp they're seein desperate fo their eating

"The count and fatter, so loss methods

published march 22, 2005

## Hypnotize your habit

Clinical hypnosis can help smokers

New York Post, Monday, September 5, 2005     nypost.com

## Hypnosis offers slim hope

In a nation where two-thirds of the population is overweight or obese, a

are getting more attention." said Jean Fain, a psychologist at Harvard

## Treatment Through Trance

Hypnosis Gains Credibility
As Powerful Aid for Patients

By Howard Wolinsky

## What's Going to Happen to You if You Don't Lose Weight?
### (Here's how hypnosis may solve all of your weight loss problems.)

178

# LIFE

**HYPNOSIS**
OLD 'BLACK ART' IS NOW
ACCEPTED MEDICAL TOOL

DARWIN'S INSECTS: JEWELS
HIS JUNGLE PARADISE

## The BIG Story

A.M.A. VALIDATES USE OF HYPNOSIS
and LIFE Magazine tells the story—

Complete article from November 3, 1985 reprinted
as a memento of the
1993 National Guild of Hypnotists
Annual Convention and Educational Conference,
Nashua, NH August 13-15, 1993

NOVEMBER 3, 1958   **25** CENTS

LIFE Magazine ©
Time Warner
Reprinted with Permission

# OUT OF ANCIENT MAGIC COMES NEW MEDICAL TOOL

## *HYPNOSIS*

Hypnosis has finally gone medically legitimate. Because it traditionally has been the secret of the stage magician, the public usually has looked on hypnosis as black magic, picturing its practitioners as spell-casting Svengalis. But in the past 10 years some 900 U.S. doctors, dentists and psychologists have been quietly employing hypnosis to help their patients. Their success has so impressed the American Medical Association that it has now endorsed hypnosis as a therapeutic aid for doctors and dentists properly trained in its use.

This significant vote of confidence means that more and more Americans soon will be experiencing the feeling of drifting into a vortex of sound — the reassuring, repetitive sound of the hypnotist's voice. They will find that the suggestions his voice plants in their minds can help them through crises that range from the extreme stress of undergoing open heart surgery without general anesthesia to the problem of gagging at the dentist's. They will discover that hypnosis can put them into a contented, relaxed frame of mind, allay their panic and help them forget their ordeal.

As an anesthetic in surgery, hypnosis persuades the patient he feels no pain, prevents the vomiting, fatigue and loss of appetite that often follows operations. It is specifically useful in operations where general anesthetics should not beused and in childbirth where too much anesthetic can harm the baby. In relieving cancer pain, it is often better than opiates, for it is not habit-forming, does not lose its effect, as narcotics do.

While medical hypnotists are gratified by its new legitimacy, they are afraid hypnosis may stimulate the fad-loving public to clamor for it as everybody's cure-all. This could cause tragic disappointment, for at least one out of 10 patients cannot be hypnotized at all and one out of six will not go into the deep trance needed for painkilling in major surgery. What is more, hypnosis does not cure anything. Compulsive overeating in obese patients, for instance, can be stopped through hypnosis. But this does not remove the cause of the compulsion — the patient may stop eating candy and start chewing his nails.

Research in hypnosis is still so new that its potentials are not fully understood. Startling new findings on the psychiatric uses of hypnosis and its potential threat in psychological warfare will be discussed in future issues of **Life**. Meanwhile hypnotism's most striking present applications, in the field of childbirth, surgery and therapy, are shown on the following pages.

*"Open your eyes, Shirley. Look — look at your baby." At these words, uttered by a Chicago obstetrician, Shirley Mucci came out of a hypnotic trance and saw her minutes-old son. Hypnotized before going into labor, she was conscious of no discomfort during delivery.*

*Months before, she had shed the anxieties of pregnancy by attending a group clinic for prenatal training where a doctor taught her to hypnotize herself by repeatedly assuring her under hypnosis that she would be able to put herself into a light trance at will when she got home. For 15 minutes each day Mrs. Mucci had done so, closing her eyes, telling herself she was very relaxed and that her arm was as numb as if it were anesthetized. Then she had said to herself over and over, "I'm completely calm. I am not at all worried."*

*At the hospital she hypnotized herself again as labor began. Next morning the doctor came by, said, "Now it's time to go under." Immediately she did. Her husband came in. "Ralph will now put his hand on you," said the doctor, "Ralph will reinforce you." In the delivery room the doctor murmured, "Think of yourself doing something very pleasant. Maybe you're gardening . . . I want you to pant like a dog. Grunt. Pant." At delivery he said: "You don't feel anything." And Mrs. Mucci did not.*

*Not all pregnant women can be as fully hypnotized as Mrs. Mucci. Nor should all cases be hypnotized. But for many women the elimination of tension through hypnosis is a blessing. And for those who have to be delivered by Caesarean section yet cannot tolerate required anesthetics, this is an ideal way to have a baby.*

*For Fred Heywang, five hours of what might have been living hell went by in peace. At Dallas' Parkland Memorial Hospital, Psychologist Harold Crasilneck, the hypnotist, kept him relaxed during the awful stress of operation while part of his skull was removed and a needlelike instrument inserted deep into his gray matter.*

*Heywang, who had been suffering from crippling limb tremors for 20 years, had to undergo this without general anesthetic. Surgeon Kemp Clark had to be able to watch his reactions as he penetrated the brain to discover which part was the area controlling spasms and then treat it to stop the spasms. Under hypnosis Heywang was conscious enough for Dr. Clark to see when the tremors stopped. Only once did Heywang sense mild pain, saying, "Oh, brother! It feels like a thousand bites." When he awoke, he recalled little of his trial, raised his arms and gasped, "My palsy's gone!"*

*For Dorothy Haralson, hypnosis meant the end of torture. Her body had been burned when a gas heater exploded in her Irving, Texas home. As healing began, dead tissue had to be cut away, and she was supposed to exercise her badly injured right arm. But even with opiates the pain was so excruciating she refused to move the limb and its muscles contracted.*

*At Parkland Memorial Hospital her surgeon suggested that Dallas psychologist Harold Crasilneck try hypnosis. Under it she felt nothing during tissue removal. Later he hypnotized her for therapy. "You are getting drowsy," he suggested. "Your eyes are sealed tight, though you are very relaxed. We're going to exercise that arm. Stretch it, stretch it. When you awake you will continue to move it but this will not be painful." Awakened, she moved her arm. "How do you feel?" asked Dr. Crasilneck. "Just fine," she beamed.*

## HUMBUG IN THE PAST, DANGERS IN PRESENT

The widest use of hypnosis in modern times has been for entertainment, and the medical profession views with considerable alarm the stage magician who puts members of his audience into trances. Both physical and mental harm come from his act. "The use of hypnosis for entertainment purposes," the A.M.A. has flatly stated, "is vigorously condemned." Medical hypnotists hope state governments will pass bills banning hypnosis in the amusement field, but the opposition from entertainers is powerful. In 1957 the city council of Buffalo, N.Y. considered such a resolution. It was opposed by Ring Twelve of the Buffalo Magic Club on grounds of discrimination and was quietly dropped.

Hypnotism has a long history of misuse. Its earliest uses were religious and medical at the same time, for primitive man correlated faith with healing, considering the witch doctor both priest and physician. As far back as the old Stone Age, anthropologists believe, religious leaders awed their caveman audiences by going into hypnotic trances. Ancient soothsayers who gazed into crystals to divine the future undoubtedly fell into trances, believing this gave them foresight. Persian magi and Hindu fakirs practiced self-hypnosis, claiming supernatural healing powers when in this state. The priests of ancient Egypt brought their patients to temples and, using a form of hypnosis, told them the gods would cure them as they slept.

In later centuries certain religions retained self-hypnosis as a spiritual aid. During the 1880's the Christian monks of Mt. Athos in Greece practiced it as part of their devotions. So do Hindu yogis of today. But in medicine hypnosis was not recognized in modern times until the end of the 18th Century. The Franz Anton Mesmer revived and expanded an old and erroneous theory that sickness was due to an imbalance of "universal fluids" which, he believed, could be readjusted by man through a magnetic force. He used a type of hypnotism to control this force and treat patients. Europe's aristocracy took up mesmerism as a fad until a scientific commission, which included Benjamin Franklin, denounced his practices as humbug.

One of Mesmer's disciples, the Marquis de Puysegur, accurately described Mesmer's "magnetism" as artificial somnambulism. The British Surgeon James Braid said it was a state of mind and named it hypnotism. In 1821, in France, the first operation under hypnotic anesthesia was performed. It was followed over the next 60 years by thousands of other operations carried out by European surgeons. Dr. James Esdaile even persuaded the British government to set up three hospitals in Britain and India where hypnosis would be used.

At the turn of the century, hypnosis received a crippling blow. Sigmund Freud tried it to treat hysteria but discarded it as ineffective and turned away from it in favor of psychoanalysis. This nearly ruined hypnotism's reputation. It was not considered valid treatment again until World War I, when it was briefly used to treat "shell shock." But doctors did not understand it and lost interest in it. In World War II the old tool was tried again for combat neuroses. This time doctors began to study its complex nature and to prove its worth.

Today most practicing medical hypnotists are not full-time hypnotists but are doctors who use hypnosis as an aid to their practice. In the U.S. there are about 400 dentists well trained in its use, 250 general practitioners, 150 specialists such as obstetricians, internists, surgeons and anesthesiologists, and 100 psychologists and psychiatrists. Some of these men were recently trained at medical schools but more than half learned techniques by themselves years ago when no good courses were available. Only two U.S. universities now offer extensive training in hypnosis, giving it as a graduate course which is open to any doctor, dentist or psychologist.

Hypnotism's increasing popularity will almost certainly create a shortage of trained practitioners. The first and oldest organization of medical hypnotists in North America today, the Society for Clinical and Experimental Hypnosis, recommends at least a year of training for any doctor or dentist who wants to use hypnosis in his specialty. It fears some doctors will try hypnosis after only a cursory course and, unaware of its limitations, will do more harm than good. "Quickie courses," warns Dr. Milton V. Kline, editor of the society's journal," give the men the tool but not the appreciation of how carefully it must be used." He points to the case of a patient who came to him after having been hypnotized by a dentist. With hypnosis the dentist had stopped the man from grinding his teeth. But the man was neurotic and when he could no longer find a teeth-grinding outlet for his tensions, he started to overeat. When Kline got him, his weight had soared from 145 to 288 pounds.

181

Hypnosis is now being tried in many cases other than major surgery — to treat asthma, hay fever and multiple sclerosis, relieve pain in minor surgery, help patients hold awkward positions for skin grafting and substitute for the needle at the dentist's. But as these applications become more and more varied there is danger that the public will take to hypnosis as heedlessly as it has welcomed tranquilizers. Doctors may be pressured into using it unwisely. To avoid this, Southwestern Medical School in Dallas permits hypnosis only after the case is discussed at a conference of several different specialists.

Dr. Harold Crasilneck advises that hypnosis "should be used only with specific cases that no longer respond to standard treatment." Some doctors may not heed this advice. Having used hypnosis to relieve physical distress during a patient's ulcer operation, for instance, a too ambitious doctor may try to get at the psychosomatic reasons for the ulcer. Unless he is grounded in clinical psychology he can botch this and drive the patient into hysteria.

Unfortunately, healing by untrained hypnotists flourishes in the nation today and the situation may get worse now that hypnosis is medically respectable. Many reputable hypnotists now warn their patient under hypnosis: "You will never under any condition allow yourself to be hypnotized by anyone who is not qualified to do so."

The true nature of hypnosis is still debatable, but in general it acts in the following manner. Usually, for a person to "go under," or be induced into a trance, he must be willing. No one normally can be hypnotized against his will, nor will anyone who is hypnotized perform an act that goes against his best interests. The best subjects are those who want it most — those in great pain.

Induction works only if the person concentrates completely on one repetitive stimulus, somewhat in the way an infant falls asleep to the repeated rocking of his cradle. This stimulus can be sight or sound or, as in the case of the whirling dervish, motion. In a typical hypnosis session, the subject responds to only one of his five senses. As he stares fixedly at a small object or a light, his vision becomes fuzzy with fatigue and he is unaware of any sensation except hearing. He pays attention to only one sound, the hypnotist's voice murmuring repetitively, "You are sleepy, so very, very sleepy." The voice gets the brain's undivided attention and literally talks the brain into a sleeplike trance.

As he drifts off, the subject may feel slightly dizzy, as though swaying, floating or falling down a shaft. Objects around him may seem to waver, as if seen under water. His temperature may fall slightly. He may see streaks of light, gaudy kaleidoscopic patterns or complementary colors — a green wall may look yellow. Patients have described such temporary illusions as "I feel as if my body were not here, only my head," or "I am an egg-shaped disk, and you (the doctor) are like a luminous crescent hovering over me."

The illusions and strange feeling of unreality come from the fact that during induction the personality that the patient had when he was awake — his consciousness — becomes temporarily altered. With many inhibitions released, he may feel intense emotion — generally elation, but occasionally anger and terror. Then his ability to perceive sensations and to conceive ideas about them change. He will take unreal things for reality, but only if this is suggested to him as an image. For example, one subject had no reaction whatever when informed under hypnosis: "Your temperature is falling." But when told that he was going up into the stratosphere in a plane, the image made him start to shiver and his temperature dropped to 92°.

When a patient is in a trance his subconscious can be influenced. He lacks volition, feels that resistance is too much effort. He is extremely susceptible to suggestion, reacts to what he is told without question or criticism. If he has to undergo surgery, he will, under hypnosis, be convinced that he is pain-free. Physically he will be receiving pain, for damaged nerves will be sending signals to his brain. But psychologically he will not be feeling pain, for his brain will refuse to perceive these signals and coordinate them into the feeling of pain.

How far suggestion, which is intensified in hypnosis, controls the reactions of the human body becomes of increasing importance to doctors as they use hypnosis more widely. Recent experiments indicate that hypnosis may affect more than the brain and may actually reduce the nerves' pain signals.

Other tests give startling evidence of hypnotism's power over physical functions. Some subjects were given constipating doses of opium under the guise of castor oil; the results were cathartic. A patient whose leg was immobilized with anesthetic was told under hypnosis that he could walk — and he did, as though his leg were normal. Another was advised he was swallowing spoonfuls of honey, and the sugar content of his blood immediately rose and one man, assured he was eating tenderloin, chewed up a blotter with great satisfaction.

LIFE magazine © Time Warner
Reprinted with permission.

# Index

Alphabetically in order

Calvert, John - 19, 20, 97, 111
Cannon, Georgina - 62, 72, 105, 145, 172
Charles, Herbert - 26
Churchill, Randall - 47, 54, 55, 75
Collins, Pat - 3, 45, 46, 91, 109, 111, 121
COPHO - 28, 72, 86, 89, 90
Coué, Emil - 5, 16, 17, 35, 125
Council, Dr. James - 143
Damon, Dr. Dwight - 24, 31, 49, 50, 51, 78, 79, 116, 171, 174, 176
Dante, Dr. Ron - 58, 59, 60, 111
Davis, Trent - 84
Deavers, Dewey - 36, 37, 38, 39, 117, 118
DeMarco, Anthony - 5, 7, 70, 83, 90, 145, 156, 172, 176
Deutsch, Ernie - 40
Directory of Occupational Titles - 4, 48
Durbin, Chaplain Paul - 41
Eastburn, Drake - 126
Eastburn, Lynsi - 73
Eichel, Steve K.D. - 141, 143
Eldridge, Elsom - 5, 7, 75, 77, 78, 83, 116, 172, 176
Ellison, Milford - 26
Ellner, Michael - 145, 178
Elman, Dave - 19, 22, 28, 33, 48, 176
Elman, Col. Larry - 22
Erickson, Dr. Milton - 1, 147, 167, 173
Eslinger, Ron - 62, 145, 176, 178
FAPH - 67
Fiore, Dr. Edith - 7, 104, 105, 176
Flint, Herbert - 19
Francis, Charles - 40, 41, 44, 83, 116, 176
Furst, Arnold - 21, 55, 75, 80, 176
Furst, Bruno - 15, 26, 32, 34, 176
Garrett, Larry - 5, 7, 42, 43, 112, 116, 145, 156, 176
Gatto, Dr. John - 70, 83
Gibson, Walter - 15
Gilboyne, Mark - 47
Giles, C. Scot - 5, 7, 76, 81, 82, 83, 84, 86, 87, 89, 116, 119, 145, 151, 156, 176
Godrottis, Betty - 40
Goodwin, Michael - 86
Gordon, Marilyn - 7, 62, 176
Graves, Sandi - 7, 151
Grippo - 35, 36, 125
Hadley, Josie - 122
Halpin, John - 36, 125
Halpin, Lisa - 84, 86, 176
Hammond, Dr. D. Corydon - 66, 101, 141, 147, 151, 152, 153, 161, 167
Harrison, Martha - 7

Harte, Dr. Richard - 5, 7, 11, 64, 75, 116, 145, 171, 173, 176
Hayes, Edward - 117, 118
Hayes, Virgil - 7, 69, 151, 152, 153, 154,176
HECI - 71
Henderson, Florence - 53, 97
Hickman, Dr. Irene - 122
Hightower, Edward - 57, 116, 176
Higley, Jeff - 7, 53, 118
HIN - 69
HMI - 53, 84, 86, 97, 118
Horton, William - 62, 126, 176
Howell, Marx - 7, 99, 100, 116, 173, 176
Hughes, Dr. John C. - 2, 7, 41, 44, 55, 63, 78, 79, 116, 145, 173, 176
Hunter, C. Roy - 7, 71, 116, 176
HypnoBirthing - 73
IACH - 68
IACT - 70
IAPH - 70
IHHFG - 70
IMDHA - 69, 70, 122, 141
ISPH - 67
James, Matt - 54
James, Tad - 51, 54, 62, 67
Journal of Hypnotism - 3, 25, 31, 32, 35, 36, 37, 39, 40, 44, 63, 64, 78, 89, 100, 105, 125
Kappas, George - 53, 67, 84, 86, 176
Kappas, John - 47, 48, 53, 67, 97, 118, 177
Kashiwa, Dr. Lester - 21
Katz, Zoe D. - 141
Keck, Layne - 7, 122
Kein, Gerald - 7, 40, 54, 62, 83, 116, 145, 173, 177
Kein, Shirley - 7, 40, 116
Kenney, Dr. George - 132
Kershaw, Maurice - 2, 7, 26, 32, 57, 67, 72, 78, 79, 145, 173
Kopelman, Dave - 22
Krasner, Dr. Al - 7, 49, 51, 53, 54, 67
Kroger, Dr. William S. - 99
LaVelle, Jill - 70, 75
LaVelle, Steven - 70, 75, 78, 177
Leidecker, Arthur - 42, 82
Leitner, Konradi - 15
Levison, Dr. Arnold - 2, 7, 26, 31, 79, 145, 174
Lewis, Sol - 43
Loder, Wendal - 44, 45, 82
Lustig, David - 15
MacIsaac, Patricia - 7, 8, 100, 116, 145, 156, 174, 177
Maltz, Dr. Maxwell - 5, 47

## Not the end - just a rest stop on the way—

That's my story as I recall it—
I've developed some close, lifetime friendships because of hypnotism.
I've met some wonderful men and women because of hypnotism.
I can hardly wait to see what the future has in store for me—for us.
I believe that success is a journey not a destination.
Although it hasn't always been smooth going we've overcome
the obstacles for the most part.
It sure has been interesting and exciting!

Dwight Damon

In the beginning
1949

Seventy + years later
2019
And still going . . .

Dr North — my mentor